HOW TO GET A PhD
Fourth edition

HOW TO GET A PhD
A handbook for students and their supervisors

FOURTH EDITION
revised and updated

ESTELLE M. PHILLIPS
and
DEREK S. PUGH

Open University Press

Open University Press
McGraw-Hill Education
McGraw-Hill House
Shoppenhangers Road
Maidenhead
Berkshire
England
SL6 2QL

email: enquiries@openup.co.uk
world wide web: <*www.openup.co.uk*>

and Two Penn Plaza, New York, NY 10121-2289, USA

First published 1987
Reprinted 1988 (twice), 1989, 1990, 1991, 1992, 1993
Second edition first published 1994
Reprinted 1994, 1995, 1996, 1998, 1999
Third edition first published 2000
Reprinted 2000, 2001, 2002, 2003, 2005
First published in this fourth edition 2005

A catalogue record of this book is available from the British Library

ISBN–10: 0 335 21684 6 (pb)   0 335 21685 4 (hb)
ISBN–13: 978 0 335 21684 6 (pb)   978 0 335 21685 7 (hb)

Library of Congress Cataloging-in-Publication Data
CIP data applied for

Typeset by RefineCatch Limited, Bungay, Suffolk
Printed in the UK by Bell & Bain Ltd, Glasgow

Dedicated to
SHELDON, JEROME AND BRADLEY REBACK
and
THE PUGHS and THE ARIELS

CONTENTS

Preface to the fourth edition   xiii

1 On becoming a research student   1
The nature of doctoral education   2
The psychology of being a research student   4
The aims of this book   5
Action summary   5

2 Getting into the system   7
Choosing the institution and field of study   7
The scientific research programme   9
Eligibility   10
Grants and research support   11
Distance supervision?   12
Choosing your work context   13
Selecting your supervisor   14
Starting out as a research student   16
Myths and realities of the system   17
    The 'ivory tower'   17
    Personal relationships   17
    Teamworking   18
Action summary   19

3 The nature of the PhD qualification   20
The meaning of a doctorate   20
Becoming a fully professional researcher   22

Differences between the MPhil and the PhD 24
Aims of students 25
Aims of supervisors 26
Aims of examiners 28
Aims of universities and research councils 29
Mismatches and problems 30
Action summary 31

4 **How not to get a PhD** 33
Not wanting a PhD 33
Not understanding the nature of a PhD by overestimating
  what is required 35
Not understanding the nature of a PhD by underestimating
  what is required 37
Not having a supervisor who knows what a PhD requires 39
Losing contact with your supervisor 40
Not having a thesis 41
Taking a new job before finishing 43
Action summary 44

5 **How to do research** 46
Characteristics of research 46
Intelligence-gathering – the 'what' questions 47
Research – the 'why' questions 48
Characteristics of good research 48
Research is based on an open system of thought 48
Researchers examine data critically 49
*Researchers generalize and specify the limits on their
  generalizations* 49
Hypothetico–deductive method 50
Basic types of research 51
Exploratory research 51
Testing-out research 52
Problem-solving research 52
Which type of research for the PhD? 52
The craft of doing research 54
Action summary 55

6 **The form of a PhD thesis** 56
Understanding the PhD form 56
Background theory 57
Focal theory 58
Data theory 58
Contribution 59

Detailed structure and choice of chapter headings   60
The concept of originality   61
Writing the thesis   63
   Writing as a process of rewriting   63
   Different types of writers   64
   Getting down to it   65
   The thesis itself   66
Alternative thesis styles   67
To publish or not to publish prior to submission?   68
Action summary   70

7 **The PhD process**   71
Psychological aspects   71
   Enthusiasm   71
   Isolation   72
   Increasing interest in work   73
   Transfer of dependence from the supervisor to the work   74
   Boredom   76
   Frustration   76
   A job to be finished   77
   Euphoria   78
Others 'getting in first'   79
Practical aspects   80
   Time management   80
   The duration of the process   82
   The stages of the process   82
Redefining long-term and short-term goals   86
The importance of deadlines   87
Self-help and peer support groups   89
Internet groups   90
Teaching while studying for a PhD   91
   Casual teaching   91
   Teaching assistantships   92
Action summary   93

8 **How to manage your supervisors**   94
The supervisory team   94
The supervisory team's limitations   95
What supervisors expect of their doctoral students   97
   Supervisors expect their students to be independent   97
   Supervisors expect their students to produce written work that is
     not just a first draft   98
   Supervisors expect to have regular meetings with their research
     students   99

*Supervisors expect their research students to be honest when
reporting on their progress* 100
*Supervisors expect their students to follow the advice that they
give, especially when it has been given at the request of the
postgraduate* 101
*Supervisors expect their students to be excited about their work,
able to surprise them and fun to be with!* 101
The need to educate your supervisors 103
How to reduce the communication barrier 105
Improving tutorials 105
Changing supervisors 108
Inappropriate personal relationships in supervision 110
Action summary 111

9 **How to survive in a predominantly British, white, male,
full-time, heterosexual academic environment** 112
Part-time students 112
Overseas students 114
Settling in to Britain 115
Expressing yourself in English 116
The culture of British doctoral education 117
Ethnic minorities 119
Racial harassment 120
Women students 121
Difficulties concerning legitimacy of topics and methodology 122
Problems of communication, debate and feedback 123
Scarcity of academic role models 124
Sexual harassment and exploitation 125
Gay, lesbian, bisexual and trans-gender students 127
Heterosexist harassment 128
Mature students 129
Students with disabilities 130
Disability legislation 130
Harassment of people with a disability 131
Action summary 131

10 **The examination system** 135
Upgrading to doctoral student status 135
Giving notice of submission 136
The appointment of examiners 136
Submitting the thesis 136
The oral examination – the 'viva' 137
Preparing for the viva 138
The results of the examination 140

The appeals procedures 142
Litigation 144
Action summary 144

11 How to supervise and examine 145
What students expect of their supervisors 145
Students expect to be supervised 145
Students expect supervisors to read their work well in advance 147
Students expect their supervisors to be available when needed 148
Students expect their supervisors to be friendly, open and supportive 149
Students expect their supervisors to be constructively critical 150
Students expect their supervisors to have a good knowledge of the research area 151
Students expect their supervisors to structure the tutorial so that it is relatively easy to exchange ideas 151
Students expect their supervisors to have sufficient interest in their research to put more information in the students' path 153
Students expect supervisors to be sufficiently involved in their success to help them get a good job at the end of it all! 153
Establishing a role model 154
Teaching the craft of research 154
Giving effective feedback 155
Introducing a structured 'weaning' programme 160
Maintaining a helpful 'psychological contract' 162
Encouraging students' academic role development 164
Supervising non-traditional students 165
Part-time students 165
Problems of access 165
Organizing work 166
Overseas students 166
Ethnic minorities 169
Women students 170
Gay, lesbian, bisexual and trans-gender students 171
Mature students 172
Disabled students 173
Supervising your research assistant 173
Outcomes of good supervision 174
Training for supervision 175
How to examine 175
The oral examination 178
Action summary 179

12 Institutional responsibilities   181
     University responsibilities   183
     A university-wide graduate school for doctoral students   183
     Participation in a regional hub   183
     Support for students   184
        Facilities for departments to support doctoral research activity   184
        A university-wide structured induction procedure   185
        A handbook for university research degree students   186
        English language support where necessary   186
        Support for non-traditional students   187
     Resources for supervisors   187
        The training of supervisors   187
        Teaching credit for doctoral supervision   188
     Faculty/departmental doctoral research tutor   189
     Providing appropriate regulations   189
        Selection of doctoral students   189
     Monitoring of students' progress   190
     Upgrading from MPhil to PhD registration   191
     Appointment of external examiners   192
     A forum for review of the PhD   192
        The PhD as a series of projects   192
        *Intellectual copyright and appropriate recognition for doctoral
           students' work*   193
        The PhD in a practice-based discipline   195
        Professional doctorates   196
     Departmental responsibilities   198
        The departmental research tutor   198
        Improving the selection of students into the department   200
        Selection of supervisors   201
     Guidelines on appropriate supervisory behaviour   202
     Support groups for research students   203
     A departmental doctoral programme   204
     The doctoral cohort system   205
     Action summary   206
     Conclusion   206

Appendix   207
References   211
Index   215

PREFACE TO THE FOURTH EDITION

The gratifying response to the previous editions of this book testifies to the need of research students and their supervisors to understand the processes of effective doctoral education. The number of translations into other languages – Reformed Chinese, Spanish, Portuguese, Classical Chinese, Russian, Arabic and Korean (in chronological order) – demonstrates that the issues covered here are highly relevant in many countries. This need to understand is reinforced by the considerable institutional change taking place in the higher education system in the UK. Since our first edition in 1987 opened up the subject for debate, many of the developments we have advocated have come about: greater university recognition and support for doctoral students, effective monitoring of student progress, training for supervisors in teaching the craft of research and so on. And the changes are continuing apace. It is therefore appropriate to offer a fourth edition, revised and updated to the present situation.

One comment made in the generally favourable reviews of the first edition deserves attention here. In our analysis of the complex tasks of PhD study, we describe the difficulties which may be encountered. This is in order to enable both students and supervisors to avoid such problems or to overcome them. It has been suggested that this inevitably gives too great a focus on the 'pathologies' of the doctoral process. We fear that this may be true, and so we should like to reiterate here the positive aspects of being a PhD student. The joys of doing research are considerable, and anyone in a position to carry out research is indeed privileged. Feelings of exploration, excitement, challenge, involvement and passion are frequent and are commented on in this book. The enormous feeling of achievement on the award of the degree lasts for many throughout their whole lives. Clearly the process is very rewarding, otherwise so many would not have carried it through to success.

Similarly it has been pointed out to us that our discussion of the particular issues concerning women, part-time and minority group students, which looks realistically at the special problems that these groups face and how they may be ameliorated when they occur, may give the impression that discrimination is the norm. This, of course, is not so, and as we note, many universities have procedures for dealing with any that occurs – although it is not possible to be complacent about the situation.

This book has grown out of EMP's own PhD research, a continuing series of studies of research students, our experience of supervising and examining doctoral students and the seminar on the process of PhD-getting conducted by DSP for a number of years at the London Business School and subsequently by both of us at the Open University. We should like to acknowledge the help of all those who contributed to those activities over the years and who, together with those who currently participate in our seminars, form the 'cast of characters' in this book. We learned a lot from all of them and we are most grateful.

For the fourth edition we received much information, suggestions and constructive criticism from Hilary Burgess (Open), Iain Cameron (EPSRC), Linda Conrad (Griffith, Australia), Chris France (Surrey), Jackie Green (Leeds Metropolitan), Graham Hankinson (London Metropolitan), James Hartley (Keele), Craig Johnson (Bradford), Shalom Lappin (KCL), Hugh Matthews (Northampton), John Sparrow (York), Wendy Stainton-Rogers (Open), Alison Struselis (Northampton), Emma Wakelin (AHRB), Robert Westaway (Brunel) and Robert White (Southampton). Shona Mullen, our publisher at Open University Press, gave her usual stalwart support. We are grateful to them all.

We should like to thank Janet Metcalfe and the UK GRAD Programme, who are the joint holders of the copyright with DSP, for permission to reproduce the 'Self-evaluation questionnaire on research student progress' on pp. 207ff.

Finally, DSP would like to thank EMP for her generous hospitality during the writing of this edition of the book.

ON BECOMING A RESEARCH STUDENT

This book is a handbook and a survival manual for PhD students. If you are intending to embark on a research degree it will introduce you to the system and, by increasing your understanding, help you to improve your choice of university, college, department and supervisor.

If you have just picked this book up and you are already a research student, then you should read it thoroughly – and hang on to it so that you can refer to it frequently. You will need to do this because we shall be discussing the skills and processes that are crucial to obtaining the PhD degree.

If you are a supervisor, or contemplating becoming one, the book is highly relevant to you too, because it deals with the educational processes that it is your responsibility to encourage for the successful completion of your students' research degrees.

If you are a senior academic administrator, the relevance of this book is that it provides a guide to procedures and systems concerned with research degrees which will enable you to evaluate the adequacy of the provision your university is making for research students.

The book focuses on process issues which are not discipline-specific. It cannot help you to design an investigation or an experiment as these activities require professional knowledge of your particular field. Similarly it does not deal with the financial difficulties of doctoral students, which will vary depending on your circumstances. Nor does it con-sider factors impinging on you after you have completed your course such as the employment options available to PhDs. (Delamont and Atkinson 2004 discuss developing a postdoctoral research career.)

But the book does suggest that you ponder on some basic questions before embarking on a course of study leading to the PhD degree. Do you want to spend three to four years of your life doing research on one topic? Will you be satisfied to live on a student grant for that time? Are you committed to a PhD or would a professional doctorate (e.g. EdD, EngD) suit you better? (The differences are discussed on pp. 196ff. of this book.) Are you able to tolerate regular periods of intellectual loneliness when only you are responsible for producing 'creative thoughts'? It is vital that you give a firm 'yes' in answer to all those questions. You must make the decision to study and work for your doctorate based on the sure knowledge that it is the right thing for *you*. If what you really want is to write a bestseller, then conducting research for a thesis is *not* the optimum way to go about it. Perhaps you don't really know what you want to do with the rest of your life and continuing in the university system seems a good way of putting off that decision. If this is so then you have chosen an extremely difficult way of solving your particular problem.

■ The nature of doctoral education

Acquiring the skills and understanding the processes necessary for success cannot be done at a single reading. As a research student you need continually to use the ideas in this book to develop your own insight into your own situation. In this way your professional learning will develop as it should – under your own management.

'Under your own management' is the key to the nature of doctoral education. In undergraduate education a great deal, in academic terms, is organized for the student. It may not have seemed like that to you at the time, because you were required to do a considerable amount of work, but, for example, syllabuses were laid down, textbooks were specified, practical sessions were designed, the examinations were organized to cover a set range of topics in questions of a known form, and so on. You could quite reasonably have complained if asked about an extraneous subject, 'But no one told me that I was supposed to learn that topic (or methodology or theory or historical period).' For the most part you were following an academic course set by your teachers.

In doctoral education, you have to take responsibility for managing your learning and for getting yourself a PhD. Of course, there will be people around to help you: – your supervisor(s), other academics in your department, fellow students and so on. Some of them will even tell you what, in their opinion, you have to do to obtain the degree, but the responsibility for determining what is required, as well as for carrying it out, remains firmly with you. And if it turns out that you need a particular topic or theory for your work, then it is no excuse to say, 'But nobody told me it was relevant.' It is your responsibility.

So you will not be traversing a set course laid out by others. You will be expected to initiate discussions, ask for the help that you need, argue about what you should be learning, and so on. You are under self-management, so it is no use sitting around waiting for somebody to tell you what to do next or, worse, complaining that nobody is telling you what to do next; in the postgraduate world these are opportunities, not deficiencies.

The overall university framework for research students ensures that there is a basic similarity for all doctoral candidates as they progress through their studies. But there are also some notable differences between the research cultures of university disciplines, particularly between the culture of the laboratory-based sciences and that of the humanities and social sciences. To a considerable extent they stem from the large capital investment in equipment and materials required in scientific research.

Supervisors in science have to take the lead in obtaining the physical resources and the research personnel required. A studentship may be allocated and a doctoral student recruited specifically to work on a designated line of research. In this situation the 'apprenticeship' aspect of being a doctoral student is emphasized. The student's research topic will be clearly defined to fit in with the innovative thrust of the supervisor's research programme, and this will set limits to the level of research creativity that can be shown. The student will be required to do 'dogsbody' work in the laboratory or on the computer as part of professional training. In these situations there develops what might be called a 'joint ownership' of the doctoral research between supervisors and the students. Supervisors will have a strong interest in getting the research work done and using the results obtained. Joint papers will be the norm. The danger to watch for in this culture is the exploitation of the student, leading to the feeling of being just an extra pair of hands for the supervisors' research. It must be remembered that there has to be a sufficient amount of autonomy for the student to be able to make an original contribution. It is this which justifies the award of the PhD degree.

In contrast, in the humanities and the social sciences students often come with their own topics within the field in which the supervisor is expert, and academics give a service of research supervision. Being busy people, supervisors often have to ration the amount of attention they can give. Research supervision has to compete with the supervisor's own current research (which can be considerably different), undergraduate teaching and administration. Supervisors will have only a general interest in the results of the student's research, and will act more as role models than as apprentice-masters. The danger to watch for in this culture is the neglect of the student for long periods of weeks, months, even years. It must be remembered that students need the regular support of supervisors if they are to develop sufficiently to achieve the PhD degree.

These descriptions are of extreme situations; there are many shades of grey in between. There are scientists who give an individual service to their doctoral students and social scientists who build up a team of students all working on related aspects of the same topic. You must work to understand the situation into which you are entering.

In recent years universities have found that it is not in a student's best interest to rely on only one supervisor for each student. Supervisory teams with two or three members are being established in many departments, with a lead (or main) supervisor and one or two associate supervisors. This team must contain a subject specialist and someone responsible for pastoral support. The team system can allow for new supervisors to learn how to supervise more effectively under the guidance of an experienced member of the department. Others involved in supervision, perhaps at times of upgrading or controversy, might be the departmental head and the research tutor.

■ The psychology of being a research student

New research students enter the system determined to make an outstanding contribution to their subject. By the time they start the final stages of thesis-writing for the degree they are determined to 'get it and forget it!' During the intervening years their enthusiasm has been dampened by the demands of having to concentrate on a specific topic and conduct routine and repetitive tasks in an atmosphere where nobody seems either to understand or to care about their work.

They come into the university or college knowing precisely who they are: successful and intelligent holders of well-earned qualifications. It is not long before they lose their initial confidence and begin to question their own self-image. This is the result of contacts (no matter how sporadic or from what distance) with academic discourse. Such contacts could come from members of staff, postgraduates who are further into their research than the first-year students, and papers published in journals or presented at conferences. These challenge the assumptions and conceptions that the young graduates had accepted as inviolable. From this period of self-doubt and questioning, the successful postgraduates emerge with a new identity as competent professionals, able to argue their viewpoint with anybody regardless of status, confident of their own knowledge but also aware of its boundaries. This new identity permits them to ask for information when they are aware that they don't know something and to express a lack of understanding when this is necessary, instead of pretending that there is no difficulty for fear of being thought stupid. To arrive at this point is what being a postgraduate research student is really all about.

■ The aims of this book

The necessity for personal academic initiative is the key cultural change that doctoral students will encounter compared with their undergraduate days. It requires a different style of operation, which is why it is not sufficient just to state the issue as we did in the previous sections. Students need information and insights to develop the capacity to operate successfully in the postgraduate environment. We have seen many students take long periods (one year or even two!) in adjusting to the environment, at considerable jeopardy to the achievement of their doctorates. Some students never come to terms with it and go away indignant, bitter – and without PhDs.

All new postgraduates have to be prepared to unlearn and rethink many of the doctrines which they have had to accept up to this point in their student career. A vital aspect of this rethinking is to take the initiative in discussing with your supervisor the whole range of your ideas, including any that might even appear to be 'off-beat' or 'illegitimate' but may in fact turn out to be surprisingly useful leads.

The first aim of this book is to explore such issues in a realistic way in order to help you understand and achieve the tasks necessary to complete the PhD successfully. Our second complementary aim is to help supervisory practice in managing the process better. The third aim is to put the whole activity in its context, since the recognition by universities of their institutional responsibilities in improving the effectiveness of doctoral education is a key factor in promoting necessary change.

In attempting to achieve these aims we shall be drawing on our experience in doctoral supervision and our systematic research into PhD education. We give real-life examples of students and their supervisors. The ratio of men to women in the illustrations is consistent with that in higher education today and covers a range of faculties including Arts, Business Studies, Science, Social Science, and Technology. We shall be examining the characteristics of the educational system, the nature of the PhD qualification, psychological aspects of the PhD process, and how to manage your supervisor, among many other practical topics.

On pp. 207ff at the end of the book we have included a self-diagnostic questionnaire on student progress to help you focus on issues that are relevant to you.

■ Action summary

1. Be aware that in doctoral education you are under your own management and have the responsibility for determining what is required as well as for carrying it out.

2. You will experience periods of self-doubt which you must come through with the clear aim of becoming a competent professional researcher.

3. Read this book for insights into the PhD research learning process, to help you manage it better.

2

GETTING INTO THE SYSTEM

Once you have decided to continue within the higher education system and conduct research for a higher degree, you have other decisions to make. First you have to be accepted by a university department to work in your chosen area of study. But which university? In what area? And how to apply?

■ Choosing the institution and field of study

If you are a postgraduate who is a candidate for a research studentship, the offer of such a studentship is likely to be the determining factor in your choice of institution and field of study. You should, though, satisfy yourself on two important counts:

1 That the research discipline or area in which the studentship is offered is genuinely one on which you can see yourself concentrating very closely for the next three or four years of your life and maybe more. Many PhD students have come unstuck simply because they have lost interest or belief in the area that they are investigating.
2 That the university department in which you are being offered the studentship has an established reputation in research and a real commitment to the development of doctoral students. You should not hesitate to ask about these issues, so important to your success, when you go to a department for interview. You should collect whatever literature is available about the department, the staff engaged in research and the precise nature of that research. Find out the departmental rating in the

British University Research Assessment Exercise, and how the department intends to develop research in the future. Obtain copies of research papers and discover as much as you can about the scope of existing work being done by staff and doctoral students and the possibilities of developing that work into areas of interest to you. Ask to speak to current doctoral students and obtain from them a description of the adequacy of the set-up from their point of view.

Accept a studentship only if you are optimistic on both counts – of the suitability of the institution and of the field of study. This optimism will fade soon enough as we shall see later on in this book, so it is important to have some to start off with.

If you are not dependent on a studentship (or if you are fortunate enough to be offered more than one and have to choose) then you have a wider range of options, but you will have to work harder to acquaint yourself with the available possibilities.

One direct way of finding out about the relevant academic activities is to go to a university library (or look on the Internet) and systematically review the current issues of journals in your subject. This allows you to locate the researchers who are publishing relevant work. Remember, all libraries in higher education will allow readers to have access to their stock for use on the premises; you just have to ask for permission. You can obtain good preliminary information through the Internet by using your search engine to explore the general introductions to a variety of relevant topics. All universities have websites and all departments have web pages describing the research that they are currently undertaking.

It is always a good idea, once you have narrowed down your options to a few departments that appeal to you, to contact those who seem most likely to be able to discuss your own plans in the light of what they know to be happening in their unit. You can initiate this contact by letter or email, followed by a telephone call and – if you are still interested – an arrangement to meet at the university. You will find that most academics will be happy to discuss research issues with you. A good way to make contact with different people and departments is to take advantage of the open days that so many universities now advertise.

Having got this far, your top priority should be defining more clearly your field of study. To do this you need to give some thought to your own interests and how they interact with what you have found out about the work of the department you are visiting. While it is premature at this stage to have a complete project worked out, you will need to be able to talk convincingly about the type of research that appeals to you and why you are considering applying to that particular department. If you are considering creating a draft proposal, it may be that the department to which you are applying may be prepared to give you some help in developing it.

Other issues to be borne in mind at this point have to do with the mechanics of getting the work done, for example, access to laboratory equipment (and what kind of equipment), computers, library facilities, potential samples and their availability and ease of access, amount of support from secretarial staff (if any), photocopying facilities and, in the case of survey research, the potential for help with postage, etc. In addition, the compatibility of the people with whom you will be working is an important component in your choice.

If you are contemplating part-time doctoral research, perhaps due to family responsibilities, essential work commitments or are otherwise subject to geographical constraints in your choice, remember that nowadays most regions have several institutions of higher learning where research degrees can be taken. For example, in the West Midlands conurbation there are at least six universities. You should also consider that you can do a PhD under the Open University system, which has considerable geographical flexibility. In Chapter 9 we look in more detail at the situation of part-time research students.

Other universities too offer opportunities for students to conduct research without having to be resident. They normally require a number of visits to the campus during a year and even, in some cases, attendance at residential weekends. Email and Internet technologies have encouraged the development of more flexible registration arrangements. For these reasons you must explore thoroughly the range of provision which might be available for you.

■ The scientific research programme

If you are a scientist you should consider whether participating as a doctoral student in a major scientific research programme would suit you. Research students in such a programme are treated as the most junior level of employee contributing to the overall work, in fact as junior research assistants. The director of the programme sets very clear constraints on the work that is to be carried out and submitted for the doctorate and the student's contribution is correspondingly restricted in range.

Viewed in educational terms, this type of programme has both advantages and limitations. The three major advantages over the position of the individual research student are that: the environment continually demonstrates that research matters – a great benefit as compared with the situation of students who have supervisors for whom research cannot be the top priority; the laboratory is well funded; and the training in professional practice and the academic issues tackled will be state-of-the-art.

These programmes do have limitations though. First, supervisors tend to discount the necessity for tutorial support as distinct from managerial supervision, since they believe that much of that support is being given by the group. The close contact that they have with the students in the laboratory on a day-to-day managerial basis leads many supervisors to neglect the educational practices that we advocate throughout this book.

Second, directors of research programmes and other senior members tend to accept the illusory picture of teams of happy researchers working together toward a common end. This view takes no account of the students' competitiveness and their fear of having their ideas or results stolen by one of their colleagues working on a very closely related problem. The tensions and distrust that can arise among such a group of beginning professionals – physically close but psychologically isolated – can be very unsettling.

■ Eligibility

The first question here is: do you have the academic qualifications to be accepted as a student for a research degree? Most universities require first or upper second-class honours in a relevant British undergraduate degree; some universities will accept lower seconds. If you already have a master's degree it is usually acceptable, whatever the class of your undergraduate degree.

These are the general requirements which will allow you to go through straightforwardly. If you do not have them it does not mean that you will not be accepted, only that a special case has to be made, which will require the strong backing of your potential supervisor. For example, if you do not have a British degree, the university will have to satisfy itself that your overseas degree is of a standard equivalent to a British one. Or you may have a non-degree professional qualification plus considerable practical experience, on which a special case could be made for your acceptance.

In general we would say that you should not be immediately deterred if you do not have the typical formal qualifications for acceptance. Always explore with potential supervisors whether a special case can be made. It may be, for example, that you could be accepted subject to doing certain extra study, or passing a qualifying examination. Remember too that if one institution rejects you, it does not mean that all will. However, if you have had several rejections it may not be wise to pursue registration. You may need to review your likelihood of success and come to a more realistic estimate of your abilities.

The second question is: what degree are you going to be registered for? If you are a beginner in research and do not already have an MPhil or an MRes (i.e., a master's degree awarded for research) you will, in the first place, be registered as a general research student or for an MPhil degree. You will often be required to take some taught courses before embarking on your thesis work. You may be required to complete successfully a one-year taught programme leading to the award of the MRes degree. The decision on formal registration for the PhD is then taken after the first year of your research when there is some indication that the work is progressing satisfactorily. You and your supervisor(s) must, therefore, be in close contact to ensure that the case can be made for full PhD registration. At this stage a title for the thesis and the intended programme of research are presented.

The third question is concerned with the limits of the period allowed between registration and submission. For full-time students there will be a formal minimum time (three or four years) and a formal maximum (four or five years) after which registration will lapse and a special (and very persuasive) case will need to be made for reinstatement. Because of this maximum limit, if you are having to abandon your research work temporarily but intend to return to it, you should obtain a formal suspension of the period of study.

For part-time students the time limits are set roughly pro rata: four to five years minimum, seven to eight years maximum. Don't forget that if you are employed by your institution as, say, a research assistant, you may find that you can be counted as a full-time student even if you are working only part-time on your PhD. This fudge is allowed because the basic nature of the PhD is as a professional training, and research assistants get a great deal of this training as part of their jobs.

When registration has been completed you should be informed formally of: your supervisor(s); the topic or field of study for which you have been accepted; the minimum length of study time required before submission of your thesis.

Continuing registration in succeeding years is usually dependent on adequate progress being made each year, and a report to this effect has to be submitted by your supervisor. Do ensure that it is sent at the appropriate time.

■ Grants and research support

It may be that you will qualify for a grant from the government, a university or a private foundation. The availability of grants is variable, and the regulations on eligibility detailed. Nevertheless if you are British or from the EU or have lived in the UK for three years or more, it would be worth your while investigating the possibilities. You may find that you fall into a category for whom special grants are available. The best place to start to explore these possibilities would be with your university careers service who will help you to discover what may be available. There is a Grants and Trusts Directory (which includes benevolent funds) to look at, and the website <*www.funderfinder.org.uk*> is a useful starting point for further exploration. If you find that you meet their criteria, you would be well advised to apply far in advance of their advertised cut-off date. However, do not build up too much hope at this stage because many of these grants are *very* specific indeed and can be quite small.

You must obtain and study the regulations of the formal system concerned with these topics. You should also be aware that exceptions can be made, and this may be worth exploring. Your financial situation should be part of your initial discussion with your potential supervisor.

If you are awarded a studentship, it will be for a set period (three or four years). There are considerable variations in the operation of grants. Some are tied to specific research projects, some come from research councils and may require you to take particular courses in the first year (which may lead to an MRes, the so-called '1+3 system'), some are linked to industrial collaboration. Remember that in certain circumstances it may be possible to obtain an extension of the grant. You have to keep your supervisor aware of this possibility and make sure that a strongly supported application is made at the appropriate time.

Grants are quite low in value, and it may be that you will be hoping for some casual work. Try to obtain some professional work which helps your academic development if at all possible. It is much better to tutor your subject than to work long hours serving behind a bar.

While academic institutions are no longer regarded as being *in loco parentis*, they may act as quasi-employers if you have a grant that they administer. Some, like any good employer, will make small short-term loans to cover an urgent financial problem. These can be repaid by instalments.

Find out from your university what you are statutorily entitled to in the way of research resources. These might include a desk, lab space, equipment and consumable resources (for example, chemicals for your project). You should ensure (via your supervisor, if necessary) that you have them. You also need to be aware that there are often discretionary opportunities available. You may be able to call on technical support from departmental technicians and computer staff, and you may be entitled to apply for financial support for travel to conferences or to visit other institutions.

■ Distance supervision?

There have always been people who, while wishing to study for a higher degree by research, are unable physically to attend regularly at a university. These include potential students who live in areas with no university provision, people with disabilities, carers and those with young children who are able to work in their own environment but would be unable to attend university at regular required times.

With the growth of IT (information technology) it is becoming increasingly possible for research work to be carried out from your own home. Libraries can be accessed from home, the Internet carries vast information loads. You can be in communication with your supervisor, academics in your field, and fellow students from any university by email. Students may expect a much better level of supervision than would have been the case previously if they have to go abroad for any reason during the course of their studies (e.g., the fieldwork period for anthropology and geology students).

This is not to suggest that the doctoral supervision process can be carried out entirely at a distance, however. The regular interaction needed with the supervisor must inevitably take place face to face in order for student and supervisor to spark ideas off each other. It is this process which moves the research forward creatively. While IT can help the supervisory process to become more effective, it cannot completely replace personal interaction. All British universities insist on a certain period of attendance on campus during the course of study. It is therefore not realistic for a potential student to consider applying to work for a PhD degree completely at a distance.

■ Choosing your work context

An important aspect of the quality of your working life as a research student is your work context. Where precisely will you be spending most of your time in the next few years? If you are in a position to make a choice of research institutions, you should certainly find out about the physical facilities offered and take them into account.

Some universities provide study cubicles for postgraduates, some a student common room and some give their research students a desk in a small shared room similar to those used by members of staff. Since personal computers, email and Internet technologies are such an integral part of research activity, it is important to discover what arrangements are made in this area. Some universities are in a position to offer the use of a PC (personal computer) to all doctoral students. If they do not, and you do not already have a machine, you must buy one. It is a key tool of your work. All universities should offer you participation in their email network and access to the Internet.

There are universities which make little or no physical provision for doctoral students. They are expected to work at home when not in libraries, laboratories, other organizations or away on field trips.

It may be that you prefer the congenial company of others in a similar situation and like the idea of being able to find a corner in a large room set aside solely for the use of research students. On the other hand, you may find it irritating having to interact with others and listen to what they have to say about their own progress (or lack of it) whenever you want to use the common room as a base from which to get on with your own work.

Perhaps you are a loner and enjoy the discipline of long hours spent poring over books or documents when not engaged in experimentation or other forms of data collection. You favour a clear dividing line between working hours and time spent socializing and are able to organize this division of activity satisfactorily yourself. Once again, you may discover that the isolation this type of work context imposes on you results in feelings of alienation and a lack of contact with others who could stimulate discussion and collaborate in the production of new ideas.

Some people believe that being given a desk in a room shared by only one or two other research students is an ideal arrangement. They have their own personal corner where they can keep their books and writing materials, interview others and chat with their room-mates, as well as having easy and constant access to their supervisors and other members of staff. However, the reality is not always like that, and you may find that you are thrown into close contact with people whom you find quite intolerable for some reason or other. Perhaps one of them leaves chewing gum all over the place, while another is constantly talking or entertaining friends when you wish to concentrate on your work. One is very untidy and continually 'borrows' your possessions without returning them, as well as spreading items that do not belong to you all over your designated work area. Another is intrusive in other ways: perhaps there are too many questions about your personal life or too much discussion of others' problems and successes.

In addition, your presence and absence are easily noted by others, and you may have to account for your movements rather more than you would wish. Also, your supervisor 'just along the corridor' may not be quite as accessible as at first appears.

■ Selecting your supervisor

This is probably the most important step you will have to take. In general students do not select their supervisors: their supervisors are allocated by the department or, in fewer cases, their supervisors may have selected them.

However, it is not impossible to influence the selection yourself and you should certainly attempt to do so. There is certain basic information that you need in order to be confident that a particular academic is an appropriate person to supervise you. The key factor is whether they have an established research record and are continuing to contribute to the development of their discipline. The questions you need to ask yourself include the following: Have they published research papers recently? Do they hold research grants or contracts? Is the lab efficiently organized? Are they invited to speak at conferences in Britain and abroad? Positive answers to at least some of these questions are desirable.

Another important aspect that you should be considering when selecting your supervisor is: how close a relationship do you want? The supervisor–student relationship is one of the closest that you will ever be involved in. Even marriage partners do not spend long hours every day in close contact with each other, but this could be the case with a student and a supervisor. Some people need to have their supervisors around a lot (especially in the beginning), while others feel it oppressive to be asked what they are doing, and to be told continually what they should be getting on with next.

There are at least two patterns from which to choose with regard to working with your supervisor. The first has already been mentioned: the student needs constant support and reassurance, and the supervisor needs continual feedback in order to give instruction, thus providing direction for the research. The second pattern is a relationship in which the student needs time to think about the work to be done and needs the freedom to make mistakes during early attempts to get started, before discussing what has been happening with the supervisor. In this relationship the supervisor must feel relaxed about giving the student time to learn by trial and error. Such supervisors are content to give guidance at regular intervals rather than the direction provided by those who stay much closer to the students and their work.

Research has shown (Phillips 1994a) that when a student who needs time to plan work and to continue unhurriedly until satisfied that there is something interesting to impart is paired with a supervisor who constantly asks for worthwhile results, the student becomes irritated and feels that the standards required are unattainable. The supervisor feels that the postgraduate is too cautious and unable to work alone. Conversely, when a student who needs constant feedback and encouragement is paired with a supervisor who wants to be kept informed of progress and ideas only at intervals that allow for some development to have occurred, the student feels neglected and the supervisor resents the student's demands for attention (if the student is actually confident enough to ask for more time).

Good communication and rapport between students and their supervisors are the most important elements of supervision. Once the personal relationship has been well-established, all else falls into place. If interpersonal compatibility is missing everything else to do with being a research student is perceived negatively. Therefore, it cannot be stressed too strongly that you should discuss this relationship at the very earliest opportunity, and a tentative agreement about working together should be reached.

■ Starting out as a research student

In general, universities put very limited efforts into induction procedures for newcomers into the higher degree system or into the role of research student. Those who have recently attained a high-quality first degree share with their peers who have returned to university after some years of working the confusion and disorientation that comes from not quite knowing what is expected of them.

Often new research students have the idea that people who possess a PhD degree are outstandingly brilliant. This idea inhibits their own development as they are equally sure that they are not outstandingly brilliant, and therefore cannot really expect to be awarded a PhD. Similarly, if they actually read any completed theses (this is not the norm and will be discussed in detail later) they often emerge convinced that they would never be able to write anything even remotely resembling such a document either in length or quality.

The world that the new research student enters, classically portrayed as an 'ill-defined limbo' (Wason 1974) involves making a traumatic intellectual transition. It also involves the phenomenon of 'unlearning existing expertise' and having to start from the very beginning in order to discover slowly what one is supposed to be doing. During this period students might question the whole point of their being in the university.

You should, therefore, make every effort to mitigate these unpleasant beginnings by agreeing a small initial project with definite deadlines at an early interview with your supervisor. The agreement should include the understanding that, once the work has been completed, you will discuss with your supervisor both the work itself and your feelings about it. This exercise will help to clarify any doubts about your ability to undertake research and written work. It will also help to reveal the evolutionary process (corrections, drafts, rewritings, etc.) inevitably involved in the production of theses, articles and books to publication standard which you have just read with such admiration.

It is also a good idea to talk to other research students about their experience of the role as well as their work. Sharing apprehensions helps to resolve them through the knowledge that the problem is not an individual one, but one that is inbuilt into a less than perfect system. There are indeed guidelines which universities are advised to follow in providing support for their doctoral students. Your student representative can help you in accessing these should it ever be necessary.

■ Myths and realities of the system

The 'ivory tower'

One of the commonest misconceptions about research is that it is an 'ivory tower' activity, far removed from reality and from social contact with others. If you say you are doing research, people will often talk to you as though you had decided to spend a number of years in solitary confinement from which, in due course, you will emerge with your new discoveries.

It is not like that at all. Although there are considerable periods when you will be working on your own (thinking and writing, for example) this is not the whole story. There is also a considerable academic network of people with whom, as an active researcher, you must interact. These include your supervisors, other academics in your department, the general library staff, the specialist librarian who deals with computer-based literature searches, visiting academics giving seminars, colleagues giving papers at conferences – the list is very considerable. To be an effective research student you must make use of all the opportunities offered. Research is an interactive process and requires the development of social, as well as academic, skills.

Personal relationships

Another popular misconception, this time of supervisors, is to believe that so long as they are on first-name terms with their research students everything is fine and the student knows that they are friends. Some supervisors even invite their students to their homes or take them to the pub for a drink in order to reinforce this camaraderie. But no matter how far the supervisors may go to assure new students that their relationship is that of friendly colleagues, the reality is that students take a considerable amount of time to become comfortable about this degree of informality. This is as true of mature students as of the more traditional new graduate.

The reason for the students' difficulty is that the supervisors already have that which the students most want – the PhD. They have the title of 'Dr' and are acknowledged experts in the chosen field of their research students. The students have admired the supervisors' work during their undergraduate days, having come into contact with it through lectures or reading, or having heard reference made to it by others. They feel privileged to be working so closely with such individuals, and are aware of the supervisors' authority in the subject and power in the relationship.

You may be in a department with many research students or perhaps you are the only one in your discipline. Either way you will probably meet others at an induction seminar, introductory lecture or other meeting for new higher degree students arranged by your university or student union.

Even if the people you meet are in different faculties, working on topics far removed from your own, it will be helpful for you to have contact with them. Since they are at the same stage as you, they have some understanding of your own experience. Make it one of your first tasks to get the names and email addresses of a few of your peers. Use this list to get in touch with them to form a mutually beneficial support group. Throughout the whole of your course this group will enable you to compare not only how your research is progressing, but also your feelings about it. The reality of this situation is that all personal relationships within the academic community, as elsewhere, have to be worked at and take time to develop.

Teamworking

'I work alone in a lab, full of people, all research students, all working alone.' This quotation is from Diana, a student in biochemistry, who was part of a 'team' of research students who were all engaged in the search for an effective anti-cancer drug. It exemplifies the situation in scientific research in which a large programme is being funded and the professors who hold the grants gather around them several research students. Each student is working on a specific problem. Each problem is closely linked to all the others. In theory there is a free exchange of information and the whole group works in harmony. In some programmes though, research students take care to guard closely the work for which they are responsible because they occasionally fear that one of the others may discover something that will render their own research unworthy of continuation.

The PhD is awarded for original work. Postgraduates working on a programme such as the one described have two worries: first, that another student's work so closely borders on their own that it will make their work unoriginal or second past the post; second, that somebody else will demonstrate something (for which that other person will be awarded a PhD) that will at the same time show their own line of research to be false.

What is needed is collaboration, not competition, between people who should be making each other's work more comprehensible and less alienating. In well managed laboratories there are regular group meetings to ensure that there is a general knowledge of the work that is being undertaken, and good communication about the issues and difficulties involved. Yet often students experience alienation and isolation as the overriding themes of their postgraduate days. The strange thing about this is that sometimes the science students appear to feel the isolation more strongly than their counterparts in the Social Sciences or Arts faculties. This is because within the sciences there is the illusion of companionship, and the expectations of new postgraduates are that they will be part of a group of friends, as well as a work group. In other faculties new research students expect to be working alone in libraries or at home, reading, writing and thinking rather than experimenting. Any socializing that may take place as a result of a seminar, shared room or organized event is perceived as a bonus.

■ Action summary

1. Get as much information as you can before choosing your academic institution. Use the Internet and visit the places beforehand to talk to potential supervisors. Find out about the research culture: is it programme based or individually orientated? Ask to see around the area in which your work will be carried out to determine whether it would suit you.

2. Find out about a potential supervisor's research experience, publishing record and supervisory management style before making your decision.

3. Ensure that you understand the eligibility requirements both for entry into the research degree programme of the university and of grant-awarding bodies. Know whether you conform to them or can make a special case for exceptional treatment.

4. Very early on, arrange with your main supervisor to carry out a small initial project with definite deadlines to get you into the system. On completion and writing up, discuss not only the results but also how you went about it and what you can learn about the process.

5. Work at personal relationships with your supervisor(s) and fellow doctoral students. Set limited goals and achieve them.

3

THE NATURE OF THE PhD QUALIFICATION

In this chapter we shall discuss the nature of a PhD. We shall consider the objectives of the process, the part that it plays in the academic system, and the inevitably different aims the students, the supervisors and the examiners bring to it.

■ The meaning of a doctorate

We are going to start with some historical background and present in a schematic way the meaning of the degree structure of a British university.

☐ A bachelor's degree traditionally meant that the recipient had obtained a general education (specializing at this level is a relatively recent nineteenth-century development).

☐ A master's degree is a licence to practise. Originally this meant to practise theology, that is, to take a living in the Church, but now there are master's degrees across a whole range of disciplines: business administration, soil biology, computing, applied linguistics and so on. The degree marks the possession of advanced knowledge in a specialist field.

☐ A doctor's degree historically was a licence to teach – meaning to teach in a university as a member of a faculty. Nowadays this does not mean that becoming a lecturer is the only reason for taking a doctorate, since the degree has much wider career connotations outside academia and many of those with doctorates do not have academic teaching posts. The concept stems, though, from the need for a faculty member to be an authority, in full command of the subject right up to the boundaries of current knowledge, and able to extend them. As the highest degree that can be awarded, it proclaims that the recipient is worthy of being listened to *as an equal* by the appropriate university faculty.

Traditionally the doctorates of British universities have been named for the particular faculty, for example: DD (Divinity), MD (Medicine), LLD (Law), DMus (Music), DSc (Science), DLitt (Letters, i.e. Arts). These so-called 'higher doctorates' are awarded as a recognition of a substantial contribution to the discipline by published work. In British universities the Doctor of Philosophy degree is a comparatively recent concept – an early twentieth-century import from the United States. Some universities abbreviate the title to DPhil (e.g., Oxford, Sussex, York) but most use the designation PhD, which we use throughout this book. Whatever the abbreviation, the degree is the same. It represents a more restricted achievement than the higher doctorates since it envisages a limited amount of academic work (three years or so), but it still embodies the concept that the holder of the PhD is in command of the field of study and can make a worthwhile contribution to it.

There are a number of exceptions to these descriptions of the meaning of the degree titles, since British universities pride themselves on their independence. Traditionally, once an institution had become a university there were no laws that specified which degrees could be awarded, by which institutions, to whom and on what basis, as was the case in Continental Europe. This has now changed, as the Government has decided to designate certain Higher Education Colleges as 'Teaching Universities', without giving them the right to award research degrees.

Historically this independence has allowed, for example, the arts faculties of traditional Scottish universities to use the MA title for their first degree, but the science faculties use BSc. Traditionally there was no extra examination for an MA degree at Oxford and Cambridge, only a requirement to continue attendance at a college for a further two years. Nowadays this has been reduced to paying a registration fee after two years and obtaining the degree without attendance. In medicine the practice is even stranger: general medical practitioners are given the honorary title of Doctor although they do not have a doctorate from their universities. Indeed, on the basis of their university course they are credited with *two* bachelor's degrees, although having a licence to practise they exemplify the concept of a master's degree. There are, of course, good historical reasons for these anomalies.

■ Becoming a fully professional researcher

Thus the holder of a PhD is someone who is recognized as an authority by the appropriate faculty and by fellow academics and scientists outside the university. In modern terms it is useful to think of this as becoming a fully professional researcher in your field. Let us try to spell out what becoming a full professional means:

1 At the most basic level it means that you have something to say that your peers want to listen to.
2 In order to do this you must have a command of what is happening in your subject so that you can evaluate the worth of what others are doing.
3 You must have the astuteness to discover where you can make a useful contribution.
4 You must be aware of the ethics of your profession and work within them.
5 You must have mastery of appropriate techniques that are currently being used, and also be aware of their limitations.
6 You must be able to communicate your results effectively in the professional arena.
7 All this must be carried out in an international context; your professional peer group is worldwide. (It always was, of course, but the rate of diffusion is infinitely faster than it used to be and with the World Wide Web is still accelerating.) You must be aware of what is being discovered, argued about, written and published by your academic community across the world.

This list clearly represents quite a tall order, not least because, as you will have spotted, most of the list concerns the learning of skills, not knowledge. The crucial distinction is between 'knowing that' and 'knowing how', as the philosopher Gilbert Ryle put it. It is not enough for someone to *tell* you that this is a fruitful area for study, that this technique is available for use, that you should write a clear paper communicating your contribution. You have to be able to carve out a researchable topic, to master the techniques required and put them to appropriate use, and to cogently communicate your findings.

So there are craft skills involved in becoming a full professional, which, like any skills, have to be learned by doing the task in practice situations under supervision. The skills required cannot easily be stated by other professionals, though many aspects can be learned from them – some consciously, others unconsciously. But there have to be the twin elements of exploration and practice, which are basic to all learning of skills. This is why the PhD takes time.

As though this were not enough, there is a further complication. When you are doing a PhD, you are playing in a game *where the goalposts are continually being moved.* Obviously, what is good professional practice today may tomorrow be inadequate. What is a reasonable contribution to a new topic now might be old hat by next year. So a final and crucial skill which professionals must acquire is the ability to evaluate and re-evaluate their own work and that of others in the light of current developments. They need to be able to grow with their discipline.

It is these skills that you are trying to acquire when you embark on a PhD, and the purpose of the exercise is to become a fully professional researcher and to be able to demonstrate that you are one. It is important to keep this professional concept in mind because it orientates everything that you have to do. For example, you are not doing research in order to do research; you are doing research in order to demonstrate that you have learned how to do research to fully professional standards (more about the implications of this later in this chapter).

You are not writing a review of your field of study because that would be an interesting thing to do, or because 'everybody does one' (although both of these may be true). You are writing a review because it gives you an opportunity to demonstrate that you have learned how to take command of the material with the maturity and grasp of the full professional (more about this in Chapter 6).

Notice that the key concept is to demonstrate that your learning is to professional standards. How will you know whether it is? This is probably the most crucial thing that you have to learn – from your supervisor and from published work in your field. It is indeed a vital responsibility of your supervisor to ensure that you are given every opportunity to become familiar with appropriate professional standards. It is only through this familiarity that you will be able to recognize and achieve them.

One thing is clear: you cannot get a PhD unless you do know what the standards are. This is because of the aims of the whole doctoral process. These are not just to allow you in due course to have the title 'Doctor', pleasant though this is and proud though your family will be. When the examiners, on behalf of the university and the academic community, award the degree and recognize you as a fully professional researcher, what they are primarily concerned with is that you should 'join the club' and continue your contribution to developing your discipline through research and scholarship throughout your career. They hope that you will publish papers from your doctoral thesis and continue to research and publish in the field to establish your academic authority, so that, in due course, you will supervise and examine other people's PhD theses.

This is in fact the aim of the whole exercise: to get you to the level where you can supervise and examine others' PhDs with authority. Thus clearly you must have the professional skills and you must know the standards that are required. Two immediate corollaries of this fact are:

☐ Quite early on in the process you must begin to read other PhD theses in your field so that you can discover what the standards are. How else will you know what standard you ought to aim for?

☐ If you have to go along to your supervisor after you have done your work and ask if it is good enough, you are clearly not ready for a PhD, which is awarded as a recognition that you are able to evaluate research work (including your own) to fully professional standards.

■ Differences between the MPhil and the PhD

The MPhil is clearly a less advanced qualification than the PhD in which the student is expected to master a content area and can be completed in two years' full-time study. The MPhil dissertation is normally shorter than the PhD thesis. It is often used as a training course in advanced research work, and can be a preliminary stage for the PhD where it is necessary to learn the fundamentals of research and acquire new techniques, although more and more the newly introduced MRes is being used for this purpose. The MPhil is also a legitimate higher degree qualification in its own right.

As with the PhD, it is not possible to spell out in bureaucratic detail what is required to obtain the MPhil in your subject now. You need to read successful dissertations in order to discover the standards expected. Here, but only in very general terms, are some ways in which the MPhil has been held to differ from the PhD.

A candidate for an MPhil must undertake an investigation but, compared to the PhD, the work may be limited in scope and the degree of originality. Considerably more emphasis is put on original work in the PhD and the PhD thesis involves greater depth than an MPhil dissertation. Greater synthesis and critical ability and also a more detailed investigation of any practical illustrations are expected from doctoral candidates.

The MPhil can be limited to the replication of research already published. It is also acceptable for secondary sources to be used. This means that for an MPhil it is legitimate to quote some authority quoting somebody else, for example, 'Francis gives several definitions of originality (Phillips and Pugh 2005)'. This would not be acceptable for a PhD thesis where the candidate for the degree would be expected to have read and evaluated Francis in the original publication.

In addition, although a full summary of literature is required, it does not have to be an *evaluative* review as in the PhD. The difference here is in the breadth and depth of the review as well as in the amount of critical appreciation that is expected. In a high quality MPhil, evidence is required of the ability to test ideas; understand appropriate techniques; make use of published work and source material; and show familiarity with different theories and empirical studies.

Each university will have its own regulations concerning the MPhil degree and you must study carefully those which apply to you.

■ Aims of students

There are many reasons why people decide to work towards a PhD. One of the most common aims at the beginning is the wish to make a significant contribution to the chosen field. In these cases students have become particularly interested in a topic during the course of their undergraduate degrees (or perhaps while working in their profession) and wish to add something to the current state of knowledge. For example Adam, who after graduating in architecture, had spent some years both teaching and working as an architect, explained why he had returned to university in the following way:

> I wanted to do more theoretical work as my interests were with the value problems in designing a building. How does the architect make decisions about features that will affect the behaviour of those using the building without ever having a consultation with the prospective users? This interest was an extension of my direction as an undergraduate and my observations during my working career. I saw it as a serious problem and a major issue in professional practice.

Greg, a history student, said he wanted to gain a PhD because:

> It was an opportunity to continue research I had started for my MA. To me a PhD means that the candidate has made some new contribution to his field and that's really what I want to do. Up until now I've never really considered doing the next degree until I had almost finished the previous one. I don't need the PhD for my work – it might even be a disadvantage.

Greg's sentiments are not echoed by all research students, as another important aim for many postgraduates is to enhance career opportunities and future earning capacity through possession of the PhD degree. Some decide on this course of action when considering plans for the future. Others, like Freddy, who was studying industrial chemistry, decide on research when they find it more difficult than they had expected to get a job in industry straight from university:

> The head of department where I did my first degree offered me a research post, so I agreed after he gave me an outline of the research area.

There are other career reasons for wanting to take a doctorate. Some students find that they are being called 'Dr' by people coming in to the laboratory or hospital department where they work and feel guilty at accepting the title they have not yet achieved. Others feel that relationships with their medical colleagues may be easier if they too have the title. Some are embarrassed at being alone in their academic group without a title and succumb to their feelings of peer pressure in order to conform.

Another reason for undertaking a research degree after doing well at undergraduate level is simply taking up the offer of a studentship as a form of employment and without having any real career aims. All of these motives are far removed from the idealistic view of the PhD student as somebody dedicated to advancing knowledge and potentially worthy of becoming an undisputed expert in a given field.

These diverse aims of students do not remain the same throughout the period of registration for the higher degree, however, not even for those students who *do* start because of the intrinsic satisfaction of actually doing research and because of their interest in the work for its own sake. The following description of his decision to work for the PhD was given by Bradley, who was studying in the English department of a university:

> I couldn't think of a more fulfilling or pleasurable way of spending my time. It's almost instinctive. I haven't weighed up the pros and cons, it was an emotional decision really.

As we discuss fully in Chapter 7 on the PhD process, all these students, together with very many more enthusiastic new recruits, change their way of talking about their PhD as the years of learning to do research and become a full professional pass by. Towards the end their aims become narrower: simply to reach the goal of the PhD – 'got to get it' – or else to complete an unfinished task – 'must finish'.

It is important that research students eventually realize that it is determination and application, rather than brilliance, that are needed. The sooner you learn this the better. Conducting a piece of research to a successful conclusion is a job of work that has to be done just like any other job of work. Also, just like any other job of work, an important objective should be to make a success of what you have set out to do.

■ Aims of supervisors

In the same way that students begin a PhD for a variety of different reasons, so too supervisors undertake supervision with different aims in mind. There are those who wish to add to their reputation for having a large number of successful research students of high calibre. With each additional success their own professional status is raised. Of course, the converse is also true: it is possible for academics to go down in the estimation of their peers by having a succession of students who drop out, do work of poor quality or take an exceptional amount of time to complete their theses. But those supervisors who have one or more ex-research students who are now professors speak of the achievements of these graduates as though they were their own.

There are at least two kinds of supervisor. Some supervisors believe that postgraduates should be encouraged to become autonomous researchers. Others believe they should be encouraged to become extremely efficient research assistants. Some supervisors have not really thought about this matter specifically but nevertheless treat their research students in such a way that it is relatively simple to deduce which implicit theory of doctoral education and training they hold.

Some supervisors are dedicated to developing their favoured area of research by having several people exploring different, but related, problems. These people aim to build centres of excellence around themselves, which will attract visiting academics from other universities and other countries. In this way they are able to spend some time discussing their work with other specialists. They may also be able to arrange an occasional seminar given by a well-known expert. Students of these academics are likely to find that they are given small, well-defined problems that closely border the research problems being pursued by other researchers attached to their supervisor.

There are also those few senior academics who aim to become eligible for a Nobel prize or other senior honour. What this means for their students is that they will be treated as research assistants and expected to do the work set out for them by the professor, in the limited manner of a subordinate.

As well as those who wish to get the work done as speedily and efficiently as possible, there are those supervisors who are genuinely interested in producing more and better researchers. They are prepared to offer a service of supervision to research students in the same way as they offer a service of teaching to undergraduate students. What this means for students is that they will be expected to develop their own topics for research and to operate in a more individual manner. This approach gives more autonomy but entails a more restricted academic peer group.

Thus supervisors have many different reasons for agreeing to add to work already being undertaken by engaging in the supervision of research students. Not all of these aims are mutually exclusive. It is necessary, however, for students to discover which approach a prospective supervisor favours in order to evaluate the implications for what will be expected of them.

It is also important for incoming doctoral students to be clear whether they wish to become autonomous researchers or superior research assistants, as well as for supervisors to become aware of which type of researcher is best suited to help them further their own aims.

Of course, we realize that it will be difficult for you, as a beginning research student, to understand fully the implications of this discussion. It will be even more difficult to act on such considerations. Two things that you could do are: talk to other research students in the department about their experience of supervision, and introduce into the preliminary discussions with any potential supervisor an exploration of their preferred way of working with their students.

■ Aims of examiners

External examiners are academics from universities other than your own and are used to ensure that, within a given discipline, standards of quality for which the PhD degree is awarded are uniform across universities. Some examiners see the aims of the PhD to be a training for a career in research, some as an introduction to writing books, some as preparation for the academic life and some, as we have suggested, to become a fully rounded professional.

Whether examiners are more interested in the research, the thesis or the performance of the candidate in the oral examination, they are looking for a command of the subject area (or context) of the research, as well as the specific topic. The British PhD is awarded for an original contribution to knowledge. Yet, as we shall see in Chapter 6, originality in the PhD is a complex concept which has not yet been adequately defined. Nevertheless, examiners need to be satisfied that the work has a degree of originality and that it is the genuine work of the candidate.

Examiners acquire reputations for their performance in this role. Some become known as difficult to please while others are prepared to take the supervisor's evaluation of the work almost without question. Some examiners make the oral examination a real test of professional knowledge and exposition, while others allow it to be more of a relaxed conversation between friends.

The reputations that the examiners acquire do sometimes affect their selection, especially when it is left to the supervisor to choose. Some candidates find that their external examiners have been chosen on the basis of how highly their supervisors regard the students' work. For example, if a supervisor thinks that a particular student will only just satisfy requirements, a less exacting examiner may be chosen. If, on the other hand, the supervisor considers the student's work to be of considerable merit a tough examiner is chosen and the student then has the advantage of being passed by somebody who adds prestige to the new PhD's success. However, such a system is far from universal and can be extremely unpopular.

Dr George, a supervisor who also has special responsibility for research students in his department said: 'I'm against the practice of getting a lesser academic, or a friend, for a weaker student but I know it happens and it has happened here.'

■ Aims of universities and research councils

Government-funded research councils provide studentships for British full-time doctoral students in science and social science, as does the British Academy for arts students. In the past they have taken a fairly relaxed view in evaluating what happened after the studentship had been awarded, considering this a matter for the academic discretion of the particular department and supervisor involved, but this is no longer so.

The commonest way of not succeeding is to drop out. Very few people actually fail. The historically high drop-out rate of students has led the councils in the past decade to require universities to demonstrate that they have an effective student support system in place. They have issued guidelines on what is good practice in matters such as induction sessions for new students, research environments, supervisory arrangements and appeals and complaints procedures. They have issued league tables of completion rates and universities who do not perform satisfactorily run the risk of not receiving any allocation of research student grants. The universities can apply for reinstatement after a period when they have to demonstrate that their support arrangements have improved.

The effect of these policies has been to make academic institutions much more concerned to control the education which takes place during the PhD to ensure that it is of high quality. They have reviewed their supervisory practices, established doctoral programmes, strengthened the procedures for monitoring the progress of research students, and so on. Academics with overall departmental responsibility for doctoral students have been appointed. This book itself is an illustration of the way in which attempts are continually being made to make the doctoral educational process more effective.

The aim of research councils is to get a high proportion of full-time doctoral students to complete within four years, and universities work to bring this about. The criterion of a successful completion for these purposes is defined as: the submission of the thesis for first examination four years after registration as a full-time student. Any referral as a result of the examination is not taken into account.

From the student's point of view the positive effects are that much more interest and care are being devoted to making the process work efficiently, and you should make sure that you get the benefits of these developments.

A possible negative effect is that you may be forced to take a narrower view of your research than you might like in order to complete within the stated time. Always remember, though, that there will be opportunities for further research on related issues after you have obtained your PhD.

■ Mismatches and problems

Once we begin to see where the aims of the different groups involved with the PhD are not congruent, it is not too big a step to realize that certain conflicts are inherent in the system.

For example, where a student who wishes to develop an area of research and make a significant contribution to it is paired with a leading supervisor who is more interested in speedy problem-solving, both of them will inevitably feel frustrated. Diana in biochemistry started by looking for 'the truth' and spending a lot of time working on important experiments even though they would not form part of her thesis. At this stage Professor Drake, whose concern was focused on findings, showed little interest and tended to leave her alone for long periods. He became more interested in her work when she began 'churning out results'. Once this happened, quite far into her registration period, she said: 'My change of attitude means that instead of experimenting for the sake of getting answers I'm now experimenting in order to get graphs that can be published.' This was more satisfying for him but less satisfying for her.

By contrast, where a student is more interested in obtaining answers and the leading supervisor wants to develop an area of research it will not be long before they both feel irritated with the situation. Such was the case of Freddy and Professor Forsdike:

> I intend to tell the Prof. that he has to have very good justification for my working after the 31st March. It has to be something vital and important. All the poisoning work was never in the original project outline and most of the additional experimental work he gives me is quite irrelevant to my thesis.

Here the supervisor is encouraging the student to go beyond the boundaries of his thesis problem and pursue the leads that result from the original experiments. The student, however, wants no more than to complete a bounded series of experiments and write them up for a PhD.

If a supervisor is interested in discussing new ideas and exploring untested areas but is responsible merely for ensuring that the student completes a thesis of the required standard in a reasonable amount of time, the work of supervision becomes less than satisfying. Mrs Briggs, a supervisor in the Arts faculty of a university, was disenchanted with the university's perception of what a PhD means now compared to the more relaxed and longer time scales before pressures for completion became the norm, but she was very much enjoying supervising a postgraduate of whom she said:

> He's always telling me things I don't know and that's exciting – except, of course, I can't know whether the things he's telling me are accurate. I try to make up to him for not being an ideal supervisor by giving him enthusiasm. He knows I think that he's interesting. I don't want to let him down – he's such a very good research student. I introduce him to others in the field who *are* experts, and then he can approach them at any time he wishes for more specialist knowledge. He should finish the PhD in three years. He says it's a life's work, and I agree that it could easily be, but the PhD is not a life's work and he must finish it quickly.

This supervisor is admitting that supervision can be of benefit to the supervisor herself, and this is quite commonly the case. Indeed supervisors can expect their students to be able to introduce them to new developments within the field of their thesis topic, and equally they must accept that they are not the only source of academic knowledge and professional skill for the student. Another benefit to supervisors nowadays is to have the number of PhDs they have supervised to successful completion on their CVs.

These cases show the kinds of juggling that have to occur between defining the boundaries of the research and managing the time available for writing the thesis. Whether it is the student or the supervisor who takes the major responsibility for this does not alter the fact that decisions regarding what is appropriate, relevant and necessary have to be made throughout the student's period of registration.

■ Action summary

1. Set out to discover the standards and achievements for a fully professional researcher in your discipline that justify the award of the PhD degree.
2. Read others' PhD theses in your field and evaluate them for the degree of originality in the research which has satisfied the examiners.
3. Be aware that the initial enthusiasm for the research will inevitably decline eventually. Provide the determination and application (rather than brilliance) that are required to complete the work and obtain the degree.
4. Use the full range of services that your university makes available to ensure that you have proper support in your studies.

5   The tension between the boundaries of the research project and the time available to complete it should be continually reviewed and adjusted by the student and the supervisors.

HOW NOT TO GET A PhD

We want now to examine some very well-established ways of *not* getting a PhD. These tried and tested ways of failing apply to all fields and have to be pondered continually by research students. You have to be clear what your position is on each of the seven ways of failing that we shall discuss if you are not to fall into the traps they offer. As we shall see, just to have them pointed out to you is not enough to avoid them. Most offer real blandishments that have to be determinedly resisted.

■ Not wanting a PhD

The first method of not getting a PhD is not to *want* a PhD. This may seem very strange, considering that a student is likely to be starving in a garret, living on a studentship pittance, perhaps having given up a job in order to study, or relying on the earnings of a spouse to put them through the course. At the very least, you will be devoting a great deal of time and effort and energy to research. Surely, you might say, considering what I am giving up to the project, can there be any doubt that I really want a PhD?

Strangely enough, there can be. We think an analogy would help here. It is the case, isn't it, that none of us, research students and research supervisors, want to become millionaires? We should quite like it if someone gave us a million pounds and we didn't have to do anything for it, not even buy a lottery ticket – that would sound like a good idea. But we don't want to *set out* to become millionaires. Obviously we don't; otherwise we wouldn't be considering how to do research and get PhDs – we would be considering how to build a better mousetrap, to invent an innovative piece of computer software, to play the property market, to write bestselling novels . . . There are many ways of making a million pounds, but doing a PhD is not likely to be one of them.

Exactly the same phenomenon occurs in regard to PhDs. People think it would be a nice idea to do a PhD, they come with views of what they want to do and then they turn round and say: 'Please can I have a PhD for it?' And the answer is often 'No'. PhDs are given for a particular form and level of research activity (which we shall discuss in Chapters 5 and 6) and if you do not wish to carry out this work then you effectively do not want to do a PhD. It is precisely the same distinction as that between hoping to become a millionaire and setting out to make a million pounds.

Clearly the purpose of this book is to help you to set out to obtain a PhD, and for this you need a degree of single-mindedness, a willingness to discover what is realistically required, and a determination to carry it out. This is the sense in which you must want a PhD, and this 'wanting' is important in that it has to work very hard for you. For example, it has to carry you through occasions when what you are doing may seem very pointless or fruitless, or when you ask yourself the question 'Why have I got myself into this?' or 'Why am I inflicting this on my family?' You cannot expect with an activity as demanding as doing a PhD that the intrinsic satisfaction (such as the interest of doing the research, the enjoyment of discussing your subject with other like-minded researchers) will be sufficient on its own to carry you through. You must always have a clear eye on the extrinsic satisfactions (your commitment to the whole exercise of doing a PhD, its necessary place in your career progression, and so on); you must want to do it.

There are, unfortunately, many who turn up as beginning PhD students who do not want to do a PhD in this sense. Particularly vulnerable are those who lack clear career goals and those who are using the PhD process as a vehicle for a career change:

> Jason was very intelligent and sailed through his undergraduate degree course in biochemistry. He spent a good deal of his time on student union affairs and was very involved in Green Party issues. In spite of this, with intense revision in the two weeks before each year's exams, he got an upper second in his finals. He was delighted to be offered a research studentship in the department, which allowed him to research a topic in the chemistry of reduction of organic residues. But he did not cut down on his outside commitments to campaigning on green issues, seeing them as highly relevant to the 'political' aspects of his research. When he first presented useful ideas that he might study, Dr Jacobs, his lead supervisor, was impressed and she encouraged him to develop a research design. But it became clear that he was more interested in sketching out the ideas than in

buckling down to designing a viable research study and carrying it out. When challenged, he always came up with a new and better suggestion for the research and promised to develop it. He carried on like this right until the end of his first year, when Dr Jacobs indicated forcefully to him that she considered that he did not have any chance at all of obtaining a PhD unless he gave up all his outside activities and concentrated on his research work. Unless he did this, she was not prepared to support the second year of his grant. Jason was nonplussed by this ultimatum, as he had always considered extracurricular activity to be an indispensable part of student life. At this time he had the opportunity to work full-time for a period on a Green political campaign, and he left the university to pursue this activity.

Iris, a teacher for many years, developed an interest in a particular specialism (multi-ethnic curriculum development) and thought she would like to do research in order to establish herself in this new subject. She found that doing research was taking her farther and farther away from dealing with what she saw as the real issues of pupils in the classroom in favour of a measurement-orientated form of 'science' to which she was unsympathetic. She left and returned to teaching.

■ Not understanding the nature of a PhD by overestimating what is required

The words used to describe the outcome of a PhD project – 'an original contribution to knowledge' – may sound rather grand, but we must remember that, as we saw in Chapter 3, the work for the degree is essentially a *research training* process and the term 'original contribution' has perforce to be interpreted quite narrowly. It does not mean an enormous breakthrough that has the subject rocking on its foundations, and research students who think that it does (even if only subconsciously or in a half-formed way) will find the process pretty debilitating.

Of course, if you are capable of a major contribution then go ahead and make it (there are still, for example, a few scientists who have an FRS but not a PhD) – but this is a strategy for getting an honorary degree, not for getting a PhD! For those not in that position – that is, most of us – an original contribution can be rather limited in its scope and indeed should be: apply this theory in a different setting, evaluate the effects of raising the temperature, solve this puzzling oddity or review this little-known historical event. In Chapter 6 we give a detailed discussion of the concept of originality in relation to the PhD.

We find that when we make this point, some social science students who have read Kuhn's (1970) work on 'paradigm shifts' in the history of natural science (science students have normally not heard of him) say rather indignantly: 'Oh, do you mean a PhD has to be just doing normal science?' And indeed we do mean that. Paradigm shifts are major changes in the explanatory schemes of the science, which happen only rarely when the inadequacies of the previous framework have become more and more limiting. Normal science is the ordinary research that goes on between major theoretical changes. It serves to elaborate the general explanatory paradigm used and to tease out difficulties and puzzles that are not yet sufficiently well explained. It is the basic useful activity of scientists and scholars, and PhD students should be pleased to make a contribution to it.

You can leave the paradigm shifts for *after* your PhD, and empirically that is indeed what happens. The theory of relativity (a classic example of a paradigm shift in relation to post-Newtonian physics) was not Einstein's PhD thesis (that was a sensible contribution to Brownian motion theory). *Das Kapital* was not Marx's PhD (that was on the theories of two little-known Greek philosophers). Of course, while doing their PhDs Einstein and Marx were undoubtedly preparing themselves for the great question-ings that led to the big shifts, but they were also demonstrating their fully professional mastery of the established paradigms.

As we saw in Chapter 3, it is this professionalism that the PhD is about. To think it is more than that can be very debilitating. You can wait for a long time for a new paradigm to strike. Overestimating is a powerful way of not getting a PhD. Here are two classic cases:

> Bob insisted that it would not be 'real' research if he read up in books and journals what others had done on the problem that he wished to tackle; his thinking would be entirely shaped by what they had done and he would only be able to add something minor. He felt that his only chance of being really innovative was not to read anything further in the field (he had a bachelor's and a relevant master's degree in the subject) but to sit down and design an investigation into the problem he was proposing to research (concerned with adult learning of skills), which he knew well from a practical point of view as an industrial trainer. This took quite a long time, as his knowledge of research methods was not that strong.
>
> When he did present his proposal to Dr Bishop, his supervisor, she was not impressed. As this field was not her own particular speciality, Dr Bishop went to the library and looked up all the current year's issues of the relevant journals. In one of them she found a paper reporting a study on Bob's topic that (not surprisingly, since it was completed and published) was considerably better than Bob's attempt. She used this paper to support her argument that he would

have to make a comprehensive search of relevant published material if he were to have a chance of designing an adequate study which would make a contribution. But Bob saw this as a negation of what he wanted to do and withdrew.

While Phil was carrying out the fieldwork stage of his research into the motivation of managers, he became very involved with his subjects. He felt that it would be a betrayal if they were to get no benefit from his research because it was written up in a dull academic book that no one would read. Most research was like that, Phil maintained, and was therefore neglected by everyone except the next lot of researchers. What was needed was a research report that could really communicate. Why couldn't we have a PhD thesis that would read like a novel so that it would become accessible?

Phil took this idea very seriously. He wrote to a novelist whose works he admired for some suggestions on how to write his thesis. He took an extra year to write up the material, letting no one see anything on the way, on the grounds that you don't show a novel to anyone until it is completed. When he did finally present his complete thesis, his supervisor thought it was inadequate, unrigorous and indulgently subjective. He asked Phil to rewrite it, but he refused and thus did not get a PhD.

We hasten to emphasize that this example is not intended to deprecate writing research results for lay people, a very necessary activity that all researchers should take seriously. It is about overestimating what can be done with a PhD and therefore falling flat on your face. Nor does it mean that in writing for your academic peers you should neglect clear expression and interesting presentation – as we discuss in Chapter 6.

■ Not understanding the nature of a PhD by underestimating what is required

Underestimating is always a problem if not corrected, but is particularly damaging in two situations.

First, it is a problem for those researching part-time and continuing in their jobs, or for those coming back to academic life after a long period in the 'real world'. It is basically the difficulty of understanding what is meant by 'research', since the word is used much more strictly in the academic than in the non-academic sphere. We shall discuss the nature of research activity in Chapter 5, but here we can just note that the layperson's view that 'research is finding out something you don't know' is not adequate, that most of the activities described as 'market research' or 'research for a TV programme' do not fulfil the criteria of research required for a PhD.

PhD research requires a contribution to the analysis and explanation of the topic, not just description. It requires an understanding that it is as important a part of the research process to fashion the questions properly as it is to develop interesting answers. It is an underestimation of what is required to accept a lay formulation of either questions or answers – even if they somehow appear more relevant – and it is a clear way of not getting a PhD. Here is an example:

> Chris was a financial manager who thought that a research degree would be a good insurance should he wish in the future to become a management lecturer, and so he enrolled part-time for a PhD degree. He wanted to do his research on the financial control systems of his firm, about which he naturally knew a very great deal. He thought that it would be easy to do some research into a topic on which he was one of the experts, but he seriously underestimated the fact that research means finding good questions as well as good answers.
>
> Chris was not able to formulate research questions very well himself. When Dr Clapp, his supervisor, began suggesting a number of questions that he might investigate, Chris would take them up enthusiastically in discussion and give 'the answer' as he knew it to be. After treating a series of possible topics in this way, it became clear that he really did not have any need to do research since he knew all the answers anyway – at least at a level that satisfied him. After Dr Clapp impressed on him that research requires actively challenging old explanations and finding new ones if necessary, his enthusiasm waned and he dropped out.

The second form of underestimating is particularly a problem for science students working in a lab and contributing a project as part of a bigger research programme. In this situation, the programme director, typically also the lead supervisor, is very keen to get the results of the students' experiments in order to push the programme forward. Students are very happy to feel that they are contributing. But the danger is that they are not exercising the full range of professional skills required to be demonstrated in the PhD. These are spelled out in Chapter 6 on the form of the PhD thesis and include, in addition to carrying out the actual experiment, the design of the investigation, the analysis of the results, and the writing up of the results into a thesis. To obtain the PhD, students have to show they are capable of all these activities; to miss out on any of them is to underestimate what is required. Here is an example.

Gary's project was part of a research programme in plasma physics. He worked hard to collect the data that he had agreed with his supervisor were needed for his PhD. His supervisor, Professor Ganesh, was very interested in the results and on several occasions took the material and wrote it up for a conference paper. Gary was pleased with this and felt he was making a contribution on the data side. But it meant that he had no writing practice beyond completing his lab reports. In his final year Gary was faced with a pile of records and had to do his own writing. On the first occasion that he tried, he sat with a blank sheet of paper in front of him but did not manage to write anything. After half an hour, he went back to the data because he felt more comfortable tidying up the records. He tried sitting down to write on several more occasions, with no more than a few pages to show for it. He cheered up when Professor Ganesh suggested another piece of empirical work that he could do, and he busied himself in carrying it out.

The writing work still had to be done, however, and the PhD registration period was running out. Professor Ganesh was sympathetic to Gary's predicament. To show him how to do it, the professor took an inadequate draft of Gary's and wrote up a section that could go straight into Gary's PhD. But he pointed out that he could not write the thesis *for* Gary, who now had to do it himself.

■ Not having a supervisor who knows what a PhD requires

If it is important for a student not to over- or underestimate the nature of a PhD, it is equally important to have a supervisor who does not do so. We shall be discussing issues of supervision in detail in Chapters 8 and 11, and so here we will just point out that first, inadequate supervision is a major cause of not getting a PhD, and second, since the penalties to students of not succeeding are much greater than to their supervisors, in the end it is up to determined students to get the supervision they need and are entitled to.

Supervisors may under- or overestimate what is required. One key cause of underestimation is lack of research experience on the part of supervisors. In our view the most important single characteristic of effective supervisors is that of being themselves involved in ongoing research and publication. They can thus give advice from current knowledge of the field, and can act as role models through their own practice. Otherwise problems will arise.

Sophia came to Britain on a government scholarship from a country that has little tradition of empirical research in her field. She was allocated to a supervisor who had good practical experience but who had not in fact done any research himself. She worked away by herself, with occasional comments from him that he thought a particular section very interesting. But he had badly underestimated the nature of a PhD. When she submitted her thesis the external examiner said that, in his opinion, it was so completely inadequate that there was no point in having the oral examination or in allowing a resubmission. She returned to her country sadder, if not wiser.

Sophia's case points up not only the problem of inadequate supervision, but also the problem that she was not aware of the deficiencies under which she was working. As we discuss in Chapter 9, these are issues that overseas students may find more difficult to cope with. All students, however, must ensure that they discuss their work with several academics and with their peers, and that they regularly read accepted PhD theses in their field to discover the standards that are required.

Overestimating supervisors, often with best of intentions, is also a problem. Here is an example.

Professor Shepherd is a supervisor very few of whose students finish their PhDs. This is surprising, because he is a well known academic in his field, has a lively intelligence and an outgoing personality – which is why he continues to attract students to supervise. But Professor Shepherd believes in treating research students as adults, as he puts it, forgetting that students are babes in research terms. He believes that it is the supervisor's job to challenge his students, to shake them up mentally, to bombard them with new ideas. He goes on doing this throughout the duration of the research, even when more convergence, more limitations are required to complete the study. Because of this overestimation, many students find they have taken on too large a project, which they do not see becoming more focused. They get disheartened and drop out.

■ Losing contact with your supervisor

As we said above, the penalties of failure are greater for the student than for the supervisor. The relationship is not one of equality, so the student has to work harder to keep in touch with the supervisor than the other way around. As we discussed in Chapter 3, the nature of the PhD process requires continual input from the supervisor if the student is to learn the craft of research and how to apply it to the particular topic under study. The details of managing this interaction fruitfully on both sides are covered in Chapters 8 and 11. Here we will just illustrate the inevitable catastrophic effect which results if contact is lost.

Tony got bogged down 18 months into his project. After a long session with his supervisor he decided that he wanted to change direction. His supervisor said that it was impossible to do so at this stage and he should carry on – even though it was now clear that more work would be required than originally envisaged, with a weaker outcome anyway. Tony did not agree and tried to persuade his supervisor to allow greater modifications. His supervisor explained that this was not sensible within the available timescale, and pressed him to carry on with the original design. They saw each other less and less because Tony felt that they were talking at cross-purposes. After four months they ceased to have any meetings; after six months Tony was observed rushing into a lecture room to avoid his supervisor whom he saw coming towards him along the corridor. He never submitted his thesis.

David's supervisor, Professor Dickinson, was one of the leading academics in Britain in her field. She died tragically when David was at the end of his second year. His supervision was taken over by an experienced researcher whose range of concerns was different and who had only a general interest in David's topic.

David did not think it necessary to tell his new supervisor in any detail what he was doing, having it clear in his mind that Professor Dickinson would have given her approval. He thus worked without supervision for a further 18 months. When he came to submit his thesis the examiners felt that he had suffered from lack of supervision, which in the circumstances should be taken into account, but that they could award him only an MPhil, not a PhD. He appealed, but in due course the university confirmed the decision.

David's enforced change of supervisor was due to a particularly tragic event. Supervisors leave for happier reasons too, and often it is necessary to be handed on to another supervisor. In these circumstances it is particularly incumbent on the student to make good contact with the new supervisor, whose knowledge and skills are a crucial input to getting a PhD.

■ Not having a thesis

Words develop in meaning, and the word 'thesis' is nowadays commonly used to refer to the project report of the research undertaken for the PhD. Thus the regulations of your university may say that your thesis may be not more than a certain number of words in length, that it must be presented in black/blue/red binding, and so on. (Incidentally, these regulations differ for different institutions and they also change over time, so it is important for you to check those that apply to you, as discussed in Chapter 10.)

But there is an earlier use of the word 'thesis' that is very important to the task of obtaining a PhD. A thesis in this sense is something that you wish to argue, a *position* that you wish to maintain (the word 'thesis' derives from the Greek for 'place'). For example, the Reformation began when Martin Luther nailed a list of 95 theses to the door of Wittenberg church – statements of his beliefs, which he wished to maintain against the Roman Church of that time. C. P. Snow propounded the thesis that British intellectuals inhabit two separate cultures – literary and scientific – which hardly overlap. It is *our* thesis that it is crucial for students wanting to obtain a PhD that they understand fully the objectives of the exercise and the nature of the processes involved, which is why we have written this book.

Your PhD must have a thesis in this sense. It must argue a position. At the minimum this means that the study must have a 'storyline', a coherent thrust that pushes along an argument, an explanation, a systematic set of inferences derived from new data or new ways of viewing current data. Often when trying to come to grips with the tough-minded pruning of material that this involves, you will feel that you are losing useful data or important points. Relevance to the argument is the stern criterion, however. Your thesis has to organize data to increase the richness of your work and focus argument to increase its cogency. It is not enough for your thesis report to be 'a short trot with a cultured mind'.

It may be that the thesis you are arguing has been decomposed into a number of 'hypo-theses' (hypotheses) each of which will be tested for its adequacy. In this case you must relate them to each other to maintain the general thrust of your argument. If you are not working in the hypothesis-testing mode you must still ensure that your discussions add up to a coherent argument. This is how the adequacy of your contribution is judged. As with all the other ways of not getting a PhD, this is easier to say than to do, particularly if you do not have good guidance in the early stages of your research, when the temptation to spread yourself too widely and too thinly is greatest.

> Harry started out to study factors affecting industrial marketing strategies. This is a large field and he was able to tackle the issues only rather superficially. Some of the chapters in his thesis report made some good points, others were rather poor, but none of the aspects was at all related to the others in a cumulative way. The examiners said that his thesis 'did not add up to anything' and rejected it.

> Graham was the administrator of a voluntary organization. He registered for a PhD because he felt that not enough was known about

how to manage such organizations; more research was needed to make administrators in this field more professional. He spent his first year reading a great deal about administration and thinking how the ideas could be applied to help administrators in voluntary organizations. When he was asked how his research could help them, he said that he wanted to write a textbook describing good administrative practices. There then followed a long period of trying to get through to him that without a thesis his work would not earn a PhD, though it might well be a useful project to do in itself. In the end he reluctantly accepted this.

We must emphasize that it is not the notion of a textbook *per se* that makes it inadequate for a PhD but the lack of a thesis. A textbook that incorporated a well-argued, justified thesis – for example, that accepted views are inadequate when the data are critically re-examined, or that the field can be reinterpreted fruitfully in the light of a new theory – would be very acceptable.

■ Taking a new job before finishing

Doing a PhD is an intellectually demanding enterprise, and this is true at all stages of the work. It is especially true of the final stage of writing up. Most students radically underestimate the amount of time and effort that this stage will require. They somehow think that having surveyed the field, designed the study, collected and analysed the data, it is downhill from then on to the presentation of the thesis. It is not so. Writing up demands the most concentrated effort of the whole process.

There are a number of reasons for this. The first is emotional: it is difficult to avoid feeling that writing is a chore, after the 'real' work has been done. There are always ambivalent feelings about the study itself and a barely suppressed desire to run away from it all, now that the data are actually there for others to see.

The second reason is intellectual: unless you are extremely lucky and everything turns out exactly as planned, there will at this stage be quite a lot of adjustment to be done in your argument, in your interpretation, and in your presentation to put the best face on the material you have available. This is an extremely demanding test of professional competence, and it is in fact at this stage that you have really to demonstrate that you are worth a PhD.

There is a third reason concerned with limitations in writing skill and experience. Few students have written anything as long as a PhD thesis before, and to complete it requires a considerable effort.

For all these reasons, writing up is not the time to take a new job. Apart from the physical dislocation, which makes intellectual work difficult and therefore easily postponed, a new job is likely to require you to concentrate your attention on a new range of issues which, particularly if they are academic ones, will inevitably get in the way of writing up through intellectual fatigue. Here is an example.

> Martin, in his late 30s, felt trapped in his job and was desperately looking for a way out which would lead to a new career. He decided to register as a full-time research student and live on a scholarship (somewhat supplemented because of his age and two children) and his wife's earnings, but at the end of the second year he felt he could no longer stand the strain of the financial hardship. In spite of dire warnings from his supervisors, he took a job which involved a move to another part of the country and switched to part-time registration for his PhD. He fully intended to carry on writing up his research results, but found it increasingly difficult to find the time to do the work or meet his supervisors. His registration time ran out and he did not submit.

The only job it is possible to do, perhaps one that you are doing already or have done before, is one that allows you to operate in 'intellectual overdrive'. Taking a new job before finishing is a way of not getting a PhD.

Remember that, rather confusingly, the terms 'thesis' and 'dissertation' are used in different ways in different parts of the world. In the US, master's students write 'theses' whereas in Australia and Britain, they write 'dissertations'. At the PhD level, however, these terms are reversed. Hence, in America an unfinished PhD project may allow the student to join the ranks of those whom the Americans call the 'ABDs' the 'all-but-dissertation' brigade. Ex-students might put this on their CVs (or resumés) and potential employers consider it as a possible benefit. However, it means that the candidates did not complete what they set out to do. We in the UK call this 'failure'.

■ Action summary

[1] Be aware of the seven ways of not getting a PhD:

- ☐ not wanting a PhD;
- ☐ overestimating what is required;
- ☐ underestimating what is required;
- ☐ having a supervisor who does not know what is required;
- ☐ losing contact with your supervisor;
- ☐ not having a 'thesis' (as in position or argument) to maintain;
- ☐ taking a new job before completing.

2. Work to understand the implications of these traps fully in your own situation and determine not to succumb to them.

3. Re-establish your determination regularly when blandishments to stray from your programme of work recur.

5

HOW TO DO RESEARCH

As we noted in Chapter 1, this book does not consider those aspects of research design and methodology which are specific to each discipline, and even to each topic within a discipline. To explore those issues, you will need the appropriate textbooks and handbooks for your subject. The current issues of journals in your field will show demonstrations of state-of-the-art methodological practices relevant to your work.

Here we discuss some general background philosophical issues concerned with the practice of research relevant to all disciplines. We start with the basic question: What is research? This is not as simple a question as it seems. We are going to explore some answers to it and examine their relevance to the nature of a PhD.

■ Characteristics of research

Let us start with a lay view: 'Research is finding out something you don't know.' This answer is both too wide and too narrow. It is too wide because it includes many activities, such as finding out the time of the next train to London, or taking the temperature of the water in the swimming pool, which we would not characterize as research. Take a moment to consider why we would not do so. And if we were measuring instead the pH value of the water – its acidity or alkalinity – would that be research?

As well as being too wide, that definition is also too narrow, because a lot of research is concerned not with finding out something you don't know but with finding that you don't know something. This sort of research aims to reorientate our thinking, to make us question what we think we do know, and to focus on new aspects of our complex reality.

In exploring the nature of research, it is useful to distinguish it from another activity: intelligence-gathering.

■ Intelligence-gathering – the 'what' questions

There are a lot of things that we don't know and that we could find out. What are the age, sex and subject distributions of doctoral students in British higher education? What are the radiation levels in different parts of the UK? What percentage of Britain's GNP is spent on scientific research? These 'what' questions are very important. They require careful definition of terms, unbiased collection of information, meticulous statistical treatment and careful summarizing to get a balanced description of the situation that gives 'a true and fair picture', to use a phrase from the accounting profession. Inevitably some arbitrary decisions will have to be made. Conventions are developed that can help to improve comparability – in the measurement of high temperatures, the definition of the money supply, the genetic classification into male and female sexes, etc. – but professionals can and do differ on what they regard as fair, and informed judgement is called for. For example, it is a matter of considerable controversy at present as to what would be a true and fair way to define, and therefore count and categorize, the number of bureaucrats employed in government, the climatic effects on the atmosphere of global warming, and so on.

Since this work is descriptive, answering the 'what' questions, it can be considered as 'intelligence-gathering' – using the term in the military sense. Intelligence-gathering is an important activity and intelligence is a valued commodity. A profit-and-loss account of a business, a map giving radiation levels in different parts of the country, a compilation of the evaluations by doctoral students of the quality of supervision they receive, are all examples of intelligence with important uses.

We may use the profit-and-loss account as part of a financial control system, the radiation-level map to develop nuclear siting policies, the doctoral students' evaluations to make decisions on selection and training of supervisors, etc. Control mechanisms, policy formulation and decision-making are the typical uses of intelligence. These are all absolutely vital activities – but they are not research.

■ Research – the 'why' questions

Research goes beyond description and requires analysis. It looks for explanations, relationships, comparisons, predictions, generalizations and theories. These are the 'why' questions. Why are there so many fewer women doctoral students in physics than in biology? Why are the radiation levels different in different geographical areas? Why is the productivity per worker-hour in British manufacturing industry less that that of France or Germany?

All these questions require good intelligence-gathering, just as decision-making and policy formulation do. But the information is used for the purpose of developing understanding – by comparison, by relating to other factors, by theorizing and testing the theories. All research questions have comparisons in them, as the words 'fewer', 'different' and 'less' in the examples above illustrate. All research questions also involve generalization. To be useful, explanations should be applicable in all appropriate situations. These are the focus of PhD study.

■ Characteristics of good research

There are three distinct but interrelated characteristics of good research which distinguish this activity from others such as intelligence-gathering, decision-making and so on.

Research is based on an open system of thought

For you as a researcher, the world is in principle your oyster. You are entitled to think anything. There are no hidden agendas, no closed systems; in American terms 'everything is up for grabs'. This continual testing, review and criticism for its *own* sake by researchers of each other's work is an important way in which thinking develops. Conventional wisdom and accepted doctrine are not spared this examination because they may turn out to be inadequate. Of course they may not turn out to be inadequate; they may stand up to examination. This is why non-researchers often regard research results as being demonstrations of the obvious or trivial elaborations of established knowledge. This examination, however, has to be done continually because this is how we probe for what is not obvious and discover elaborations that are not trivial. The key to the approach is to keep firmly in mind that the classic position of a researcher is not that of one who knows the right answers but of one who is struggling to find out what the right questions might be!

Researchers examine data critically

This characteristic of research is clearly part of the first one. We list it separately because it is probably the most important single element in distinguishing a research approach from others and researchers from practitioners and laypeople. Researchers examine data and the sources of data critically so that the basic research approach to provocative statements ('women make less effective managers than men'; 'soft drugs are less harmful to health than alcohol'; 'renewable energy sources cannot provide for all our needs in the foreseeable future') is not to agree or disagree but to ask: 'What is your evidence?'

Researchers are continually having to ask: Have you got the facts right? Can we get better data? Can the results be interpreted differently? Nonresearchers often feel that they don't have the time for this and are thus impatient with research. Politicians and managers, for example, often need to make decisions under constraints of public pressure or time. Their need to act is more important than their need to understand. Researchers' priorities are of course different. They have to go to great trouble to get systematic, valid and reliable data because their aim is to understand and interpret.

Researchers generalize and specify the limits on their generalizations

It is the aim of research to obtain valid generalizations because this is the most efficient way of applying understanding in a wide variety of appropriate situations, but there are difficulties here. It was not a researcher but a novelist, Alexandre Dumas *fils*, who said: 'All generalizations are dangerous – including this one!' Indeed, research may be said to proceed by insightful but dangerous generalizations, which is why the limits of the generalization – where it applies and where it does not apply – must be continually tested.

The way generalizations can best be established is through the development of explanatory theory, and it is indeed the application of theory that turns intelligence-gathering into research. So to return to the question asked at the beginning of this chapter: would measuring the pH value of the water in a swimming pool be research? The answer would depend upon what we were going to do with the result, not on how complicated or how 'scientific' the measurement was. If the result were used to develop and test a theory of the factors that determine the acidity of water, it would be research; if it were used to make a decision on whether the pool was safe according to established criteria, then it would be intelligence-gathering.

■ Hypothetico–deductive method

So the examination of the adequacy of generalizations, formulated as hypotheses, is the cornerstone of research. 'Hypotheses,' said Medawar in 1964, 'are imaginative and inspirational in character'; they are 'adventures of the mind'. He was arguing in favour of the position taken by Karl Popper in *The Logic of Scientific Discovery* (1972, 3rd edn.) that the nature of scientific method is hypothetico–deductive and not, as is generally believed, inductive.

It is essential that you, as an intending researcher, understand the difference between these two interpretations of the research process so that you do not become discouraged or begin to suffer from a feeling of 'cheating' or not going about it the right way.

A popular misconception about scientific method is that it is inductive: that the formulation of scientific theory starts with the basic, raw evidence of the senses – simple, unbiased, unprejudiced observation. Out of these sensory data – commonly referred to as 'facts' – generalizations will form. The myth is that from a disorderly array of factual information an orderly, relevant theory will somehow emerge. However, the starting point of induction is an impossible one.

There is no such thing as unbiased observation. Every act of observation we make is a function of what we have seen or otherwise experienced in the past. All scientific work of an experimental or exploratory nature starts with some expectation about the outcome. This expectation is a hypothesis. Hypotheses provide the initiative and incentive for the inquiry and influence the method. It is in the light of an expectation that some observations are held to be relevant and some irrelevant, that one methodology is chosen and others discarded, that some experiments are conducted and others are not. Where is your naive, pure and objective researcher now?

Hypotheses arise by guesswork or by inspiration, but having been formulated they can and must be tested rigorously, using the appropriate methodology. If the predictions you make as a result of deducing certain consequences from your hypothesis are not shown to be correct then you must discard or modify your hypothesis. If the predictions turn out to be correct then your hypothesis has been supported and may be retained until such time as some further test shows it not to be correct. Once you have arrived at your hypothesis, which is a product of your imagination, you then proceed to a strictly logical and rigorous process, based upon deductive argument – hence the term 'hypothetico–deductive'.

So don't worry if you have some idea of what your results will tell you before you even begin to collect data; there are no scientists in existence who really wait until they have all the evidence in front of them before they try to work out what it might possibly mean. The closest we ever get to this situation is when something happens serendipitously; but even then the researcher has to formulate a hypothesis to be tested before being sure that, for example, a mould might prove to be a successful antidote to bacterial infection.

Another erroneous idea about scientific method is not only that it is inductive (which we have seen is incorrect) but also that the hypothetico–deductive method proceeds in a step-by-step, inevitable fashion. The hypothetico–deductive method describes the *logical* approach to much research work, but it does not describe the *psychological* behaviour that brings it about. This is much more holistic – involving guesses, reworkings, corrections, blind alleys and above all inspiration, in the deductive as well as the hypothetic component – than is immediately apparent from reading the final thesis or published papers. These have been, quite properly, organized into a more serial, logical order so that the worth of the *output* may be evaluated independently of the behavioural process by which it was obtained. It is the difference, for example, between the academic papers with which Crick and Watson demonstrated the structure of the DNA molecule (e.g. Watson and Crick 1953) and the fascinating book *The Double Helix* in which Watson (1968) described how they did it. From this point of view, 'scientific method' may more usefully be thought of as a way of *writing up* research rather than as a way of carrying it out.

■ Basic types of research

Research has traditionally been classified into two types: pure and applied. We find this distinction – implying as it does that pure research supplies the theories and applied research uses and tests them out in the real world – is too rigid to characterize what happens in most academic disciplines, where, for example, 'real-world' research generates its own theories and does not just apply 'pure' theories. We shall consider a threefold classification of research: exploratory, testing-out and problem-solving, which applies to both quantitative and qualitative research.

Exploratory research

This is the type of research that is involved in tackling a new problem/issue/topic about which little is known, so the research idea cannot at the beginning be formulated very well. The problem may come from any part of the discipline; it may be a theoretical research puzzle or have an empirical basis. The research work will need to examine what theories and concepts are appropriate, developing new ones if necessary, and whether existing methodologies can be used. It obviously involves pushing out the frontiers of knowledge in the hope that something useful will be discovered.

Testing-out research

In this type of research we are trying to find the limits of previously proposed generalizations. As we have discussed above, this is a basic research activity. Does the theory apply at high temperatures? In new technology industries? With working-class parents? Before universal franchise was introduced? The amount of testing out to be done is endless and continuous, because in this way we are able to improve (by specifying, modifying, clarifying) the important, but dangerous, generalizations by which our discipline develops.

Problem-solving research

In this type of research, we start from a particular problem in the real world, and bring together all the intellectual resources that can be brought to bear on its solution. The problem has to be defined and the method of solution has to be discovered. The person working in this way may have to create and identify original problem solutions every step of the way. This will usually involve a variety of theories and methods, often ranging across more than one discipline since real-world problems are likely to be 'messy' and not soluble within the narrow confines of an academic discipline.

■ Which type of research for the PhD?

Since we spent so much time in Chapter 4 discussing how not to get a PhD, let us now look on the more positive side and ask how to get a doctorate. Consider for a moment the three types of research that we have just reviewed. Which type is likely to offer the best chance of completing the degree successfully? Remember that we have already noted that the PhD is primarily a research training exercise to get you from being a mere beginner in research to the level of a full professional. All research involves working within particular constraints, but those of a PhD are very stringent. They include clear limitations on finance, physical resources, administrative back-up and, above all, time. So which of the three types of research would you choose as the best route at this stage of your career? Take a few moments to consider your decision and the reasons for it.

We hope that you will understand why it seems very obvious to us that the appropriate route is that of testing-out research. With this approach you will be working within an established framework and thus learning the craft of doing research in an environment that gives you some degree of protection by the established nature of much of the ideas, arguments, measuring equipment, etc. A degree of protection in the environment is the best situation for efficient learning: being thrown in at the deep end is all very heroic but it does tend to induce a phenomenon known as drowning!

Of course, you will have to make your original contribution – merely replicating what others have done is not adequate. So, for example, you will have to use a methodology on a new topic where it has not been applied before and therefore make manifest its strengths in giving new knowledge and theoretical insights. Or you will have to apply two competing theories to a new situation to see which is more powerful, or design a crucial experiment to produce evidence to choose between them. As a result you may produce your own innovative variant of the methodology or theory. There will always be an appropriate element of exploratory work and you may well solve some useful discipline-based problems on the way. Testing out is the basic ongoing professional task of academic research, and doctoral work done well in this framework is much more likely to be useful, and thus publishable and quotable.

On the other hand, the idea of tackling an exploratory topic which has little by way of conceptual frameworks seems very attractive. Potential employers give considerable weight to the 'real-world applicability' of the research undertaken by PhDs, as an Australian survey by Phillips and Zuber-Skerritt (1993) showed. It is also an approach that the British Government now wishes to encourage. There is no denying the appeal of tackling such topics, but you should be aware that the risks of failure are much greater. If you have a lot of confidence, stemming, say, from a great deal of practical experience and very strong support from your supervisor (who will inevitably be called upon to make a larger input) you might consider work in the exploratory or problem-solving approaches, but these are undoubtedly less structured and therefore professionally more advanced activities. Most students should be considering whether they can run before they can walk. If you are going to tackle a real-world problem, it may be that the more structured and limited project of a professional doctorate might be more appropriate for you (see pp. 196ff).

It is also fair to point out that even if you obtain a PhD for work that is completely exploratory or problem-solving, which is less likely anyway, there will almost inevitably be a considerable element of giving credit for a 'brave try' (examiners being kind people who look for ways of passing students). So in these circumstances it is less likely that your work will make sufficient impact to be publishable and quotable than if you do well in the testing-out approach. It will then serve you less well as a base on which to build a research career. It is a wise student who decides to postpone the pleasures of attempting to be totally original until after the PhD has been obtained.

■ The craft of doing research

Doing research is a craft skill, which is why the basic educational process that takes place is that of learning by doing. After you have decided on your research approach and the particular field in which you are going to learn your craft, you should be systematically considering how you are going to get the training that you require in each of the craft elements.

These are many and varied, and depend on your particular discipline. There may be courses that you may take, or may be required to take, which will develop your skills. But a key initial task is to watch established good researchers in your discipline and note down, as systematically as you can, what practices, skills and techniques they are using. Hopefully your supervisors will act as exemplar researchers, but you must examine and learn from others too.

Your second task is to practise these skills as much as you can, *getting feedback on how well you are doing*. Adults learn best in situations where they can practise and receive feedback in a controlled, non-threatening environment. So a good principle to aim for is: *no procedure, technique, skill, etc., which is relevant to your thesis project should be exercised by you there for the first time*. You should always have practised it beforehand on a non-thesis exercise, which is therefore going to be less stressful and will allow for greater learning. Your trial exercises will allow you to learn about your ability to carry out the range of professional skills that you need to develop. You will gain feedback, not only from your supervisor but also other professionals (e.g. computer people) and from your own evaluation of what you have done.

This may seem an eminently sensible principle, and you may wonder why we are labouring it. After all it is obvious that skills need to be practised if they are to be performed well. An art student doesn't expect the first oil painting she ever attempted to be exhibited at the Royal Academy, a poet doesn't expect his first poem to be publishable. They are likely to be apprentice pieces, learning experiences.

In fact, as regards PhD skills this issue is often not thought through well enough. If the thesis report, which is maybe 60,000–80,000 words long, is the first thing that the student has written longer than the answer to an examination question, a term essay or a lab report, then it is not surprising that it is a daunting task and poorly done. The skill practice has just not taken place. Analysing your data from the key experiment or survey you have just carried out is precisely not the time to discover for the first time the joys of getting your data into, and the results out of, a computer. You should have practised that craft skill beforehand. Again, it does not seem sensible to base your PhD thesis study on the first faltering questionnaire that you have ever tried to devise – but all too often people do, and later pay the price for their inevitably less than skilled performance in questionnaire design.

We could discuss many more examples of the skills that a doctoral student needs to set about acquiring. They range from the seemingly mundane but absolutely crucial ones of maintaining your lab apparatus and conducting a computer-based literature search, to the more conceptual ones of being able to evaluate quickly the relevance and value of published work. You will need to have found out what craft skills are relevant to your needs and to have practised them, so that in your thesis project you can apply them with some confidence.

■ Action summary

[1] Consider very carefully the advantage of doing 'testing-out' research for your PhD.

[2] From observation and discussion with your supervisor and other academics, construct a list of the craft practices that characterize a good professional researcher in your discipline.

[3] Aim to ensure that no procedure, technique, skill, etc., that is relevant to your project will be exercised by you there for the first time.

[4] Find out from researchers in your subject how the scientific approach actually works in practice.

6

THE FORM OF A PhD THESIS

Three of the key ways of not getting a PhD that we discussed in Chapter 4 involved either the student or the supervisor (or both) not understanding the nature of a PhD degree. This demonstration that you are a full professional requires the exercise of the craft of doing research, as discussed in Chapter 5, in such a way as to satisfy the examiners (i.e. your senior professional peers) that you are in full command of your academic field.

This you do by 'making a contribution to knowledge'. This sounds both very impressive and extremely vague, and is therefore worrying to students. In this chapter we shall examine what form of a PhD thesis will satisfy these requirements.

■ Understanding the PhD form

Once again we must start by explaining that, as with the nature of a PhD, it is not possible to spell out administratively or bureaucratically what is required – that is not the nature of the process. The university regulations for a doctorate, for example, have to apply in all subject fields from Arabic to zoology. So they are inevitably formal and are not able to catch the particular requirements in your field at this time. Indeed the aim of the training process is precisely to put you in a position where you can evaluate what is required, in addition to being capable of carrying it out.

There is, however, a certain *form* to doctoral theses – clearly at a high level of abstraction, since it has to be independent of the content and apply to all fields of knowledge. We may think of the analogy of the sonata form in music. This is a structure of musical writing, but it tells you nothing about the content. Haydn wrote in sonata form, but so did Lennon and McCartney. The range of content covered is therefore enormous *but* the sonata form does not cover all music. Neither Debussy nor Britten used this form. In jazz Scott Joplin used sonata form but Bix Beiderbecke did not. The same is the case with the PhD. It has a particular form and since not all research conforms to it, you have to be aware of what the elements of its form are.

There are four elements to PhD form that we have to consider: background theory; focal theory; data theory; and contribution. These analytical constructs run throughout the thesis and do not have to correspond directly with the chapter headings used. They have to be covered in the thesis as a whole, however, as they are the headings under which its worth is evaluated.

■ Background theory

This is the field of study within which you are working and which you must know well, that is to full professional standard. So you must be aware of the present state of the art: what developments, controversies, breakthroughs are currently exciting or engaging the leading practitioners and thus pushing forward thinking in the subject.

The standard way of demonstrating this is through a literature review. Remember that you are not doing a literature review for its own sake; you are doing it in order to demonstrate that you have a fully professional grasp of the background theory to your subject. 'Professional' means, as we saw in Chapter 3, that you have something to say about your field that your fellow professionals would want to listen to. So organizing the material in an interesting and useful way, evaluating the contributions of others (and justifying the criticisms, of course), identifying trends in research activity, defining areas of theoretical and empirical weakness, are all key activities by which you would demonstrate that you had a professional command of the background theory.

It is important to emphasize that a mere encyclopaedic listing in which all the titles were presented with only a description of each work and no reasoned organization and evaluation would not be adequate. It would not demonstrate the professional judgement that is required of a PhD. It would be the equivalent of your taking a driving test and driving at no more than 20 mph throughout. Even if you made no mistakes during the test, you would fail because you had not demonstrated sufficient confidence and competence to be in charge of a vehicle. As a PhD, you must similarly be confidently and competently in charge of your understanding of background theory, and you have to demonstrate this through the literature review.

For this part of your task you can, in many disciplines, get a good idea of the style and standard of the approach that is required by reading the literature surveys that comprise the 'annual reviews' in your subject or equivalent volumes of summaries of current research. The *Annual Reviews* of biochemistry, sociology, etc., contain such reviews of the background theory of parts of the discipline contributed by leading scholars in the field. You can discover therefore how they evaluate, shape and focus their topics in ways which encourage further fruitful research. It is that level of command to which you should aspire.

■ Focal theory

The second element in the form of the PhD is the 'focal theory'. It is here that you spell out in great detail precisely what you are researching and why. You establish the nature of your problem and set about analysing it. The generation of hypotheses, if appropriate, the examination of others' arguments, and the use of your own data and analysis to push forward the academic discussion are the key tasks here.

It is in the carrying out of your work on the focal theory (as we saw in Chapter 4) that it is vital to have a thesis in the narrow sense. This gives a clear 'story line' and enables you to relate what you are doing to the focal theory in an organized way. Your thesis and the need to support it with your data and arguments perform important work for you as the criteria for what it is relevant to include in your study. You should therefore be very careful to ensure that the argument is not blurred with extraneous or makeweight material that is not contributing to the maintenance of your thesis position. The thesis of the focal theory should always be in focus!

■ Data theory

The third element of the PhD form is the data theory. In the most general terms this gives the justification for the relevance and validity of the material that you are going to use to support your thesis. A key question in the evaluation of your work must be: why should we (your fellow academics in the field) have to listen to you? You must clearly have a convincing answer.

Just what the content of your data theory is will vary enormously from discipline to discipline, but the form will always be concerned with the appropriateness and reliability of your data sources. In the sciences it will entail the establishment of a supportable theory and justification of a particular experimental approach, as well as a demonstration that your apparatus is sensitive enough to detect the effect and is reliably calibrated.

In historical studies you will need to show that in the light of your topic and your analytical approach to it, your documents are adequate and properly interpreted. In the social sciences, in addition to justifying your methods of data collection, you might need to engage in an epistemological discussion about which interpretative framework (e.g. positivist, postmodernist) it is appropriate for you to use to maintain your position.

Identifying just what an adequate discussion of the data theory for your particular thesis involves is one of the professional tasks that you have to undertake. You do this in discussion with your supervisor, by reviewing the latest papers in your field and by examining successful PhD submissions.

■ Contribution

The spelling out of your contribution is the final element in the PhD form. It is concerned with your evaluation of the importance of your thesis to the development of the discipline. It is here that you underline the significance of your analysis, point out the limitations in your material, suggest what new work is now appropriate, and so on. In the most general terms it is a discussion as to why and in what way the background theory and the focal theory that you started with are now different as a result of your research work. Thus your successors (who include, of course, yourself) now face a different situation when determining what their research work should be since they now have to take account of your work.

It might seem strange that you are asked to evaluate your own work, pointing out its limitations, putting it into perspective, and so on. Aren't you likely to think your study is the best thing since sliced bread, or at least take a very biased view of it? Well, clearly not, and this is another demonstration of the point that we made in Chapter 3 on the meaning of a doctorate. You are not doing some research for its own sake; you are doing it in order to demonstrate that you are a fully professional researcher, with a good grasp of what is happening in your field and capable of evaluating the impact of new contributions to it – your own as well as others'. That is what you get the doctorate for.

In practical terms, this component of the thesis is usually the last chapter or so, and it is very important not to underestimate this task. We have already pointed out in Chapter 4 that it takes much longer than you anticipate to write. Indeed, in our experience its inadequacy is the most common single reason for requiring students to resubmit their theses after first presentation.

There is one particular trap to avoid. If you entitle your last chapter 'Summary and conclusions', and you have no very clear idea of what 'Conclusions' would mean except that it goes at the end, then you will inevitably spend most of your time on the summary. You will know the details of your work very well by this time, and the 'summary' could easily stretch into large amounts of repetition. Then, when you have written most of a chapter, just a short ending does not seem so bad. DSP has examined theses where, after an overlong summary, only on the final page was a conclusion attempted – in one case only in the final paragraph was this ventured. Of course this is inadequate, and such submissions are referred back for the necessary further work to be done.

It is important then to be clear that the summary and the conclusions are separate tasks, and that more effort needs to go into the conclusions than the summary. Then you must have a concept of what purpose the conclusion performs: namely, to demonstrate how the background theory and the focal theory are now different as a result of the study.

■ Detailed structure and choice of chapter headings

You may hear people telling you about the 'ideal' length of a thesis. Pay no attention. A thesis should be no longer than it needs to be in order to report what you have done, why you did it and what you have concluded from the results of your work. Don't be impressed by theses that run to two volumes: it is often (correctly) said that a lot is written in order to obscure the fact that little has been achieved. In fact you might adopt the maxim that if you can say it briefly you should do so; but not if this means using lots of long words and complex sentence structures.

As we saw above, a thesis must contain the four elements of the PhD form. Just how they are presented can vary. A possible example, commonly used, would be:

☐ introduction (including aims);
☐ literature survey (background theory as a review of the relevant literature);
☐ method (data theory including a description of what has been done);
☐ results (focal theory including what was found);
☐ discussion (development of focal theory and suggestions for future work);
☐ conclusions (summary and contribution).

These general sections can be further subdivided into relevant chapters, depending on your discipline and topic. In addition to the main sections your thesis will require, at the beginning, an abstract that summarizes the work in order to make the job of the examiners easier. There should also be a clear statement of the problem under exploration. Once they know what to expect, the examiners have a frame of reference for reading the thesis. At the end you should have a detailed list of references and any appendices such as graphs, tables, data collection sheets, etc., that do not fit easily into the body of the thesis.

Your university will have detailed information on how the finished article should look, including precise width of margins and wording of the title page. There will also be rules concerning the binding of the thesis and number of copies to be produced. Be sure that you are in possession of all this information so that you do not have a last-minute panic because you failed to adhere to some minor but crucial instruction.

Once you have all these formalities under your control you can begin to have fun with the thesis. Thinking of pertinent but snappy titles for your chapters and subsections is a pleasant diversion from churning out thousands of words which conform to the expectations of supervisors and examiners. Even the title of the thesis itself can be a source of entertainment for a while. Don't go for the dry-as-dust and long-winded descriptive title. Yes, of course the title must bear a relationship to the contents, but that's no reason for it to make what is inside the thesis sound boring. Try to whet the appetite of the reader, arouse the curiosity of the examiner.

One supervisor repeatedly told his students that he expected to be supplied with a thesis that would make bedtime reading, challenging his usual book. He expected to be so engrossed in it that he would be unable to put it down and would read it right through until 2 a.m. or later in order not to spoil the flow. This might sound like an impossible task, but that is no reason not to aim for it. What it means is that you have to use everyday English instead of jargon wherever possible, without losing the precision of definition that is essential. You should also keep to sentences that do not include complicated constructions, such as ever-increasing numbers of embedded clauses. Aim to impress with clarity as well as original and sound research. Remember that even well-established experts are human beings, and nobody enjoys turgid prose.

■ The concept of originality

The aim of this section is to help you to get used to the idea that it is easy to be original. As you read further and realize the different definitions of originality that are acceptable, you should begin to feel more comfortable about your ability to be sufficiently original to satisfy your examiners.

The PhD is awarded for 'an original contribution to knowledge' In the statements that most universities have to guide examiners on the grading of theses, there is usually some reference to 'unaided work', 'significant contribution' and 'originality'. As Francis (1976) has pointed out, however, you may be original in any one of a number of possible ways.

Francis, a professor of hydraulics working in the area of civil and mechanical engineering, observed eight ways in which students may be considered to have shown originality. We agree with only the six listed below:

1 setting down a major piece of new information in writing for the first time;
2 continuing a previously original piece of work;
3 carrying out original work designed by the supervisor;
4 providing a single original technique, observation, or result in an otherwise unoriginal but competent piece of research;
5 having many original ideas, methods and interpretations all performed by others under the direction of the postgraduate;
6 showing originality in testing somebody else's idea.

He concludes that the examiner's interpretation of this ambiguity is an important component in the decision whether or not to award the PhD degree.

In later research, interviews with students, supervisors and examiners yielded nine further definitions of how a PhD can be original (Phillips 1993). These are:

1 carrying out empirical work that hasn't been done before;
2 making a synthesis that hasn't been made before;
3 using already known material but with a new interpretation;
4 trying out something in Britain that has previously only been done abroad;
5 taking a particular technique and applying it in a new area;
6 bringing new evidence to bear on an old issue;
7 being cross-disciplinary and using different methodologies;
8 looking at areas that people in the discipline haven't looked at before;
9 adding to knowledge in a way that hasn't been done before.

A total of 15 different definitions of originality has thus been obtained from those involved. This should be reassuring. It is much easier to be original in at least one of 15 possible ways than it is to be singularly original.

The main problem is that there is little or no discussion between students and their supervisors of what constitutes originality in the PhD. Although students and staff use the same word to describe a range of different concepts, they do not discuss with each other the definitions to which they are working. Further, academics think that it is not too difficult to be original because it is not necessary to have a whole new way of looking at the discipline or the topic. It is sufficient for the student to contribute only an incremental step in understanding. Unfortunately, supervisors do not usually tell their research students this.

For their part, postgraduates' thoughts on originality change as they progress through their period of registration. In the beginning research students tend to say things like, 'I'm worried about that – I don't know how creative I am.' Students in their third year are more likely to say, 'Now I know it can be just a small advance in everyday life; before I knew this, I was worried about being original enough.' Eventually, as part of their academic development, students acquire a similar grasp of what is expected in the way of a small step forward, but do not seem to be helped towards this realization by their supervisors. Be warned that once students get over their initial worry about their ability to be original in their thesis, there is a tendency to go almost to the other extreme and decide that doing a PhD is not really creative at all. The good news for you is that, typically, students get to the point where they are no longer worried about being original enough. This section should have helped you to reach the point of feeling confident about being original sooner, rather than later. Do remember that because the PhD is awarded for 'an original contribution to knowledge' it remains an extremely important concept.

■ Writing the thesis

Writing as a process of rewriting

Your thesis is the product on which you will be assessed. Writing it is far more than merely reporting the outcome of several years of research. Students experience a great deal of discomfort when attempting to present results in written form because writing makes people think about their work in a different way. If writing leads to discovery and not, as is generally supposed, discoveries merely need to be put into writing, then it is easy to understand why writing the thesis is experienced as the most difficult part of the work. Torrance *et al.* (1992) suggest that 'think-while-you-write' strategies be consciously adopted from the start and not lapsed into when 'think-then-write' strategies have failed.

One student said,

> Obviously you don't formulate what you're going to say *completely* until you come to write it down . . . it was only when I was writing it that I realized that in one section my interpretation was completely wrong. The point I was trying to make just wouldn't embody itself verbally, so I thought it out again and rewrote the whole section.

If you are able to read what you have written as though it were the work of someone else, you will find it easier to be critical of your own imprecise phrases and sloppy style. The way to achieve this 'distance' between yourself and your work is to put it aside for a few days and then come back to it as though you had never seen it before. Alternatively, if there is no time for that, you might try doing something else – make phone calls, meet friends – and then come back to it. The psychological switch will help to create the required distance. Another technique is to read aloud what you have written, as hearing often reveals the difference between what you intended to say and what you actually did say. In the same way, recording what you have written and then playing it back can also be very helpful.

Rugg and Petre (2004) give a helpful overview of writing for a PhD thesis, including a list of the 14 or more activities involved. Rewriting is a very important factor in the writing process and it is a good idea for students to keep successive drafts of a report or a chapter and then compare them to see whether later drafts define and refine meaning more effectively than earlier ones. Computers enable you to amend the text of drafts as often as required. The final version can be used in the thesis and can also serve as the text basis for journal articles which may be published from your research.

Different types of writers

Not everybody goes about writing in the same way. Just as there are at least two different kinds of learners there are also two distinct types of writer. At school we are instructed to make a plan and then write the essay. But we are not all 'planners' – some of us are 'get it all outers'. It is not at all easy both to first, say what you want to say, and second, say it in the best possible way at the same time. It is sensible, therefore, to do it in stages.

'Serialists' see writing as a sequential process in which the words are corrected as they are written and who plan their writing in detail before beginning to write. Here is an example of the serialist approach:

It's stylistic, the phrasing of the work and the way it flows, that I'm having difficulty with at the moment. When I do write sentences I feel good about my style. I don't feel like an inadequate writer, but writing sentences is very slow.

'Holists' can only think as they write and compose a succession of complete drafts:

I write a complete first draft in longhand. As I go along I tend to revise a bit, but when I've finished I revise a great deal and it tends to look like World War III on paper. If I'm really interested in it I'll start at 8.30 a.m. or 9.30 a.m. and go on until late at night. Once I start I want to see it finished, the shorter the time between conception and finished article the better.

The serialist emphasizes the writing of sentences which is very different from the way the holistic writer talks about his work.

Getting down to it

Phillips (1991) found that research students in science disciplines showed a preference for experimental work, including keeping lab books up to date. Writing papers or thesis chapters was assigned to evenings, weekends and holidays:

> If it's time-consuming and mindless, like just repeating experiments, I like it, but if it's difficult too, like writing an introduction and conclusion, then I don't like it.

> I'd rather potter about in the laboratory during working hours – it's less taxing mentally.

Writing was not perceived as 'real work', and as it was thought to be of only secondary importance was never undertaken at the time intended. One student said, 'I'm doing bits and pieces of writing-up whenever I get a minute,' but repeatedly abandoned the latest piece of writing.

Procrastination and incoherence are often the order of the day and, until supervisors have training in providing adequate supervision of writing, you cannot realistically expect very much assistance. In fact most research students tend to postpone writing until their final year, but we advise very strongly indeed against adopting this course of action.

Our advice is always to be writing something and to write up the easiest parts of the thesis first. This may sound so obvious that it seems unnecessary to mention it, but it is surprising how many people believe a thesis should be written in the order that it will be published and subsequently read. Not true. In an article entitled 'Is the scientific paper a fraud?' Medawar (1964) explains the process of writing up research as an exercise in deception. By this he means that readers are deceived into believing the research was conducted in the way it is described and the report written in the logical and sequential manner in which it is presented. He maintains that this is misleading and might be discouraging to others who wish to conduct research and write scientific papers, but who find that nothing ever happens quite as systematically for them as it seems to do for the experts.

Consider writing the method section first. You know what you did, and how you did it, so it is a good way of getting started on the thesis, even though this chapter will come well into the body of the finished work. Alternatively you may prefer to start with the literature review, which is a safe way of reminding yourself of what has already been written about your topic. If you do start here, remember to check at the end of your work for important subsequent publications.

Our recommendation is that you approach every piece of writing in the following way: First of all, if your computer does not have a built-in dictionary and thesaurus which you can use at the press of a button, ensure that you have hard copy versions readily available together with a copy of Gowers' *Plain Words*.

- ☐ *Generate* the main points (in any order if you're a holist, and sequentially if you're a serialist), noting everything that comes into your mind, thus making a rough plan (which you need not stick to).
- ☐ *Organize* this into an acceptable structure.
- ☐ Only then attempt to *construct* the points into grammatical paragraphs made up of well balanced sentences.
- ☐ *Plan* to spend two to five hours a week in term time on writing.
- ☐ *Find* quiet conditions in which to write and, if possible, always write in the same place.
- ☐ *Set* goals and targets for yourself.
- ☐ *Ask* colleagues and friends to comment on early drafts.

It is useful practice in writing to use, from the beginning, the appropriate conventions of your discipline. Ascertain, for example, whether footnotes are encouraged, allowed or forbidden. If you are not sure, choose one of the leading journals in your subject whose articles you are quoting and follow them. If you are quoting from a range of journals using different conventions, choose the one you prefer and state at the beginning of your thesis that you are using the conventions and referencing system of the *British Journal of X*. Do not mix conventions. Make sure that all the references in the text are listed in the bibliography. Then recheck to find the inevitable few that you missed! These pedantic details do not sound important, but you should note that one of the easiest ways to irritate your examiners, and therefore start off on the wrong foot, is to get references and their citations wrong. So you must be punctilious about them.

Our final advice is not intuitively obvious, and thus all the more important. When you have to stop writing, do not carry on until you reach a natural break – the end of a section, a chapter, etc. You should deliberately leave your work in the middle – mid-design, mid-chapter, mid-paragraph, even mid-sentence. Your psychological need to complete the task provides you with extra internal pressure to return and finish what you have started. It also makes restarting easier and quicker.

The thesis itself

In the thesis it is necessary to formulate clearly in writing ideas that you will have got to know very well indeed, but which will be new to the reader. This means that assumptions have to be made explicit and ideas expressed clearly. The thinking that links one idea with others or that emerges from a particular hypothesis has to be unambiguously translated into the written language. Remarks such as 'good writing can't cure bad thought', and 'I can't clearly express in words what I have in my head', are typical of the comments made by thesis-writers. Eminent poets, authors and psychologists admit that the only time they think is when they write. This may be true of all writing.

Phillips (1996) found that students and supervisors agree that a thesis should compress a great deal of information into a highly structured and relatively short format. Supervisors see this positively, as confirmation that the student has finally managed to understand what is required in order to summarize and conceptualize their work. One supervisor said, 'Evolution of the thesis is not so much a change in length but a change from what was traditionally a large book to something that should become two or three or four separate projects tied together with a theme, all different aspects of a specific topic'. Another, speaking as an experienced examiner, talked of 'making the string of sausages into a small salami'!

Students, on the other hand, see this compression as a negative requirement which impoverishes the richness of the information they have worked so hard to acquire. They complain that lots of different areas have to be forced into one section and perceive the thesis format as constraining. But students do know what is required of them. 'To be good, work needs to be relevant to some problem and valid in its methodology. It should also be clear in its expression'.

■ **Alternative thesis styles**

In some social sciences and humanities there is now a gradual acceptance of alternative styles of presentation. Instead of having to express your thinking and work in language that we might recognize as 'academic', it is acceptable to use the kind of language you might employ when writing a letter. So long as what you are saying is clear and unambiguous, there should be no problem. This may apply in other subjects too but you will need to find out what is permitted in your discipline.

Murray (2002) distinguishes between formal and informal writing where the informal or simple, everyday style is used for free writing and notes for yourself, and the formal or more academic for drafts of sections of the thesis. Her examples demonstrate her belief that academic writing for a thesis needs to be in the past tense, passive voice and with an objective viewpoint. The writer is firmly removed from the whole venture. We do not consider this to be necessary for all topics in all subjects. Different ways of describing your work and thought in writing are often subject-specific with disciplines having their own conventions. Reading accepted journal articles and theses in your field will make these clear but do bear in mind that changes are occurring.

Murray discusses how understanding what you have written for yourself helps you to express the ideas in more specialized language and stresses the importance of defining terms carefully and defending what you have written. While we agree emphatically that it is very important to define your terms thoroughly and to defend what you have written with good supporting arguments, we do not believe that this is only possible using technical terminology. For example, think how you would explain a significant point in your work to your family, as opposed to your colleagues, and then check whether you have actually said the same thing in both cases. If so, you have mastered, in part, the highly skilled task of being able to communicate equally well with laypersons and professionals in your field – as Einstein advocated.

Hartley (2004) used a standard method to measure the ease of readability of texts (called the Flesch Reading Ease score) to show that articles which had proved to be more influential over a period of years were written in a more accessible, easy to read and understandable style than less influential articles. He found that this was true of classic texts such as Einstein's first paper on relativity and Watson and Crick's (1953) paper on the structure of DNA. Of course, if a particular term is used in a specific way in a specialist context, then the technical word is essential but it is not necessary to make thesis writing overcomplicated and difficult to penetrate.

Disciplines also vary in how much your personal voice can be heard or the extent to which your thesis can support the 'writing in' of the researcher. This becomes important when there are issues of impartiality, involving making decisions about how you present ideas with which you disagree. If you wish to include your own subjective point of view, it is vital that you make clear both that it is indeed your own interpretation and that you are completely aware of the objective way of describing the theory, idea or 'fact'. One way of doing this would be to use different fonts for different voices. Now that anyone can select any font they wish with a click of a computer mouse this should present no difficulty.

We applaud this notion of making your thesis reader-friendly for your professional peers. Look at the latest edition of any journal in your field, and notice how, though all are within the current conventions, some are much more readable than others. Those are the ones you should emulate.

■ To publish or not to publish prior to submission?

Should students publish academic papers during their doctoral studies? This is an important and recurring question. The task of a PhD is to carry out research on a particular subject. This involves doing background reading and data collection, collating and analysing results and coming to a conclusion. During the course of the research you are writing an account of your work. Our view is that until you actually sit down and try to write a paper you do not think your way through logically. Writing helps understanding of your own topic and encourages you to keep up with the latest literature. A PhD is not just about getting results. It is also about developing the thought processes required to work through and explain problems, and subsequently to present the results in a coherent manner.

So writing is a necessity, but there are advantages and disadvantages attached to publishing a paper in an academic journal prior to completing your PhD. There is no rule that publications are required for a PhD degree. They are an added bonus. The arguments for publication include getting experience of the important professional skill of writing papers and getting your name on your work and into the public sphere at the earliest possible opportunity and thus begin to establish yourself as an academic.

The argument against is primarily that it is a misuse of thesis time. A strong concern is that it can be used to divert time that would otherwise be spent on writing the thesis. Because the thesis is a daunting document some research students experience panic symptoms at the mere thought of trying to write it. These panic symptoms vie with feelings of guilt when the student is not writing. One way of stemming both these emotions is to write – but not to write the thesis. Therefore, the legitimate activity of writing a paper for publication is used to evade the inevitable duty of confronting the actual thesis writing.

If the paper writing is approached professionally, if not too much time is spent on it, if it is sent off for refereeing and then attention is returned to thesis writing, it would be time well spent. But, if the paper writing continues indefinitely, if it is never quite good enough to be sent to a journal, if it always requires just a little more work, time and attention, then it only succeeds in distancing you even further from your thesis and the work that requires to be done. For these reasons, any writing aimed at publication must be agreed with your supervisors and closely monitored throughout the process. They should give advice on the form of publication and put you in touch with publishers where appropriate.

Ultimately, however, whether you write any papers during your time as a PhD student is really up to you. If you consider the PhD to be a period of professional training, then learning to write papers, as well as learning to teach and do research is an important component. Provided you know what you want to get out of it, and what you want to do at the end, you can choose your own specific objectives. The criteria for obtaining a PhD are the same for everybody (presenting and defending an original piece of work). If you meet those criteria, you are free to develop the skills you want to develop.

■ Action summary

1. Ensure that the four elements of the PhD form (background theory, focal theory, data theory, contribution) are adequately covered in your thesis.

2. Do not make your thesis (that is, the report) any longer than it needs to be to sustain your thesis (your argument).

3. Remember that you need only take a very small step indeed with regard to the 'original' part of your work.

4. Discuss with your supervisor the many different ways in which a thesis may be presumed to be 'original' and come to some agreement about the way that you will be interpreting this requirement.

5. Write your thesis in readable English, using technical terms as appropriate but avoiding jargon.

6. From the beginning, use the footnoting and referencing conventions of your discipline.

7. Take every opportunity to write reports, draft papers, criticisms of others' work, etc., during the course of your research. Do not think that all the writing can be done at the end. If you do avoid writing you will not develop the skills to write efficiently, or even adequately, for your thesis.

8. Write up your final thesis in the order which is easiest for you. It does not have to be written in the order in which it will be read. The method section is often a good place to start.

7

THE PhD PROCESS

The activity of getting a PhD is inevitably a complex one. Students often embark on their research with the naive view that, having identified their topic, they will follow a predictable path to its conclusion. Unfortunately this is totally misleading. As we have already discussed in Chapter 1, even within the framework of the scientific method there will be the need for guesses, reworkings, backtrackings, corrections and, above all, inspiration if the PhD is to be achieved. Other conceptual paradigms provide even less structure. Uncertainty is inherent in the doctoral process, and a degree of tolerance of ambiguity is a prerequisite for successful research work. You therefore need some signposts for understanding to help you along the way.

In this chapter we are going to consider two aspects of working towards your PhD. First we will discuss the psychological nature of the experience, placing emphasis upon the fact that it has a significant emotional component in addition to the recognized intellectual one. Second, the practical issues involved in managing the work in the time available will be analysed, including the vital role of setting goals and establishing deadlines.

■ Psychological aspects

Enthusiasm

Postgraduates begin the period of their research full of enthusiasm for their new undertaking. This changes during the time that it takes to complete the course. The main reason that initial enthusiasm diminishes is the length of time that has to be spent working on a *single* problem. In this chapter we refer to interviews that were conducted by EMP with students over three years of their PhD research in order to give the flavour of how they were feeling during the different stages.

Freddy, studying industrial chemistry at a technological university, said that during the years of his research he had become more remote and detached:

> In the beginning I had to concentrate hard on what I was doing, it completely occupied my mind. In some ways I've got less enthusiastic, at first I was full of enthusiasm for work and work was going to be very important, but at the end other things gave me much more satisfaction.

In general the students' early enthusiasm revealed itself in the form of overambitious estimates of what they could accomplish during the first year. As time went by and deadlines came closer they felt the stress of time constraints and the monotony of focusing on a particular problem for an extended period.

At first Adam (architecture) was very excited about the direction in which his work was taking him, but 'I have more enthusiasm than organization and I hope my supervisor will help me to decide what to do next.' Later on he found that writing helped him to organize his thoughts, but this meant that he could not explore all the avenues that had begun to open up for him.

Isolation

Postgraduates discover what not to do for their PhD after they have spent some time struggling with their own topic. Generally they have experienced disappointments in the amount of work they have managed to get done during this period and usually feel that they should be much farther ahead than they actually are. Some examples from students illustrate this point.

Greg (history) said:

> I don't feel I've got very far after a year. I think I could have done more. I'm frustrated at not making as much progress as I hoped but don't know how I could have achieved more.

Adam (architecture) said:

> It's difficult to know how well I'm doing as I'm working well but progressing really slowly.

Charles (astronomy) referred to contact with others during the course of his work:

Most of the time communication is artificial. Conversation is just polite, you do it all the time with people. Communication, if it's real, is more between two minds. So I don't think of conversation as communication any more.

Charles was dissatisfied with the amount and quality of his interactions with his supervisor. He also felt that he had very little in common with others in his department; in addition, he was not talking with anyone about his work. This resulted in a period of isolation, even though he shared a room with other postgraduates and came to the university every day. The lack of intellectual stimulation and exchange of ideas with either peers or supervisor eventually led to a loss of interest in his topic, which he thought was of no importance or interest to anybody else. Once again, work slowed down almost to a standstill.

In Chapter 2 we mentioned that Diana (biochemistry) complained that she was working alone in a laboratory full of people who were working alone. Bradley (English) provided an alternative viewpoint with 'I'm utterly alone but don't feel isolated. I'm happy to get on in my own time.' Although one might think that Diana and Charles are less isolated than Bradley, for them the experience is one of total isolation; while Bradley's perception of spending so much time on his own is not as extreme as theirs, or for that matter Adam's. Some months later Bradley had changed his mind; he reported: 'Postgraduates are treated scandalously. We're not treated in any way as members of the academic community. The pleasures of isolation are wearing rather thin.' We can see that the subjective perception of research students is as important a component of the experience as the objective situation.

Intellectual isolation is a necessary and desirable component of successful research. But as Delamont *et al.* (2004) argue there is no need for this to be accompanied by social or emotional loneliness.

Regardless of discipline, topic, or university the postgraduates interviewed were suffering from the effects of the social circumstances in which they were working rather than from the work itself. Nevertheless, the effect of these feelings was to dampen their initial enthusiasm and slow down their pace of work almost to nil.

Increasing interest in work

As students develop self-confidence and gradually become independent of their supervisors, so too do they become more involved with their work because of its own intrinsic interest. Once you have learned how to interpret the results of your own efforts you will find that you can grapple with problems as they arise instead of turning immediately to your supervisor for advice. When this happens you will find that you become increasingly absorbed in the work that you are doing, and that the problem you are investigating demands more and more of your time and attention.

In fact Bradley (English literature) explained that he needed to feel that he had rounded off a schedule of work in the three years and that it was this inner drive that had kept him going. At first he had 'gravitated into research because I couldn't think what else to do'. By the third year he said that his 'natural inclination' to do anything other than work hard on his research and complete the thesis had become much less pressing. The thesis had become one of the most important things in his life, but this had certainly not been the case in the beginning. He described 'a lot of chafing and inner rebellion' at the start of his three-year period of registration, and dissatisfaction with the department and with supervision. Gradually, although he still did not admire the way things were done, these external irritations grew less important as he became more and more absorbed in his work. He commented on the relationship between a lack of direction from outside and the development of his own personal autonomy.

Transfer of dependence from the supervisor to the work

As students become more involved with their work, so there is a lessening of the need for external approval. In fact your supervisor should be engaged in a kind of 'weaning process' to enable you to become more independent, as we describe more fully in Chapter 11 (p. 160).

For example, Adam (architecture) said towards the end of his period of research: 'In the beginning I wanted immediate feedback and was afraid to ask. When I got it plus the confidence, I stopped working so hard and felt secure.' Here he is talking about the way that his own increasing independence in his work is related to a lessening of dependence on productivity. It is from the student's output that the supervisor is able to evaluate progress in the explicit terms necessary for giving feedback. Therefore this comment from Adam indicates a simultaneous growth in independence from external approval coupled with reliance on the information he was receiving as he worked on his topic. The more he felt he could rely on his own judgement of the quality and standard of his work, and the longer he could develop his thinking, the less he needed to turn to his supervisor for comment, criticism or interpretation.

As Adam became his own supervisor, by evaluating his efforts without needing a third party to act as mediator between him and his work, he felt less pressure to produce something tangible to show Professor Andrews. This meant that, although it might appear that he was doing less, he was in fact working steadily without forcing himself to complete a piece of work before he was ready to do so, merely in order to be seen to be producing.

He may be compared to Ewan (nuclear chemistry) who did not continue to develop the confidence in his own work that was necessary if he were to be able to rely on the feedback provided through his own achievements – or lack of them. Near the end of his registration period Ewan said:

> I don't think that my early relationship with my supervisor was good and he wouldn't give me information first-hand. At first I had to do all the work without any lead, but later that changed. If you begin to enjoy the relationship with your supervisor then positive feedback is obvious. Some supervisors would opt for the student to dig up the research themselves; it would make you approach the problem differently and is a better training for later work when you have to cope alone.

Dr Eustace had started to supervise Ewan by referring to articles he should read but leaving him to develop his own thinking about the subject. Later he realized that Ewan needed more direction than the guidance that he had been giving and continued to increase the closeness of his supervision right up to the end of Ewan's period of registration. In order to take some of the effort off of himself he also introduced, as a second supervisor, a postdoctoral researcher who was working in the same lab.

Ewan had been happy to depend on his supervisors but finally commented on how the spoonfeeding he had ultimately received had affected his work. He linked his considerable dependence on his supervisor with his lack of intrinsic work satisfaction and involvement. He was convinced about the importance of external control while, at the same time, being aware that his own training may not have been the most efficient for later autonomy in research.

These two examples describe quite different relationships between research students and their supervisors, and differing perceptions of what they considered important to their progress. The examples also illustrate the importance placed on the need for information concerning their progress that students expect to receive from their supervisors. Equally important, as the examples show, is the need for students to understand and accept the feedback that is constantly available in their own work.

At the end of his postgraduate days Ewan said: 'It's important to get good guidance, and I feel my supervisor is doing this.' But Dr Eustace, the lead supervisor, said: 'Following superhuman efforts to get sense into him, he's got experimental results as good as anyone.' In fact his supervisor continued to see Ewan weekly right up to the end of his period of registration. He edited, corrected and rewrote large sections of Ewan's thesis, and the student never did manage to discard his dependence completely and rely on the information which resulted from his own efforts.

Boredom

About halfway through the period of research postgraduates tend to get fed up, confused and feel completely stuck. This 'getting nowhere syndrome' has been remarked on by many creative people, including those who discuss it as part of their own experience of doing research. Supervisors too commented on it during the interviews. Professor Forsdike (industrial chemistry) said of Freddy, 'During the next six months he'll get through the sticky patch and results should just pour out.'

Freddy himself reported, however, 'It's the boring part now, essential to the thesis, just plodding on. Just churning out results with no thought, no challenge.'

Bradley said, philosophically, 'I see it's always darkest before dawn, it's just me and it [the thesis] now.'

Adam said, 'Now that I know that what I'm doing is good enough for a PhD I've lost interest; there's no challenge.'

Greg (ancient history) said, 'I'm really fed up with it right now, doing the mechanical things just goes on.'

The monotony and repetitiveness of concentrating on the same thing for an extended period of time are quite common. Both seem to be an integral part of learning how to be systematic about research and disciplining yourself to continue, despite the fact that everything seems eventually to become predictable if the work is proceeding as it should.

Frustration

As the research progresses, new ideas about how to follow up the results of work that you have already done are constantly being generated. It is very tempting to pursue some of these new avenues, but if you are to complete the agreed research programme in time it is important to concentrate on the problem in hand and not be sidetracked. This becomes increasingly frustrating as the original problem becomes more and more familiar. Not being able to follow up results, ideas and theories is a constant source of dissatisfaction and frustration for most research students during the thesis stage of their PhD.

So do beware lest these common feelings and reactions against what might have become mechanical and repetitive work prevent you from continuing. It is only by understanding the need for precision and having the ability to apply yourself in a disciplined way that you will eventually get to the point where you have the right to follow up interesting leads and explore a series of ideas that arise out of the work in hand. We suggest that, for the moment, this should be after your doctorate.

In his autobiographical novel *The Search* (1958), C. P. Snow gives an excellent account of how he coped with the kinds of frustrations that result from a systematic programme of research. He explains that he spent years of his life doing 'bread and butter' work until he had made enough of an impact on the scientific community to enable him to undertake some fascinating but seemingly irrelevant research:

> I could not expect the authorities to take me as a rising scientist on trust. I had to prove myself . . . To begin with I was going to work on a safe problem. It was not exciting but almost certain to give me some results . . . With the future temporarily assured, I turned eagerly once more to the problem which had enticed me for so long. I had done enough for place and reputation and I could afford to gamble on what might be a barren chase . . . I had gained a good deal of experience and technique in research
>
> (Snow 1958: 55, 90–1)

We cannot do better than offer those words of a well known and perceptive scientist as advice on how to approach the research you undertake for your PhD degree. Don't let your frustrations allow you to deviate. Remember that once you have your doctorate you will be in a far better position to experiment with your ideas.

A job to be finished

In Chapter 3 we described the different ways in which research students talk about their PhDs as they come to the end of their period of registration. It seems to be important for the morale of most postgraduates that they think in terms of a goal – 'got to get it!' – or an unfinished task that needs completion – 'must finish!' You will recall that, by the time they were reaching the end of their period as research students, the postgraduates being interviewed realized that it was determination and application, rather than brilliance, that were needed to complete what they had started.

In Chapter 2 we mentioned the way in which this idea of 'brilliance' inhibits the development of new postgraduates. Because they believe that people with a PhD are outstandingly clever, they admire those who have them – especially those in their own field whose work they have read. In the same way they do not see themselves as outstandingly clever and so are sure that they do not now, nor will they ever, merit the coveted degree. Once they are firmly embarked on their research career they gradually come to understand that the requirement is not for any outstanding abilities – other, of course, than those to do with persistence and overcoming feelings of boredom and frustration.

This realization is a step towards a changed perception of the PhD. It is necessary to come to the eventual description of research work as just that – work. If you have not managed to make this switch in the way you think about your research by your third year, do spend some time analysing precisely what it is that you realistically hope to achieve in your research. If you *have* got to the point of realizing that your work, just like any other kind of work, needs to be planned and developed and *completed* in a given period of time, you will have entered the final crucial motivating stage of the process. There is a job to be finished: the time has come when you must set a deadline for completion. As with other jobs, you will be rewarded at the end of it; not in this case by a financial bonus, but by a higher degree.

You will by now have become more skilled in the techniques and mental attitudes that this work demands. You will, too, have come to terms with the anxiety that all research students experience. The most pervasive of all the psychological aspects of doing a PhD is the anxiety that accompanies you through all the stages. At first it is very high and exemplified by such concerns as, 'Am I clever enough?', 'Will "they" realize what a fraud I am?' and so on. As you progress, you go through periods of higher or lower anxiety but you are never completely free of it. It comes in bursts, and one of the reasons for feeling that a great weight has been lifted from you once you have successfully completed your PhD is the nagging anxiety that has been your constant companion for so long has finally been lifted.

As your perception of the postgraduate situation changes, you will find that your behaviour will adjust to match it. You will have discovered that you are *not* destroyed by criticism and that you have developed a new confidence in yourself, which will stand you in good stead in the oral examination. The job of work started so long ago is about to be finished; the end is in sight.

Now you are actively progressing towards this goal in a very matter-of-fact and routine manner. There are discussions to be held with your supervisors; writing to be completed; decisions to be made about which publications can be excluded and which must be referred to; final checking of statistical calculations or experimental results; a last look at data that have not yet been incorporated into the story you will be telling; and some theoretical concepts to be mulled over. All of these loose ends need to be tied up in order for the job to be ready for inspection. The aim is for your PhD to be a high-quality product.

Euphoria

After submission of the thesis there is a period of anxiety and expectation that you have to live through waiting for the day of the viva. There is then, when you are no longer constantly confronting your thesis, the feeling of a gap in your life – a burden that has been lifted from your shoulders. Those feelings are mitigated, however, by the knowledge that all is not yet over.

This final stage is that which occurs *after* you have had the viva and been told that you have been awarded the doctorate, or that you will have the doctorate once you have made specific alterations to the text of the thesis within a limited amount of time.

Then you are overwhelmed with feelings of joy, lightheadedness and achievement. You gain enormously in confidence, the kind of confidence that allows you to ask questions in a crowded room in the belief that if you need clarification from the speaker then many others do too. No longer do you think that you are the only nitwit who is too stupid to comprehend what is being said. No longer do you refrain from making a comment at a meeting because it might not be appropriate, only to hear someone else say the very thing that you were wondering about 10 minutes after you thought of it. The delight may gradually lessen; the gap will inevitably be filled with other work – perhaps a book – but the confidence is there forever.

The years you have been working now seem worthwhile just to get to the feeling of euphoria that permeates your whole being once you have succeeded in what you set out to do all those years ago. This is truly an example of delayed gratification, but anybody who has been through it will tell you just how rewarding it is to come out the other side.

■ Others 'getting in first'

A recurring anxiety of many research students is that someone else will publish something on the same topic, even taking the same approach and obtaining the same or similar results. It would be most discouraging to find that another researcher had got in first. This other person may live many miles away, even be working in another language.

It is no accident that researchers, unknown to each other, make similar discoveries at the same time. Kuhn (1970), referred to in Chapter 4, has a very nice explanation of this phenomenon. He describes how scientific evolution prepares society for the next step – the latest discovery. This stage cannot be reached until the scientific basis for it has been laid, but once everything is in place then researchers all over the world have the opportunity to make the breakthrough. Therefore there are regularly shared Nobel prizes for researchers in different countries who have never met, but who have made the same important discovery or invention at precisely the same time.

Once the relevant published research has appeared, many students believe that their own painstaking work is rendered null and void. Even supervisors seem to be unsure about the position of their student's work when this happens. There is no need to worry. You have not wasted your time.

If your own work is similar to the published work but the results are different, you (or your supervisor) may think it a good idea to establish contact with the author and enter into a discussion that can help to develop and improve the research of you both. If your own work is similar to the published work and the results are consistent with those found by the author, then you have an early opportunity to support those findings and add credence to the new work. You might want to do this via an early publication of your own. Whether your findings support or disconfirm the published work, your own work is still useful to whatever happens next in that particular field of research.

The worst that can happen is not that someone else publishes on your topic, but that someone else publishes on your topic and you are not aware of it. What is important for you, as a postgraduate research student, is that you show an awareness of developments in your field and keep abreast of the latest findings.

■ Practical aspects

Time management

The psychological aspects of the PhD process that we have just discussed develop continuously, often in recurring cycles, throughout the whole period of the research project. We now have to consider the conceptual and practical tasks that have to be undertaken to obtain a PhD. Since these have to be achieved within a limited period, timetabling and time management become crucial to success.

You will probably have three years full-time after your taught component in which to design, conduct and complete your PhD, or an equivalent amount part-time, spread over five or six years. Of course, you will have some idea of what you will be doing during those years but how much thought have you given to just how and when you will be undertaking specific activities?

These activities operate at two levels: first, the general level at which the tasks required to complete a PhD must be realistically charted if they are to be accomplished in the time available; and second, the detailed level concerned with setting timetable deadlines for particular tasks, and achieving them. In addition, the activities must be seen as both part of the research task and part of the essential structure into which the timetabling of the PhD falls.

At first you will have an overall plan such as that described by Ewan at the start of his research in nuclear chemistry: 'I hope eventually to come up with the *shape* of the molecules in solution.' He was unable to be more specific than that, but quickly discovered that before he could proceed several preliminary steps had to be taken. First he had to calibrate the viscometer that he would be using. In order to do this he had to read the literature on viscosity to see how such calibration had been done previously. Once he started to read, he realized that there was a confusion in the literature, which had to be sorted out. In order to do this he had to check the calculations reported in the journals; this involved engaging the help of a mathematician. Therefore, his overall plan could more accurately be described as: 'to find the shape of the molecule in solution by making measurements with a viscometer, calibrated according to verified equations'. This more sharply defined overall plan was gradually formulated as Ewan thought about what he had to do and began the work.

This situation is not unusual. New research students enter the system with a vague overall plan that will get them to their long-term goal of a PhD at the end of three to four years. Their short-term goals may be more clearly defined: starting work on the problem, discussing what they want to do with their supervisors and gaining access to equipment or samples. Beyond that, however, goals are very fuzzy indeed. This is because there is a tendency to take an unstructured approach to the project regardless of the time constraints and interim tasks to be undertaken and completed.

At first three years (or six years part-time equivalent) will appear to be an extraordinarily long time for completing a single piece of research. Beware of this illusion. If you trust it and behave accordingly, you will be in very deep trouble later on. A postgraduate in biochemistry learned this the hard way. At the end of her second year of research into anti-cancer drugs, Diana said:

> I'm aware that I've only a year left and two years have already gone. Three years doesn't seem half long enough; it seemed a long time in the beginning. Now I'm trying to finish off groups of experiments and say 'that's the answer' rather than exploring it more fully, which is what I used to do.

The importance of not losing sight of the time constraints on each part of your project is clear.

It is useful to look on the total process as a series of tasks which lead to the *progressive reduction of uncertainty*. As we saw in Chapter 6, there is a form to a PhD that structures the overall amount of work to be undertaken. This form generates a series of stages that have to be gone through. These stages, in turn, will point to a series of tasks that you will have to do. Going from 'form' to 'stages' to 'tasks' in planning what needs to be done becomes more and more specific to the individual research project and is an important part of your interaction with your supervisor (see Chapters 8 and 11). In principle, as you carry out each of the tasks that comprise the stages you should be reducing the uncertainty involved in your thesis. So you start with a wide field of possible topics and end, after some years of work, with the very specific report of your particular PhD research.

The duration of the process

Overleaf is a suggested model for the form of the thesis and the stages of the process. The form, as we have seen in Chapter 6, is constant. The stages are fairly standard but there will be some variation according to your discipline. For the purposes of discussion the figure represents typical stages within the usual timescale for a PhD, not including the taught element.

The figure is, and is intended to be, quite crude in that it uses timeblocks of 'terms' (i.e. four months of full-time work or six months of part-time work) and outlines only six stages of the PhD process. However, it does illustrate the sort of programme that you will need to develop in conjunction with your supervisor. You need this framework in order to be continually aware of how your current work fits into the overall time allocated. Otherwise you will find, like Diana, that you wake up one morning to discover that half of your time has gone and you haven't 'really' started.

The aim of the exercise is to reduce the areas of uncertainty as we go from left to right along the timescale shown in the figure. At the overall level blocks of time are allocated to the background theory, focal theory, data theory and contribution elements of the thesis. More specifically, six stages of the process are identified, the first four being allocated one 'term' each, the fifth two 'terms' and the last stage (writing up) three 'terms'. In our experience this is a fast, but not unrealistic, timescale; some have achieved it, many fallen behind. An appropriate adaptation of this figure for you should serve regularly to locate your current work in the overall process, and therefore enable you to make realistic plans which motivate you to keep going until you have completed the work.

Of course, it is unrealistic to expect that you would go through these stages in a straightforward linear way. You may lag behind, you may have to revise earlier stages, you may have to jettison earlier work altogether and replace it. Although the main weight of writing will come towards the end, you should regularly be writing all the way through the period of the research because writing is an integral part of researching. So you may well find that you are having to work in more than one place on the figure at the same time. All the more reason for keeping a time-based framework such as this to enable you to locate your activities in an overall perspective.

The stages of the process

Most of the stages of the figure will be relevant in some way to your work, although the detailed working out may vary. Some comments on them:

☐ *Field of interest.* Some departments may require prospective students to present a preliminary research proposal in order to make a decision on

The PhD process
as the progressive reduction of uncertainty

PhD stages		WRITING						Final writing up	

Maximum uncertainty

Minimum uncertainty

| Field of interest | Possible topics | Pilot study | Thesis proposal | Data collection and analysis | | Final writing up | | |

Timescale in 'terms'
(1 term = 4 months full-time,
6 months part-time)

0 1 2 3 4 5 6 7 8 9

Thesis form

Background theory

Focal theory

Data theory

Contribution

An example of a time-based programme of work. The diagram is intended to help in objective setting and does not show all the iterations in which earlier stages may have to be revised or replaced. You need to develop, in agreement with your supervisor, an appropriate version for yourself.

whether to accept them. If you are in this position and need help, then ask the departmental research tutor (see p. 198). Your proposal can only indicate the general field of interest which you intend to research. It is important that the field should really be of interest to you. You are going to spend a lot of time saturating yourself in it over the next few years. It should have some intrinsic attraction for you to help along your motivation, since you need all the boosts that you can get.

You may not be in a position to make choices about your field. This might come about because, for example, of the availability of apparatus, research sites, or funding. Then you have to work to kindle your interest in the area that *is* available to you.

Through your own choice or enlightened recognition of necessity, you have to develop during this period a commitment to your field of work capable of carrying you through to the end.

☐ *Possible topics*. This stage is concerned with getting ideas that are worth researching and researchable in the time available. The fact that it is not until the next stage that a choice of the actual thesis topic needs to be made does not mean that you can float through *this* stage having no specific topics but only general ideas – quite the opposite! You should be working up two or three topics in some detail to enable you to make a realistic professional choice at the next stage.

You should be thinking of two or three research proposals, each about, say, four pages long. These should form the bases of discussions with your supervisors in which you test out how viable they are in research terms, and how realistic in time terms. The capacity to spot worthwhile openings and fashion them into researchable topics is the key professional skill of the whole doctoral learning process, so practice at this stage is vital.

☐ *Pilot study*. The precise nature of this stage will vary considerably across disciplines. It may involve testing apparatus, data collection methods, sampling frames, availability of materials, etc. Essentially we are asking here: will it work?

☐ *Making a thesis proposal (including the design of the investigation)*. At this stage, which may be linked to upgrading to PhD status, you are going to work in much greater detail to establish that your proposed research investigation (a) will address the problem convincingly and (b) is likely to make a contribution. You will therefore need to examine the current focal theory fully and survey the background theory to estimate the likelihood of contributing.

A key point to bear in mind here is that an ideal design will involve 'symmetry of potential outcomes'. What this means is that ideally the thesis will not stand or fall by *a particular result*, but will be able to make a contribution whatever the outcome. Thus a high mean value or correlation will support one argument, while a low mean or lack of correlation will be equally interesting because it fits in with another line of approach. This symmetry cannot always be obtained, but it is worth exploring carefully to see whether you *can* obtain it. If present, it is a great advantage in establishing at a later stage the contribution of the research work.

☐ *Data collection and analysis.* The collection and analysis of data are activities clearly specific to each discipline and, within that, to each topic. One generalization that we would make though, is that good researchers at this stage are very close to their materials. They know their *raw data* practically by heart, let alone the analytical results that are derived from them. They are in no sense laid back but are living, eating and sleeping data and results. This involvement is very important as it is the psychological basis that gives researchers the facility to see the data from different angles and in terms of different theories. It enables them – often unconsciously – to 'test' their material against new, innovative, offbeat ideas. They conceptually play with their data, intuitively trying lots of 'what-ifs', and often can come up with a new, interesting conception that makes a contribution to the subject.

☐ *Final writing up.* For reasons already discussed in Chapter 4, the final writing-up stage always takes longer than intended. A period of three terms is not generous, even though it has been done in less time by determined and able students. Anything less than two terms full-time or a year part-time is unrealistic considering the nature of the task, which includes the 'contribution' component as described in Chapter 6.

Rightly or wrongly, the doctoral regulations do not explicitly preclude students from engaging the help of a professional editor to work on their thesis. There is a degree of ambiguity here, but it is clear that those students who are aware of the existence of professional copyeditors, know how to contact them and can afford to pay them, have an advantage over those who are more naive. Students who have never heard of copyeditors, are unaware of the legitimacy of using their services and would not, in any case, have the financial means at their disposal to engage them, are at a disadvantage.

The responsibility of a professional copyeditor is to contribute to the thesis only in terms of improving writing style, grammar and spelling. Any other changes – of meaning, for example – would not be a fair use of their services. But as supervisors are not usually told that an editor has been working on the student's thesis there is no control over the editor's input.

■ **Redefining long-term and short-term goals**

If you do not take this kind of structured approach to planning your PhD work, then one result will inevitably be a much greater dependence on your supervisor for feedback concerning your progress. Evaluating your own work will also be more difficult.

If you define short-term goals it will be less necessary to rely on external sources of information, such as supervisors, because the step-by-step structure will be clear. This clarity results in information on progress that you can interpret for yourself with very little difficulty. First, you will know whether you have managed to do what you said you would do; next, you will know whether you managed to do it in the time allocated. If – exceptionally, we must say – both these aspects of your work are as anticipated, then it is only the *quality* of the work that needs to be evaluated by your supervisor. In time you will be able to do this evaluation for yourself; but the best way of learning how to judge your own efforts is to pay careful attention to your supervisor's comments.

If, on the other hand, you discover that you have not managed to complete the projected work in the time assigned to it, you will be in a good position to analyse the reasons. You might estimate how much was due to circumstances that could neither have been foreseen nor prevented, and how much was due to your own inexperience, inactivity or inability to estimate the amount of work accurately. This last is the most usual discovery.

Typically, research students gradually realize that progress is slower than they had expected. This realization eventually leads to a reassessment of what may, realistically, be achieved. As this happens with short-term goals the related longer-term goals can be adjusted too. Once you know what it is you have to get done in the immediate future, it will not matter so much that your more distant goals are rather fuzzy. As you progress through a series of related goals, either the long-term ones get closer or, if they do not, you rethink what you want to achieve.

Sometimes the rethinking results in the overall goal of the PhD being changed to that of an MPhil. This is usually both unfortunate and unnecessary. The decision is based on panic, unless, of course, the original selection was incorrect or the supervisors have completely neglected their own part in the undertaking. More often the rethinking results in a narrowing and redefinition of the research problem. When such a redefinition occurs, which involves coming to terms with the limitations of research for a higher degree, it is a very good sign that one important lesson has already been learned.

An example of such positive redefinition as a result of disappointment with progress towards short-term goals comes from Adam. At first he said that his thesis would deal with the problem of 'how to transmit the building rule system of a culture in a way that can be used to accommodate change'. He knew precisely which books to read and that only very few of them would be in architecture. But his reading and note-taking became much more extensive and took many months longer than he had anticipated, primarily because he became very interested in a structuralist approach to social anthropology and cognitive development. His thesis eventually became a contribution to the controversy raging in design education concerning whether the designer is a tabula rasa who 'creates' according to inspiration, or whether there is a starting point with an existing lexicon of known forms.

The redefinition was possible because Adam had set himself short-term goals of writing specific sections within set time limits. As he repeatedly failed to achieve these goals, he decided to look at the long-term goals in the light of what he had discovered during the course of his reading, writing and note-taking. In this way his thesis became redefined. If he had just continued with his research without any kind of monitoring in the light of pre-set constraints, he would inevitably have had a last-minute panic. He would then have had to decide whether to take a much longer time to complete his thesis or, alternatively, to put together whatever he had managed to achieve in the time available and hope that it would be adequate.

■ **The importance of deadlines**

Where, you may ask, are the supervisors in all this? Well, of course, supervisors have a very important role to play in the negotiating and setting of short-term and long-term goals. However, many supervisors accept postponed appointments or long gaps between meetings with their research students without putting much effort into persuading them that they need a tutorial. This is often due to concern on the supervisors' part that they may be pressing their students and so causing undue stress. Sometimes it is because they assign too little importance to the task of supervision in comparison with their lecturing loads, developing their own research and keeping up their writing output.

It may be that supervisors are not really aware of just how important it is to ensure that goals are set and deadlines met. Students need a goal closer than 'a thesis some time in the future', but not all supervisors realize that even good students often lack confidence.

Many supervisors have difficulty in understanding that their students find it hard to create and work within a structured timetable. It seems clear to the supervisor, particularly if the work requires a series of experiments or interviews, that there is a natural structure which it is straightforward to follow. But very often students are confused and cannot decide what to do next. Despite the guidelines on student/supervisor meetings, supervisors may hesitate to take the initiative in setting up a programme of regular appointments when they believe that part of what characterizes successful PhD candidates is being able to organize and administer their own working pace.

Yet PhD students have supervisors because they need guidance and support. The relationship between them is the basis for a social approach to knowledge. What is often lacking is communication regarding expectations and needs, in fact anything relating to the process of doing a research degree. If you have followed the suggestions contained in Chapter 2 you will have already set up some kind of verbal agreement regarding the working relationship and the way in which you will each carry out your role. Such an agreement will lessen the ambiguity and confusion for both parties to this relationship and make it easier to discuss how to arrange meetings and the setting of deadlines.

Deadlines create a necessary tension between doing original work and reporting its progress, either orally or in writing. Very few people are able to work well without some pressure (either internal or external). Knowing that a deadline is looming is usually sufficient for most people to get on and do whatever it is they are supposed to do. In fact it is not at all unusual for people to leave things until the very last minute because they find it difficult to work well if they are not under pressure – a strategy not to be recommended. But neither is it desirable, when you have a long period of time in which to complete something, to have no steps along the way. Such a lack of structure in the task or its timing is not conducive to effective working.

For these reasons it is crucial to ensure that you have firm deadlines all the time. As we have seen with both Ewan and Adam, deadlines met and left behind provide a valuable index of how realistic the longer-term goals are. As you move towards them, those once-distant deadlines become short-term goals.

In fact for some students deadlines are very real external constraints. For example, for many biology students the seasons set clear time limits to experiments, with a year's penalty for failure to observe them. For many students, though, the timing of the work that they have to complete is not marked except by the final submission of the thesis. In such cases it is imperative that *pseudo-deadlines* are created.

Pseudo-deadlines are time limits accepted by the student as a motivating device. They may be set by your supervisors, agreed between you, or set by and for yourself. Even if this last is the case, you must ensure that you have somebody to report to once the deadline has been reached. The public commitment that you have set up in this way strengthens your motivation. It may be that a friend, colleague or relative will agree to help, but this should be only in order for you to take smaller steps than you have agreed with your supervisor. Your overall agreement with your supervisor must include provision for regular reporting meetings. While it may not always be necessary to provide a written report for such occasions, it is certainly advisable, as one of the most important things that you have to do during the course of your research degree is to keep writing.

Deadlines are as important for monitoring the development of thinking as they are for ascertaining that an agreed amount of reading or practical work has been completed. Whatever the short-term goals, regular opportunities to discuss progress and exchange ideas are vital to the development of the project and your continuing enthusiasm.

■ Self-help and peer support groups

Working towards the PhD is often experienced as an isolating and lonely time. This need not be the case. If you can arrange to meet regularly with others in your situation you will find that you can help yourself and them in several ways.

The first, and most obvious, is that you are no longer in solitary confinement, with nobody interested in your work, aware of what you are doing, or concerned about how you are feeling with regard to the research degree. You will discover, when you feel depressed and discouraged and are thinking seriously about dropping out, that this is part of the general malaise of postgraduate life and not peculiar to you and your inadequacies. Once you become aware that such feelings are experienced by the majority of research students from time to time, you will be able to put them into perspective as part of the process that has to be got through, instead of seeing them as proof of your own incompetence.

Further, once you are able to share these feelings and to talk about them and their effect on your work, you will all start to feel better. As one of the group confronts the problems, the others will be able to help, and when it comes to their turn they will remember how it was and know that it is possible to get through it. This may sound a little like Alcoholics Anonymous and that is precisely what it is, but the difference is that you are trying to continue doing research and writing it up, rather than trying to give up doing something.

A more pragmatic function for your group or peer (just one other postgraduate at your stage of the PhD is sufficient) is to help in keeping you to deadlines. Each of you states what work you want to do and sets a time limit for its completion. This commitment serves as a motivator. When that date arrives you meet, as already arranged, and talk about your progress. If you have done what you intended, then set another time limit for the next piece of work. If you have not done what you intended, discuss with the other(s) why this is so, what the problems were and how you feel about not having got to where you were aiming. Sometimes it is acceptable not to have continued because of things that have been discovered en route or because of overambitious planning. As long as these reasons are not just rationalizations, then there is nothing to be concerned about. If, on the other hand, you are dejected because of your failure to produce on time, then you need to talk about what happened in some detail. Once things have been clarified and you and your peer group are satisfied that the way is now clear to proceed, you can set new deadlines for the same, or a somewhat modified, piece of work.

Another positive function for this group of two or more people is to provide feedback on written work. It is not even necessary for you to be working in the same discipline. As long as your areas of research are reasonably comprehensible to each other, which is usually the case within a faculty, then there is no need for any real knowledge of the topic. For example, Evelyn, a social psychologist, and Joyce, a geographer, helped each other with drafts of their thesis chapters even though neither knew anything about the other's discipline. They were both social scientists, understood research methodology and statistics appropriate to the social sciences, and were able to read and understand English. This was sufficient for them to be of great help to each other until quite an advanced stage of thesis writing. They questioned that which they did not understand, which helped the writer to clarify her thinking and explain it more simply. They criticized complicated sentence structure and confusion in the structural development of a line of thought. They queried quantum leaps from the results of the research to interpretations based on the results, and generally learned from each other how to improve their own work, while also becoming interested in the other's research for its own sake. They are both convinced that they would never have completed their theses and gained their PhDs within the time they set themselves if they had not formed this self-help group of two. They are still firm friends several years later, and each proudly has a copy of the other's thesis.

■ Internet groups

You are also able to reduce your isolation by making contact through email and the Internet. Scanning the Internet will enable you to find a number of research conferences in your field of study which you can join and, in due course, contribute to. The World Wide Web allows you to make contact with others working in your field in other universities or even other countries. There are often specialist conferences for doctoral students in particular fields. In addition, with the help of your university library, you can locate theses at <*www.theses.com*>. You can also use your search engine (for example 'Google' or 'Ask Jeeves') to find other sites of interest to you, and of help to your work.

In Britain an important general contact that you should make early on is that of the National Postgraduate Committee. The Committee aims to discuss all issues of relevance to research students, and can be very helpful in making you aware of what is happening in other universities. It produces guidelines on a number of issues to help you in your discussions with your supervisor or departmental head. These include: codes of practice for postgraduate research, employment of postgraduate students as teachers, research degree appeals, and accommodation and facilities for postgraduate research. It has a website, <*www.npc.ac.uk*> and an electronic conference (<*postgrad@mailbase.ac.uk*>), runs an annual conference and sponsors the *Journal of Graduate Education* which reports research on doctoral students.

Another useful British support group is the UK GRAD schools. In addition to their website, <*www.gradschools.ac.uk*>, they run activities such as an annual conference and regular week-long courses which will help both in completing your PhD and in making a successful transition to a post-doctoral career. They are supported by the Research Councils, and, particularly if you are on a grant, you should explore your entitlement to attend their sessions.

■ Teaching while studying for a PhD

Casual teaching

Larger student numbers have resulted in university departments needing extra teaching staff. Many research students need both additional funding and experience of teaching in preparation for a future career. There has thus arisen a long established tradition of casual teaching by doctoral students which benefits all those involved. The teaching normally consists of taking seminars, marking essays, tutoring undergraduates and even giving lectures. In science subjects having to demonstrate in lab classes is standard practice.

The positive view of this arrangement is that it serves three useful functions. Overworked academics get the help that they need, undergraduate students get enthusiastic teachers and up-to-date information, and research students, in addition to earning some much needed money, get practice in some of the skills they will be required to develop if they wish to go into an academic job once they have gained their PhD.

It is clear, however, that this positive view may be somewhat overoptimistic. Research students can get little or no training in the skills needed, and be poorly paid. Teaching can require excessive amounts of time in preparation and marking and not all doctoral students intend to include teaching in their future careers.

Usually the department will give you a temporary contract of employment where the gross amount of pay for the contract is calculated on a piecework basis which clearly defines what you have to do. With such a contract you cannot be required to do more work than stated in the original agreement without extra payment. Having agreed to undertake some teaching, you should ensure that you get a letter of appointment specifying the tasks involved and their hourly rates. If these are below the rates recommended by the academic unions, then you have a basis for any negotiation in which you may get involved.

Teaching assistantships

Teaching assistants receive funding from their university which allows them to pursue a PhD in exchange for some teaching in their discipline. Teaching assistantships are welcome as they provide a source of funding for research students, but the terms and conditions of service vary widely between, and even within, universities. They often leave students significantly worse off than those on research council grants. Since assistants are employed by the university, they are taxed and they do not have the opportunity to supplement their income through casual teaching. So teaching assistants may be used as cheap labour in understaffed departments. In addition, many teaching assistantships run for the standard period of PhD registration, without allowing for the extra workload that teaching imposes on the student. In this situation teaching hampers research progress.

Sun Yi, in chemistry, is an example of a worst case scenario. Her particular arrangement was extremely ad hoc. She had to do up to 100 hours of demonstrating per semester in exchange for what was the minimum amount (paid for by the department and not a funding body.) Because the lab times were erratic, she was demonstrating far more than she had anticipated. This prevented her from having enough time to spend on her PhD research which was supposed to be full-time.

Some teaching experiments required her presence from start to finish and she would then have to work all weekend and late at night in order to get her research done. She was on a minimum income which was insufficient for her needs but, because of the time she had to spend in the lab, she was unable to work part-time to earn any more. She was clearly being exploited, and found completing her PhD a great burden.

By contrast, the National Postgraduate Committee's guidelines recommend a maximum of six hours teaching a week during term time, including all associated marking and preparation. This is equivalent to the maximum hours allowed by the research councils for those holding studentships. Many students find that their universities conform to this standard.

■ Action summary

[1] Be aware of the psychological stages that research students go through on the way to a PhD. Use discussion with your supervisor and peer support group to ensure that you do not get stuck at any one stage.

[2] Construct, in conjunction with your supervisor, an overall time plan of the stages of your research along the lines of the figure shown on page 83. This will enable you to locate your work in a time frame. Use this time plan to monitor your overall progress, and thus motivate yourself to continue on course.

[3] For each stage, construct a list of tasks that have to be carried out. This will enable you to monitor your detailed progress.

[4] With this approach, you will be in a better position to redefine any short-term goals in the (frequent) event of progress being slower than expected. It may even be necessary to redefine long-term goals.

[5] Deadlines are important. Set realistic deadlines and achieve them. If there are no external constraints acting as deadlines (e.g. nature of the research topic, conference paper, seminar presentation) then set pseudo-deadlines to report to your supervisor or a peer to act as a motivating device.

[6] Establish a peer support group with at least one other PhD student in order to give mutual criticism and encouragement and to act as monitor on time deadlines.

[7] Join Internet peer groups to widen your contacts.

[8] When accepting casual teaching work or becoming a teaching assistant, ensure you get a letter of appointment from the departmental administration stipulating rates, hours, responsibilities, etc. Be involved in any meetings to discuss the future of individual modules on which you teach.

[9] Refer to the self-evaluation questionnaire on student progress in the appendix to help you focus on the issues.

8

HOW TO MANAGE YOUR SUPERVISORS

In this chapter we shall be considering a series of strategies for handling the all-important student–supervisor relationship. The relationship is so crucial that students cannot afford to leave it to chance.

■ The supervisory team

Recommended guidelines, applicable to all British universities, state that every research student should have a supervisory team of at least two appropriate academics. Many universities indeed require a team of three to be set up for each student. The team consists of a lead or main supervisor who takes primary responsibility, plus a second supervisor to provide additional support when necessary. It may also be that a member of the team is appointed especially to give pastoral support. The team system also has the benefit of allowing new supervisors to have the opportunity of working with their more senior colleagues and thus obtain greater experience in supervision more quickly.

Supervisory teams are set up so that many of the difficulties that appear in the one-to-one supervisor–student relationship can be avoided, or at least reduced. There are many problems that can arise when the total weight of supervising is borne by a single person. For example, such a person may not be an expert in the whole range of the research topic, or may be interested in the academic field but not concerned with professional development of the student. The supervisor may be very busy with undergraduate teaching and administration, or may be on secondment for long periods. One may have had little or no experience of supervision and so may be unsure of the standards required for the PhD, another may be highly experienced but frequently out of the country attending conferences and giving papers and so not be available when the student needs attention. Or the personal chemistry between the supervisor and the student may not be right. Problems such as these will be less likely to completely impair progress if there is another academic on whom the student has a right to call for supervisory help.

■ The supervisory team's limitations

The supervisory team system does have its limitations though, and you may find yourself on the receiving end of some of them. Having more than one supervisor may seem like a good idea at first; after all, two or even three academics, instead of just one, will be involved in your research studies. But there are negative as well as positive aspects to be considered. Difficulties may stem from:

☐ *Undue predominance of two supervisors over one student.* There should be regular three-way meetings with both your supervisors. However, such meetings may present problems for you, the student, in terms of feeling overwhelmed. It is possible that you might feel that you have powerful people ganging up on you which could reduce the expression of your real ideas and feelings. Guard against this and, if necessary, let your supervisors know that you need help in this respect.

☐ *Diffusion of responsibility.* Where no distinction in agreed roles is established between members of staff, there is the clear likelihood that each supervisor will regard the other as taking the lead and having more of the responsibility. Even if this feeling is only subconscious, as it may well be, it acts to reduce the commitment of both of them. There have also been cases where supervisors use the student in order to score points off each other in their own power struggles. You must try to ensure that these problems of appropriate contribution are addressed early in the process so that all of you know exactly who will be doing what, and when. An important step is to get agreement on the unequivocal division of the areas of responsibility between your supervisors.

☐ *Getting conflicting advice.* The probability of seeing all your supervisors at the same time is considerably less than that of seeing them separately. They almost certainly will not have had a chance to confer beforehand, so it could happen that you are regularly given conflicting advice. If the conflict is not major, the commonest way out for you is to do what they suggest, in the end doing considerably more work and delaying the progress of the project.

☐ *Playing one supervisor off against another.* It is not only the supervisors' behaviour that might lead to problems – you, the student, also have a dangerously seductive avenue available. If you feel frustrated, alienated, trapped into doing something not of your choosing, then you can spend (waste) a lot of time and emotional energy playing one supervisor off against another. Beware, be warned, avoid such a course of action. For this reason, it is more useful for you to have a first supervisor who takes the lead and a second supervisor who gives support – rather than two equals.

☐ *Lack of an overall academic view.* Probably the most important difficulty associated with supervisory teams is that there is less likely to be one person who is willing to take an overall view of the thesis. Who will evaluate and criticize it as a whole in the same fashion as the examiners? The weight of the necessary self-evaluation that you have to do is therefore considerably increased.

☐ *Lack of the supervisors functioning as a team.* There are cases where lead supervisors feel very possessive of their students and dislike the whole idea of sharing them with others. They resent the participation of even a second supervisor as diluting their authority, and freeze them out.

For example, one professor of engineering science in an old traditional university said of the establishment of supervisory teams:

> It will never work. All it would do is ensure that students are not looked after. The student–supervisor relationship is both intense and personal. Students need to know that they can depend on their supervisor, although of course they are encouraged to take every opportunity to talk to others. Supervisors need to know that they have responsibility for a particular student. It is also important for staff development that they can personally claim a number of successfully completed PhD graduates to put on their CVs.

By contrast, in other cases it is the second supervisor who is happy to remain purely nominal, hardly making a contribution at all. Or you may find that you do not have a team to supervise you because you are in a department where the staff are not committed to this way of working.

These are some of the pitfalls to be avoided with a supervisory team, and it is very important indeed that considerable care be given to its operation. Be prepared to confront problems as soon as you notice any signs of their existence.

In spite of these potential difficulties there is every reason to expect team supervision to work well, provided it is given sufficient thought. To increase the likelihood of success, bear in mind the following two golden rules of communication:

1 *Meetings*: Arrange a preliminary joint meeting where all of you discuss how the project should develop. Arrange further meetings at least once a term (always remembering to be aware of the cautions given above).
2 *Reports*: Ensure that all your supervisors are kept on board. They should be made fully aware of your progress by sending each of them a copy of what you are currently writing, but make it clear whether it is for 'information only' or 'for comments'. Ensure that they know of each others' reactions to your work if there are differences. This enables you to call on them for their special knowledge and skills and thus obtain good supervisory support.

Finally, remember that even if you have more than one supervisor, it does not mean that you cannot have access to the expertise of other academics for particular aspects of your work. You can, and certainly should, go to them for help, advice, and criticism as often as you need them. Your supervisors are not going to object as long as you make sure that they are kept informed of any developments in your work.

■ What supervisors expect of their doctoral students

So the student–supervisor relationship is a key element in your success as a PhD student. As we have seen above, it must be managed. If you are to do this well, you must understand what your supervisors expect of you. Once you have this inside information, you will be in a better position to develop the skills necessary to reduce any communication barriers and sustain the relationship for mutual benefit. In a series of interviews EMP found the following set of expectations to be general among supervisors regardless of discipline.

Supervisors expect their students to be independent

This is not as straightforward as it may at first appear. Despite the emphasis put on independence throughout the whole period of working for a PhD degree, there are still very important aspects of the process that demand conformity: conformity to accepted methodologies, to departmental and university policies, to style of presentation, to the ethics of the discipline, and to all those things which your supervisors consider to be important. They are in a powerful position with regard to your work and to your own progress through the system. For these reasons it is no simple matter to balance the required degree of conformity with the need to be independent. The difficulty is compounded when we remember that many research students come directly from a university and from schools that encourage obedience. The problem was made explicit by Dr Chadwick when he spoke of his first-year research degree student in theoretical astronomy:

> Charles asks too frequently, 'What do I do next?' I prefer a student to think for himself. He's not among the very best people we've had, but his progress is reasonably satisfactory. The only slight hesitation I have about him is an indication of lack of original thought shown in an obedient attitude, which results in his doing whatever I say.

Here we have a situation where the student needs to be given the structure necessary for organizing his work, but the supervisor considers that to direct his student to such an extent would be making him too dependent. In this case Charles went to several members of staff in the department asking for their advice on what he should be doing. In an interview about his progress he said: 'Nobody cares if you come in or you don't, if you work or you don't. There's no point in making any effort – it's important to have someone standing over you.'

Charles was emphasizing the fact that, as he saw it, it was not necessary to do any work that was not being closely monitored. He needed more direction than his supervisor was prepared to give and wished to rely more on Dr Chadwick's assessment of his work than on his own judgement. Charles should have spoken more openly to his supervisor about his difficulties in becoming instantly independent in his new situation. Of course, this is easier said than done. First, a student has to identify the problem and, secondly, pluck up enough courage to raise the issue in discussion. (It might help to take this book in – opened at this page!) If Charles had managed to raise the subject, a lot of unhappiness on the part of the student and disappointment on the part of the supervisor would have been avoided.

Supervisors expect their students to produce written work that is not just a first draft

Having actually written something, you may well feel such a sense of achievement and relief that you want to get it in to your supervisor's hands immediately – especially if you have already missed a deadline or two! However, it is no more than a matter of courtesy to take the time and trouble to present it properly. Do not expect your supervisor to act as a copyeditor for your thesis.

Seeking advice and comments on your work from others is an excellent method of ensuring that you optimize the time spent in discussing your work with your supervisor. It also ensures that you maintain contact with others who are interested in you, your work, and how you spend your time. One of the major dissatisfactions with the lifestyle of a research worker is that nobody else either understands or cares about what it is that the researcher is doing. This leads to almost complete isolation and a feeling that perhaps it really isn't worthwhile after all. An effective means for combating this and, in addition, gaining helpful input into your work is to keep one or two other people in close touch with what you are doing.

These people can either be other academics, research students with whom you form an exchange self-help relationship, or they can be significant people in your life. The best way of keeping them in touch with what you are doing is to talk about your work from time to time. Surprisingly you avoid the risk of becoming boring and making your work dominate the relationship by offering drafts of written work for them to read and comment upon. This has two benefits: it allows you to spend the rest of your time together on other topics of conversation. Also it boosts their morale to think that somebody who is doing a PhD values their opinions. What this means is that you must be prepared (and willing) to accept criticism from your peers and not only from your supervisors and others in more senior positions than you. Hopefully the feedback will be constructive and you will be able to select from it those points which seem to you to be of help. This might be in rethinking an idea, restructuring some paragraphs or generally clarifying items that were not initially well presented by you because of your close association with the draft.

If you choose your readers carefully, you will probably find that you want to redraft some sections, if not all, of what you have written before giving it to your supervisor for comment and discussion. By these means you will (a) achieve a relationship with, at the very least, one other person who will be able to talk coherently and knowledgeably with you about what you are currently doing, and (b) offer to your supervisor work that has been trimmed and developed to a more sophisticated level than your initial rough draft.

Presentation is a very important component of both the final thesis and of any interim conference papers or journal articles that you will wish to submit. Therefore, having the discipline to ensure that all reports to your supervisor leave you in a clearly printed form is a necessary part of your training and good practice for the future. To maximize the time you spend with your supervisor and to get the best you can in the way of comments and suggestions from any readers of your paper, is a valuable reward for having made the effort to present your ideas in an easily readable way.

Supervisors expect to have regular meetings with their research students

Regular meetings can occur daily, weekly, monthly, termly or even half-yearly. The more frequent the meetings, the more casual they are likely to be, helping to create a climate for discussion. Formal tutorial meetings are less frequent and need to be prepared for on both sides. Usually supervisors expect to meet with their research students every four to six weeks. It is a good idea to discuss the frequency of meetings when you first agree the kind of student–supervisor relationship you are going to have. We have already considered (in Chapter 2) the advantages and disadvantages of more and less frequent meetings, so you will realize the importance of ensuring that a principle is established that is satisfactory for both your own and your supervisor's way of working.

Your supervisor has to fit tutorial meetings with you (and other postgraduates) into what is probably an already full work schedule. In order to be of most use to you, your supervisor will have had to spend some time prior to the meeting thinking about you, your research and any problems connected with it, reading anything that you have written and preparing a focus point for the tutorial. In order for you to get the best out of your supervisor it is essential that you allow ample time between setting up the meeting and the actual date. It is a good strategy to agree dates for the next tutorial during the course of the previous one. It is also important that you do in fact turn up at the appointed time and date. If you are late it produces additional difficulties for the meeting. Either it will be cut short or your supervisor will be worrying about work that should be attended to but is being neglected because of the time given to you. If you cancel a meeting at short notice, the time and thought that your supervisor has already invested in it is wasted, nor does it augur well for your future relationship or the seriousness with which future meetings will be treated.

A very important part of managing your supervisor is to set a good example. If you find that your supervisor is not as exemplary as the above model suggests, you can provide encouragement by behaving in an exemplary way yourself. By doing so you demonstrate that you expect tutorials to be well prepared and treated with equal respect on both sides. You may even wish to phone or email a day or two before the planned meeting to confirm with your supervisor that everything is in order for it and to ask whether there is anything else you should be thinking about or preparing that may not have been mentioned previously. At the end of the tutorial, be sure that both you and your supervisor have noted in writing what has been agreed as the next stage of the work.

Supervisors expect their research students to be honest when reporting on their progress

Supervisors are not idiots – at least, not many of them – and they are not fooled by absent students who leave messages saying that everything is fine and they will soon be needing a meeting or sending in a written draft. Neither are they taken in by the student who does put in an appearance from time to time, talks volumes about work in hand, new ideas and the next steps about to be taken in practical work, and then disappears again, never submitting anything tangible in the form of precise figures, graphs, experimental results or, of course, written work.

If there is a problem, if you are blocked, if you have lost confidence, if you are experiencing domestic troubles of whatever kind, or if anything else at all is interfering with the continuation of your work, then do let your supervisors know about it.

Supervisors expect their students to follow the advice that they give, especially when it has been given at the request of the postgraduate

Now this really does seem to be a most reasonable expectation, yet it is surprising how often it is contravened. For example, when Bradley asked whether his reading was going along the right lines, Mrs Briggs told him that he needed to know the romantic literature. She explained that it was not enough to know the area only through two writers. But Bradley decided to concentrate on four works and read them thoroughly and carefully, rather than following up a lot of leads at the same time. He could not see the point of reading the works of other authors when his PhD was to focus on a specific work of a specific writer. In other words he had not received the answer he was hoping for when he requested the advice – and so ignored it.

This upset Mrs. Briggs. She had believed that she had an excellent relationship with Bradley, but she now interpreted his behaviour to mean that he had no respect for her as a supervisor. She felt unable to work with a student who believed he knew what was best regardless of having asked for guidance and so requested that he be transferred to someone else. The result of this was that Bradley wasted a year trying to find another academic who was competent in both Italian and English literature. When he did find a new supervisor, she looked at what he had done to date and then, just as Mrs Briggs, recommended that he familiarize himself more widely with the romantic literature!

Supervisors expect their students to be excited about their work, able to surprise them and fun to be with!

If you are not excited about your research who else will be? How can you expect to arouse anybody else's excitement, enthusiasm, interest? When postgraduates are really excited about what they are doing, it stimulates those around them. Excitement is infectious. It works to the advantage of the student concerned if other people want to know what is happening and encourage conversation around the research. It is invigorating to be in the centre of a hub of energy and enthusiasm. There is a world of difference between working away for the sake of getting on with something (in an environment where there is little communicable interest in what is happening) and wanting to tackle the next task because of the desire to push ahead and then let everyone else know about your progress.

Of course, there is a line to be traversed here between becoming unbearably boring and pompous about what you are doing and maintaining that element of excitement. If you succeed in maintaining this level of motivation then not only will your postgraduate days be days of enjoyment and anticipation, but you will also have a headstart on managing your supervisor to fit in with your own ideas of how the relationship between you should operate.

Being able to surprise your supervisor stems from the fact that, if you are to be successful, it should not be too long before you know more about your area of research than your supervisor does. To be awarded a PhD means that you must have become expert in your research topic. Therefore, although your supervisor is an expert in closely related areas, such expertise will fall short of the depth and detail on your own topic that you yourself are now developing. For these reasons your supervisor will expect to be constantly surprised by new information, evidence and ideas that you are able to supply. Supervisors do not expect to be shocked by their students' failure to conform to a professional code of conduct, or a moral approach to their subjects. To manage your supervisor successfully be sure that you steer a course between surprising them and shocking them.

Be fun to be with! Perhaps you think this is asking too much, but just imagine how much more enjoyable your own work is when you actually like the people with whom you are working. Three years plus is a very long time indeed to spend with somebody who makes you feel ill at ease. In other words, it is wiser to select your research topic to match the supervisor of your choice, than to select your topic and then be allocated to the relevant academic specialist. Just as you may take an instant dislike to somebody, so too may your supervisor. It may not be as extreme as that of course, but doing a PhD is an intense and emotional experience that continues over a very long period of time.

What this means in interpersonal terms is that any irritant, no matter how minor it may appear in the beginning, becomes exaggerated and distorted over time until it is well-nigh intolerable. This works in both directions so that the supervisors' expectation of enjoying the time they spend with their students has its payoff for you too. It is not that you have to spend your time thinking up witticisms and novel ways of entertaining supervisors, in the hope of being invited to spend more of your out-of-work time with them and their social group. It is merely advisable to follow the instructions given in Chapter 2. If you have chosen your supervisors carefully and discussed the way that the supervisory relationship will work, then you have a headstart over those who have not gone to this trouble.

Like any relatively long-term relationship, the one that you have with your supervisor will change over time. If you begin cautiously then you increase the probability that the two of you will gradually grow to appreciate each other and so get to the point where you might even discover that you too expect your supervisor to be fun to be with. You might even find that in working well together, you manage to have fun too.

■ The need to educate your supervisors

We have already discussed the importance of keeping your supervisors informed of new developments and findings as your work advances. Earlier in this chapter we mentioned that you will gradually become more expert, better informed and perhaps more skilled in specific techniques, methods and areas of investigation than your main supervisor.

Managing your supervisor efficiently involves an educational programme as well as a training course. The training course involves fulfilling the expectations of supervisors and moulding them to fit with your own needs and requirements. The educational programme need not be so subtle, as it is more acceptable to acknowledge that you will know more than your supervisor about your research topic, given time, than it is to admit that you have a supervisor who does not know how to supervise effectively. Nevertheless, it is recommended that you enhance the education programme by presenting information to your supervisor in as surprising and stimulating a manner as you can, thus maintaining an optimum level of excitement about your findings. All this will help to make you fun to be with too.

So much for the style. The content is important and not quite as uncomplicated as it may at first appear. You might find yourself in murky waters if you assume too little knowledge on the part of your supervisor or, alternatively, if you show that you have realized from your discussions that there are gaps in your supervisor's knowledge of the specialist field. It is fine to mention any new findings that are a direct result of your research, and indeed they must be mentioned in order to demonstrate the progress that you are making. Any readings or discussions with others that teach you something you did not previously know may also be mentioned easily to your supervisor. But beware of doing this in such a way that it becomes clear that you believe that your supervisor was also unaware of this information. In other words, it may be necessary to educate your supervisor by giving information in a manner that assumes that your supervisor already knew about the things that are only now becoming accessible to you.

Such measures will become less necessary as time passes and your own work becomes more advanced. You will find, if you have handled the situations described here sensitively, that your relationship with your supervisor has changed from one in which the supervisor is guiding or directing your work to one where you are in control of what you are doing. Instead of being someone from whom you need information and approval, he or she gradually becomes someone with whom you can discuss new ideas and develop your thinking. You will be more inclined to use your supervisor as a sounding board, as an expert with the ability to proffer the reverse argument to be countered. Instead of a teacher, the supervisor becomes a colleague and the relationship becomes less asymmetrical than it was. In fact, this is the central aim towards which your relationship with your supervisors should be working.

It may be that you will have specialized in a particular technique or method so that your supervisor will not be able to test or replicate your investigations without considerable new learning and practice. It will then be more likely that your own findings and results will be accepted as correct, even if they seem doubtful, than would otherwise be the case. In such circumstances your reasoning as to why you think you should have got these results becomes an important focus in your discussions. Your interpretation of the evidence will also have to stand up to very strong inspection. All this is to the good because it gives you practice in arguing your case, which is an essential skill both for your viva and for any conference papers and seminars that you give on the topic.

The learning that goes on in such a situation is very much two-way. You learn from your supervisors what kinds of questions are important and how to respond to them; your main supervisor learns from you about the new methodological development and how it might be expected to affect the discipline.

Once your supervisors see that you have confidence in what you are doing and begin to respect your work, it will become easier for you to educate them. Supervisors do benefit from having research students and they are aware of the role these students have in keeping them, the busy academics, in touch with new developments and at the forefront of knowledge in their field. All you have to do to keep your supervisors in a position to be of help to you throughout the whole period of your research is to ensure that they are aware of what you are discovering, more or less as you are discovering it.

If you are at this stage and feel that your supervisors are not taking your work as seriously as you would wish in giving comments, a good tactic is to ask whether the report, etc. warrants presentation in a conference paper. This makes it more likely that the work will then be fully evaluated.

■   **How to reduce the communication barrier**

It should be clear by now that it is necessary for you to educate your main supervisor to become the kind of person that you find it easy to talk to. It should also be clear that there are a variety of ways in which you can begin to do this. Some of them have already been mentioned, but now let us look at them a little more closely.

It is first necessary to realize and remember that there is usually a difference between what supervisors actually do and what their students believe them to have done. For example, the time that supervisors allocate to their students includes time given to thinking about you, the student, as well as the obvious time allocation needed for reading what you write and the tutorial meeting.

It is important to show that you are aware and appreciative of the hidden time and effort that your supervisor gives to you. Showing your appreciation of this will make it easier for you to talk to each other more frankly, not merely gearing the conversation to purely technical matters. In fact, all too many supervisors feel that in discussion they need to keep closely to the actual work, thus avoiding the all-important PhD process which includes your relationship. They may not have any experience of discussing openly and freely what they perceive to be 'personal matters'.

An example of this comes from Professor Andrews and Adam. The supervisor said of their tutorial meetings, 'He always seems to go off in a more contented frame of mind than when he arrives', but Adam reported, 'I haven't found a way of telling him how very frustrated I am with these meetings.' Here we have misunderstanding and a clear breakdown of communication between them. The misread signals resulted in the student being unable to follow any advice that he was given. This is partly due to the student's disappointment that Professor Andrews did not say what he, Adam, wanted him to say but merely assumed that everything was in order between them. If Adam had been better at managing his supervisor, he would have told the professor how he felt, which would have opened up the way to a more honest and trusting relationship between them.

Improving tutorials

The most basic lesson to be learned in managing your supervisor is the necessity of encouraging very broad-ranging discussions. By doing so you reduce the communication barrier. It is a good idea for you, the student, to take responsibility for the content of your tutorials. You may wish to enter a tutorial with a proposed list of topics for discussion. If necessary, ask your supervisor for an equivalent list so that a joint agenda can be agreed. There are almost always misunderstandings to be clarified.

The way to get your supervisor talking about what may be perceived as taboo topics is to ask direct, but positively constructed, questions revealing that you are assuming good intentions on their part. It is always a good idea to start from a general question that is not focused directly on the actual work, but neither should it be too personal too soon. For example:

Am I making enough use of the learning opportunities available?

Do you think that I am managing to get enough work done in the time between our meetings?

Are you satisfied with how I use your comments?

Are you satisfied with my attitude towards your supervision of me?

How do you think we might work together more effectively?

Such a series of questions should lead naturally into a conversation about the relationship itself. If supervisors do not feel unfairly judged, they will be more open. There will be no need for either of you to use defensive tactics, such as hiding behind technical details.

A further component in reducing the communication barrier with your supervisor was described in Chapter 2. Discussing your expectations and hopes for the working relationship between you is of prime importance. If you agree an informal contract that includes the amount and type of contact that would be acceptable at different times during the course of the work, you will have an effective basis for discussing any deviations. Your needs change over time, so part of the contract should be an agreement to review at agreed intervals, probably annually. With such a contract it is also easier for any party to request a change if the relationship is not working well.

In Chapter 7 we talked about the importance of deadlines. Here again is an important step in managing your supervisors. You must ensure that every time you leave a tutorial meeting there is another one agreed and written into your diaries. It is less important how near or far into the future the next meeting is; what is vital is that a date should have been fixed on which you know that you have to face your supervisor again.

We have seen how essential it is for you to receive effective feedback, so do make sure that when the date fixed for a meeting arrives you help your supervisor to make the most of the time available. Once again, ask the right questions for eliciting the information that you need. If your supervisor says 'This section is no good', you should respond – tactfully, of course – with 'What precisely is wrong with it?' It may be that the grammatical construction is unacceptable, or that the conceptual design is misleading or confused, or that the section is irrelevant, or any of a dozen other things. You have to establish exactly what it is that is being criticized and what you can do about it to put it right. You may need to omit the section completely, or move it to another part of the report, or rewrite it, or rethink it before rewriting it. You must help your supervisor to express clearly, and with as much information as possible, what it is that is wrong. Once you have the information, you will be in a position to do something about it. You might want to discuss it further, and perhaps disagree; or persuade your supervisor of the correctness of the point you were trying (but apparently failed) to make; or go off and do whatever has been agreed.

Be sure to make a short summary of what occurred during each tutorial. This single sheet of paper should be photocopied with student and supervisors keeping a copy. In this way all can refer to what has been agreed, and have a continuous record of how the work and the supervision is progressing. There are several advantages to this systematic method of keeping track of the development of the research process. The student has an aide-mémoire of what was discussed. Ideas suggested by a supervisor are less likely to be forgotten, and work agreed to be done in preparation for the next meeting is recorded. For the supervisor, the summary serves as a reminder of the work of that particular student, thus greatly reducing confusion when more than one student is being supervised. In addition, if, unfortunately, any serious dispute arises between you and your supervisors, the summary can be used as evidence of what has been taking place.

It may even be necessary for you to help your supervisor to understand what doing a PhD means to you. For example, Mrs Briggs contrasted working on a PhD unfavourably with writing a book; she thought of it as preparation only for becoming a university teacher through creating and concentrating on artificial problems. However, as we have explained, a PhD is a thorough training in doing research and learning the criteria and quality required for becoming a fully professional researcher in a chosen field. It admits the holder to a club in which you are recognized as an authority and accepted as a person who is knowledgeable enough in a specialized area to be able to extend the boundaries of the subject when necessary. Doing a PhD is a hard training ground for a specific profession.

If, unusually, your department does not have regular seminars you can suggest introducing them. They should take the form of a meeting in which you and other postgraduates can discuss your ideas for research and the problems encountered en route. A meeting of this kind will make it easier for you and your supervisors to talk to each other on subjects not directly connected with the minutiae of your research.

Finally, if you want to succeed in managing your supervisor, you have to ensure that you do not make excessive demands and become a nuisance. Always speak honestly about anything that is bothering you and be direct in your requests and your questions. Take the responsibility for keeping the lines of communication open, because it is you who have the most to lose when misunderstandings and communication breakdowns occur. Try to make the relationship with your supervisors as far as possible a shared, if inevitably asymmetrical, partnership.

Changing supervisors

It may be that you will feel that the relationship with your main supervisor is not developing satisfactorily, and you might therefore consider changing. We are not referring here to situations where it becomes necessary to change supervisors for extraneous reasons (for example, your supervisor leaves the university) but to situations in which you wish to initiate a change.

There is usually a formal mechanism that allows for the possibility of such a change, but it cannot be emphasized too strongly that this is a course not to be undertaken lightly. In the very early period of the research, during the first few months of establishing more precisely your common areas of research interest, an obvious mismatch of interests can often be rectified with relatively little difficulty. But a change made after that period, or made for any other reason, requires considerable heart-searching.

A change of supervisors is the academic equivalent of getting a divorce. There are the formal (legal) mechanisms for doing it, but the results are achieved inevitably only after considerable emotional upset. There are important consequences for the supervisor's professional status and self-esteem if a student initiates a change. Thus it is bound to be a difficult process – often ending with metaphorical blood on the walls.

The important key to the process is to find and make use of a third party as a mediator. There should be such a person available. It might be the sub-dean for research, the convenor of the doctoral programme, the chair of the higher degrees committee, or the research tutor – the title will vary, but it will be a person who takes some responsibility for the system of doctoral supervision as a whole. If there is nobody specifically allocated to this task, then it is always possible to approach your head of department, who has overall responsibility for the academic working of the department.

The importance of the third party is in helping to improve communication so that both you and your supervisor get a better understanding of the problems. This role is also vital to finding ways of getting your current supervisor to accept a change, if that turns out to be necessary, without feeling too damaged by it. The third party is also essential for offering advice on, and making preliminary contact with, a new supervisor. The relationship between your old and your new supervisors, as departmental colleagues, will be preserved more easily with the help of the third party.

As an example, let us consider Nick. He was interested in working in a certain field of management operations in which research is not yet well developed. In his first year he attended seminars given by doctoral students across the whole range of management research. After some months he began to feel that his supervisor, Dr Newman, was not really directing the advice she was giving him to the sort of research approach he observed in his colleagues. It was far more discursive and descriptive than the analysis his peers were engaged in. Dr Newman, on the other hand, felt that Nick was neglecting her advice on how to proceed, because he did not want to put in the groundwork to make himself knowledgeable about the field. In her view this was more important than the methodology.

Like so many students and supervisors in their position, they carried on for the whole of the first academic year with this uneasy relationship: Nick thinking that Dr Newman didn't really understand research, and she thinking that Nick didn't really want to do research that was worth doing in relation to her field. Towards the end of the year, the director of the doctoral programme became aware of this mutual dissatisfaction, and in discussion with both of them separately the possibility of transfer to another supervisor was considered.

Dr Newman believed that Nick would never carry out any research in her field anyway, so somebody else might as well have him. The proposed new supervisor was prepared to take him provided Nick was willing to start again from the beginning. The change was accomplished because the third party took the initiative in making all three aware of the relevant issues. Nick had lost a year in getting it all sorted out, but did indeed eventually obtain his PhD in the new field. Even so, Nick and Dr Newman avoided each other, literally not exchanging a word, for the remainder of his time as a research student.

Monica, doing research into computer systems analysis, is another example of the difficulties involved in changing supervisors. She was so unhappy with the supervision she had received that, when asked about it a year after having gained her PhD, she started to cry and had to struggle to find the words to describe her feelings. She said:

> I knew that if I did the higher degree it would be difficult to get through it and that I needed a certain type of person – someone with a lot of grit – to supervise me. Dr Montague's a nice person outside of his role as supervisor but he wasn't the right kind of person for me. The personal relationship between us was never established. I've blotted out most of this period except the pain.

Monica never felt that her work was taken seriously by Dr Montague. He saw her for tutorials only in his own home, with his children demanding attention. His comments were always supportive, and she felt that he was not being helpful by sparing her any criticism. Nor did he offer her any suggestions which she could build on.

Clearly some exercise of assertiveness would have been useful in this situation. Monica could have said quite unequivocally that she would appreciate it if Dr Montague would arrange to see her in his office during working hours, so that he could discuss her work privately. She could also have asked him direct and detailed questions as to how her work could be improved.

In fact, Monica eventually adopted an additional unofficial supervisor whom she felt would take her thesis work seriously. Dr Montague made no comment on this. It happened that the other academic was the acting head of the department and encouraging all research initiatives. After this relationship had continued for about 18 months the change of supervisors was formalized by the university.

■ Inappropriate personal relationships in supervision

There are regulations in most institutions that preclude friends or family members from being examiners of PhD candidates, but the issue of being supervised by someone with whom you may have a close personal relationship (e.g. your spouse or parent) is not covered by the regulations. Such a situation can have considerable disadvantages, as can a developing amorous relationship between student and supervisor.

The problem is that the role of supervisor and the roles of parent, spouse, partner or lover are to a considerable extent incompatible. In the first place the supervisory role inevitably involves a considerable amount of professional criticism, hopefully constructive, but criticism nonetheless. This is most effectively given in a purely professional relationship. If there are many non-professional ties of a personal and emotional nature, the student is much more likely to be upset by criticism or, conversely, to become more and more dependent. In either case the intended development of the student into an effective, fully professional independent researcher becomes more difficult.

Second, a close personal relationship with the supervisor may well disrupt the student's other relationships in the department. For example, the student may find that others, students and staff alike, may be reluctant to involve themselves so that the student becomes disadvantaged through lack of discussion and other learning opportunities. This reluctance is due to the fact that others feel uncomfortable because they are aware that any comments they may make about their own experience in the department would get back to that particular supervisor. What might have been the development of new friends is curtailed, and even ordinary interactions and collaboration can become viewed by peers and staff as professionally dangerous, if the student is considered to have a special line to a high-status supervisor.

We firmly believe that this is a situation to be avoided as much for the sake of the personal relationship as for the progress of the work and your interactions with peers. The medical and psychological professions regard amorous relationships between practitioner and patient or client as seduction. Similarly, there is a clear argument for romantic involvement between supervisor and student to be treated as a violation of ethical professional conduct.

■ Action summary

1. Be aware that you must accept the responsibility for managing the relationship between you and your supervisors. It is too important to be left to chance.
2. Ensure that you have a first supervisor and a second supervisor, rather than two supervisors with equal responsibility. Get assurances from your supervisors that they will maintain email or telephone contact with each other, and jointly meet with you once a term at a minimum.
3. Try to fulfil the expectations that supervisors have of their students. If you cannot fulfil any of these expectations do not neglect them, but raise the issues in discussion.
4. You need to educate your supervisors continually: first on the research topic, in which you are fast becoming the expert; second on ways of understanding how the supervisory role can best help in your own professional development.
5. Look for ways of reducing the communication barrier between you and your supervisory team. In addition to research content, discuss at various times working relationships, setting deadlines, what doing a PhD means to you, the adequacy of provision for research students, and so on.
6. Ensure that every time you leave a tutorial you have agreed and noted down a date for the next one. Be punctilious in meeting appointments and deadlines, so that your supervisors will be too.
7. Help your supervisor to give you better feedback on your work. Always ask supplementary questions to ensure that you understand fully what is being required of you.
8. If you are seriously considering changing supervisors, use an appropriate third party as a mediator.
9. Avoid inappropriate personal relationships with your supervisor.
10. Refer to the self-evaluation questionnaire on student progress in the appendix to help you focus on the issues.

HOW TO SURVIVE IN A PREDOMINANTLY BRITISH, WHITE, MALE, FULL-TIME, HETEROSEXUAL ACADEMIC ENVIRONMENT

University departments in Britain are largely staffed by British white male full-time academics. Female academics are often in junior posts, or on short-term contracts; many are working part-time. Only about 1 member in 20 of academic staff is black or Asian; about 1 in 50 is disabled. What does this mean for research students who are not members of the majority group? They may experience forms of discrimination including racism, sexism, heterosexism, ageism and the barriers that we erect against the disabled. They therefore may need help through equal opportunities policies and practices.

■ Part-time students

What does it mean for part-time students that the PhD process is primarily organized around the idea of three or four years' full-time work? There are institutions that cater specifically for part-time higher degree students but arrangements can usually be made to do a research degree on a part-time basis in a conventional university. Indeed, part-time research students are in a majority overall, although there are considerable variations by departments. However there are problems experienced by part-time students that the individual engaged in full-time research does not encounter.

The main problem is that of having to switch repeatedly from everyday work to research work. This is primarily a psychological difficulty, but of course time enters into it too. Some students find that trying to work on their PhD every evening after concentrating on other things during the day is self-defeating. It takes so long to get back to where they left off that there is very little time to do any work before needing to get some sleep. Also, once they are absorbed in the task it is just as difficult to force themselves to stop in order to rest.

In order to cope with this difficulty, try your best to choose a research problem that is related to your work. As so much of your time is spent in your place of work, it makes good sense to maximize the facilities and resources that are available to you there. In addition, a carefully selected topic can help you to avoid the constant switching that is otherwise necessary for people doing two different jobs.

Part-time students have reported setting aside weekends for their PhD work to overcome these difficulties. The problem then is that they often become resentful at having to give up all their spare time to research and writing. When this happens it is not long before they decide that the work is not worth the effort and begin to change their minds about wanting a higher degree after all.

Attempt to avoid this by making a contract with yourself to set aside specific periods of time for your PhD work. This might be, for example, alternate weekends and all bank holidays plus two consecutive evenings every week, or you might be in a position to take a whole week off work for uninterrupted application to your research. Try to make all necessary domestic and professional arrangements beforehand, so that the significant people in your life are aware of the way in which you are allocating your time and attention.

It may be that you can arrange to have at least one whole weekday to spend on the research each week, the best day to choose would be one that either follows or precedes other days spent working on the research. This is preferable to the more popular habit of opting for a day that gives you a break from other work in the middle of the week. For example, if you spend a whole two-day weekend (Saturday and Sunday) on research work, then you can turn those two days into three by selecting either Monday or Friday as your one extra day. Any other weekday would mean that you have to waste time thinking yourself back to where you were when you left your academic work last time.

Another important consideration for part-time research students is the financial side of working towards a higher degree. Usually they are self-supporting, and try to arrange their employment in such a way that they can spend more time on their higher degree work. For you, this might mean arranging to work fewer hours for less money over a given period, or taking unpaid leave. Without such formal arrangements, you might be tempted to give less value for money at work than previously and find that you are in trouble with management. All these situations have been described by part-time PhD students over a period of some years.

As a part-time student, you are taking on a task that full-timers often find very difficult. Success can come – and is especially meritorious – but you must be prepared to work really hard. Having set up a programme that fits into your requirements, see that you stick to it.

Finally, follow the guidelines laid down in this book for all research students regarding contact with peers, supervisors, academic departments, and research seminars. At the very least regular telephone calls or emails to your supervisor will help to prevent you falling by the wayside. Hopefully you will be able to come up with some more ideas specifically suited to your own lifestyle, once you have started to think seriously about this situation. Ways in which you can help to overcome these problems are given in the action summary.

■ Overseas students

Overseas students pay higher fees than home and EU students because there is not a government grant towards the costs of educating them. Departments able to attract considerable numbers of overseas research students will generate more income for the university and have more resources made available to them.

In the UK there are currently three main attitudes taken towards overseas students by academic staff. It may be reassuring for you to realize that what happens to you, at least in the first instance, is dependent on how your department, or university, views its overseas students in general and is unlikely to have very much to do with you personally.

The first attitude, somewhat traditionally, views students as part of the British aid contribution to the Third World and the Commonwealth. This results in an attitude of patronizing and paternalistic benevolence being adopted towards them.

The second attitude regards them as proof that the institution is truly international. In this case overseas students are treated in a collaborative manner.

The third, focusing on the additional revenue, is as a source of fees; 'a cheque walking through the door', as one academic put it. This attitude results in treating overseas students in a businesslike way but without the support that the students would like. This stems from the fact that overseas students bring in fee income which is additional to the government allocation for British and EU students. This sometimes results in acceptable British students being refused as the quota has been filled, while additional overseas students can be accepted.

The following quotations show how the situation is seen by some supervisors:

> We're in business for overseas students. UK students can't even pay high fees if they wanted to. We can take any number of high fee students but we're limited on low fee places. (Philosophy)

> We can't accept all we'd like to accept. We reached the low fee quota very early this year and had to put good people on the waiting list. The high fee people go through the same process but don't have the barriers to acceptance of the home, low fee, students. (Sociology)

> We mustn't just take students for cash generation, it's a moral issue. (Business School)

In these cases, you will be treated helpfully but with an element of resentment from staff who may have had to pass over another student whom they would ideally have wanted to accept.

Not all departments take the view that large numbers of overseas students are preferable, however. It is also the case that some supervisors find foreign students are more work than 'home' students and do not actively seek them. It is important that you are aware of which situation you are entering as it may affect the way that you are treated initially.

Settling in to Britain

You may also find an added difficulty in getting settled into your research work because of the difficulties of settling into the country. You may feel excluded by home students who cannot put themselves in your position sufficiently to realize that the small things they take for granted, such as shopping or going to the launderette, can be major obstacles for you. It makes sense for you to anticipate these problems and find out as much as possible about Britain before coming.

One study by Hockey (1994) has noted problems with a lack of established relationships that have to be overcome by overseas students. He discusses the isolation experienced by so many research students and says that 'this social isolation, in the case of overseas students, may be compounded by a cultural disjuncture'. To illustrate he gives the following extended quotation from an interview he had with an overseas student who had been studying in Britain for a few months:

> One aspect that really makes me miss my family every night is the idea of going into the kitchen and cooking alone . . . I'm not used to that kind of feeling, I'm not used to sitting with your utensils, your food. You sit in the corner on your own and eat your food . . . Yes, it's certainly different, and you know, we have been brought up to think

of ourselves as a part of the family. Because of this aspect of our upbringing, being individualistic comes a bit difficult [for you to get used to].

(Hockey 1994: 180)

An important way of tackling problems such as these is to join university societies where people from your home country meet together. This helps to minimize the shock of accommodating yourself to the differences in culture. Getting to know non-university compatriots for social activities, particularly if they are not to be found at the university, is also helpful.

Getting finance to live on may also be a big issue for you as a research student from overseas. You may be misled by your undergraduate experience in other countries and expect to be able to support yourself by working through college. Particularly in science subjects, the amount of time that you must spend in the lab makes it extremely unlikely that you could undertake the more than 16–20 hours of paid work per week necessary to survive financially.

Overall you must realize that it takes a significant amount of time for any new doctoral student to settle in and begin useful research work. Because of these additional difficulties, you must not become impatient if it takes rather longer for you.

Expressing yourself in English

It is almost inevitable that students from non-English speaking backgrounds have problems to cope with that are additional to the usual problems experienced by other research students. For example, you may feel that you have lost part of your personality by having to express yourself in English all the time. Because of the funding situation, overseas students are often accepted into a research degree course without being given a clear idea of the standard of written English that is required for the thesis. This could have extremely unfortunate repercussions for you and you must ensure that you make it your business to be aware of precisely what is needed for a thesis to be written to the required standard. For example, one student explained that when he was told to 'read around the field', he was very confused and did not know where to go: 'What field? Where should I read?'

As well as the obvious point that ultimately the doctorate is awarded for a *written* thesis, writing is also important in the organization of practical work and in the conceptualization of the argument that links the different parts of the work together. The problem is exacerbated by the considerable discrepancy between the English demanded for academic writing and the everyday spoken English you will encounter. So, it is vital that as a student from a non-English speaking background you do something about improving your command of the English language and its grammar from the very start of your course. It cannot be stressed too strongly how important it is for this to be arranged from the very beginning and not left until the research work is almost completed. It is a sensible investment which will have payoffs in the rest of your career, as English has become the international scientific and academic language. Reading with a good English dictionary beside you has advantages for all students.

One result of inadequate English, especially on the part of good students, is that conscientious supervisors become involved in a moral conflict concerning how far they should intervene in the writing process. As their students come to the end of their period of registration and residence in Britain, supervisors feel increasing pressure to ensure their students' success by writing parts of the thesis themselves. This is unacceptable for a variety of reasons, not least because potential employers are entitled to assume that a British PhD can write acceptable English.

The culture of British doctoral education

For overseas students from many countries the self-starting nature of the British postgraduate educational process may present particular problems. Students from such countries expect major contributions from their supervisors towards the research and writing the thesis. You may come from an educational system that is built on the view that knowledge and wisdom come from the ancients; that the older a source is, the more senior in status a person is, the more valued their pronouncements are held to be. You do not argue with your father, your guru, your professor; that would be showing disrespect. You are here to learn from your supervisors by doing what you are told. If you come from a culture that accords deferential respect to elders, seniors, teachers, you will be more used to waiting to be told what to do before starting on a task. At the very least you will expect to get approval for your idea before working on it.

If you do hold this view you will have to work very hard to understand the nature of the new culture which you are entering. First, it is a scientific and academic culture that values newness and change. Everybody is striving for new conceptions, new analyses, new results that give more knowledge, more understanding, more insight, more control. Older approaches are superseded and become of historical interest only. Newton is still regarded by many as the greatest physicist who ever lived, but we no longer study his works in modern physics. We do not regard it as a paradox that we know more about the English Civil War than historians did a century ago, although they were living considerably nearer to it.

Second, it is a culture in which you are being prepared to play your role as a partner in this process. You are being helped to think for yourself, take initiatives, argue with your seniors and so on, in order to demonstrate that you have something to contribute to the continually changing academic debate.

Third, to help you on in this, you will be left to your own devices for much of the time and this is regarded as an opportunity, not as a deficiency.

If it is not conquered, this cultural difference becomes extremely debilitating by the time you get to the end of your period of research and have to face the oral examination. In this situation the student is expected to provide an assertive and confident defence of the thesis. It could happen that students from cultures where they were taught to be respectful to those in authority would find it far more difficult to engage in any real argument with an examiner. The examiner would have a high status and probably be older than the candidate, thus making a discussion between equals almost impossible for the overseas student.

It would be sensible to spend some time going to seminars and observing, and eventually participating in situations where the usual criticism, challenge and debate take place, in order to familiarize yourself with how this non-deferential activity is an accepted part of the academic process. You may also find that attending a course on assertiveness skills, in order to help you to get to the point where you feel confident enough to participate in the academic process, would be helpful. In this connection, it might help if you were able to join, or develop, a support network of both new and experienced overseas students.

There are some male students whose attitudes to women academics make it difficult for them to learn anything from a female supervisor. This is because in their own environment, women do not usually have a higher status than men in the professional sphere.

One supervisor recounted her experience with Mohammed, a new student. She found that he would accept neither work nor comments from her or, indeed, acknowledge that she was his supervisor. Eventually, in desperation, she arranged for her male colleague in the next office to act as intermediary. He received work from Mohammed, passed it to Dr Marlow and then read her comments to Mohammed who went off happily to continue as Dr Marlow had suggested. However, he believed that the suggestions were those of her colleague. This was not the best solution for any of the people concerned, nor could it continue indefinitely. It does illustrate, however, some of the difficulties that can be encountered when people from diverse cultures are suddenly thrown together without any preparation.

If you recognize that women are not usually in positions of authority over men in your own country, it would be as well to realize that there are places in the world where women can achieve the highest office. For example there are now many countries in the world where women have held the highest political post of prime minister.

Less serious, but still a problem, is the attitude of some students to using the first names of their supervisors and, to a lesser extent, being referred to themselves in what they perceive as a familiar or disrespectful manner. The difficulty of what to call each other is also experienced by supervisors who are sometimes unsure which of two names is the given, as opposed to the family, name of one of their students. This is because in countries such as Japan, for example, the family name is the first in order and in, for example, some West African countries both names sound so unusual to British ears that either one could be the given or family name. The result of all this confusion is that sometimes a member of staff will call a student from a non-English speaking background by his or her family name as though it were their given name and the student may never pluck up the necessary courage to correct the situation.

Even students who come from countries where English is the main language may be surprised to discover that differences in language use cause difficulties in understanding.

We hope that by now you are beginning to realize that there is bound to be a certain amount of culture shock – the discovery that accepted ways of behaving vary. For example, the famous English reserve can be discomfiting when you first encounter it. Ways in which you can help to overcome these problems are given in the action summary.

■ Ethnic minorities

There are clear differences between those students who come to study in British universities from overseas and those whose home is in Britain. Nevertheless, students who are members of ethnic minority groups still have problems that are specifically related to that fact, whether or not they are from non-English speaking backgrounds.

There is a 'noisy silence', as Bird (1996) put it, with regard to racism in British universities, based in part on the belief that the liberal academy is not a site of discrimination. Thus complaints of discrimination are regarded as ill-founded or exaggerated. Yet we know that one of the barriers facing ethnic minority students is a lack of comparable staff to act as role models. This lack also serves to make relationships with staff more difficult.

Winston, an Afro-Caribbean student educated in the UK, spoke of the lack of role models for disadvantaged groups. He said that one of his main reasons for wanting the doctorate was to demonstrate to other black students that it *was* possible.

Carina, a black student researching minority cultures, told of difficulties in gaining entry to a university department at research degree level. She described becoming a research student as a closed shop and repeatedly spoke of exclusion and exclusivity. Carina said that when talking to potential supervisors she had been told: 'Black research on minority cultures is biased, and therefore whites do it better', and 'It has all been done already; we know everything there is to know about the black minority in this country.'

She explained that, as an act of self-preservation, students from ethnic minority groups select the institutions to which they will apply very carefully indeed. They have to know the university and the attitude of its academic staff very well before they will put themselves into the position of even being considered. Also, she reported that she and her non-white friends had got used to being subjected continuously to administrative bureaucracy, such as being asked for identification whenever they went into the library, whereas white students were allowed in on the nod.

Similarly Salmon (1992), in an insightful set of analyses of the experiences of her research students, describes the case of Jocelyn. This black student of education wished to study racial identity and its implications for young black children by assessing the impact of positive self-reference teaching materials. At first she had great difficulty in getting this topic accepted, being pressed to adopt the 'neutral' stance of traditional developmental psychology. However, she persevered, eventually found a sympathetic supervisor, and with great personal determination carried out her project. Salmon (1992: 38–9) comments:

> But as a black woman she remained, throughout the ultimately successful progress of her work, keenly alive to the whiteness of her academic context and its ever-present possibilities for disregarding, even violating, her personal standpoint. To a white supervisor such as myself, these possibilities were not always obvious.

Racial harassment

Many forms of racial harassment are criminal offences and there are legal provisions which can be used against the perpetrators. The Commission for Racial Equality uses the following working definition of racial harassment:

> Racial harassment is violence – either verbal or physical. It includes attacks on property and on the person. When the victim believes that the perpetrator was acting on racial grounds and/or there is evidence of racism, any act suffered by individuals or groups because of their colour, race, nationality, ethnic or national origins may be construed as harassment.

It can take many different forms, ranging from violent physical abuse to more subtle ways of making people feel uneasy, uncomfortable or angry because of their race. Racial harassment intimidates people from ethnic minority backgrounds in such a way that they often miss out on experiences and opportunities to which they are entitled.

It includes:

☐ offensive jokes and comments that degrade particular races;
☐ referring to members of ethnic minority groups by insulting epithets or by making ignorant statements about them, undermining the self-confidence of the individual;
☐ bullying, humiliating and patronizing behaviour directed at a person because of their race;
☐ rudeness – while rudeness is not encouraged generally, in the context of race relations at work this kind of behaviour may be racial harassment if unconsciously the instigator feels that the victim, because of their skin colour, is inferior.

Consciously most bullies would assume that they are only acting within the hierarchy, within the rules of the game. For the student on the receiving end it is usually all too clear that they are experiencing racial harassment, but challenging it can appear an impossible task. Do try though to use assertion techniques to introduce the topic of discrimination with the person most directly concerned, as soon as you feel it to be necessary. Contact your student union representative for help if you think that you need formal support for a specific grievance or to establish an ethnic monitoring system.

It is essential to investigate whether there are institutional customs, practices or procedures which overtly or covertly discriminate against students from racially and culturally different backgrounds. You would be well advised to ascertain that the university of your choice has formal policies in place which monitor student admissions and progress as well as staff appointments and promotions (see pp. 189–191). You might also join or, if necessary, set up a peer support group of other similar students across colleges or institutions. Ways in which you can help to overcome problems directly related to discrimination are given in the action summary.

■ Women students

Numbers of male and female research students in our universities are now roughly equal. In some disciplines, such as social sciences, women outnumber their male colleagues, but in others they are in a minority. Indeed in some departments a woman may find no other female students. The proportion of staff potentially able to supervise research degrees who are female still averages less than a third. The percentage of professors who are women has been increasing by only 1 per cent per annum over the last few years and is now in the mid-teens. Many women therefore will inevitably be supervised by men.

In this situation many women students find their postgraduate studies to be fulfilling and experience no problems that are significantly different from those of their male colleagues. Indeed, there are some who find being in a minority in their department an advantage, delighting in their difference.

A male academic with institutional responsibility for research students said 'leaving aside the attitude of a very small number of my male colleagues who talk down to women in a way that they wouldn't to men students, women don't have any more problems than men do' (Phillips 1994b: 141). This is, however, a rather shortsighted view. There are situations where women students face obstacles that are not encountered by men. In this section we shall explore some of these barriers to the smooth progress of women doctoral candidates in order to enable you to understand and overcome any such difficulties.

Difficulties concerning legitimacy of topics and methodology

The lack of women on decision-making committees is important because it affects what subjects are thought to be worthy of serious research, which methodological approaches are acceptable to investigate them, and whether the theoretical frameworks which are employed to explain the results are perceived as legitimate.

The position of the researcher in relation to what is being studied is also an issue for some women. The problem of finding a supervisor who believes that the work that the student wishes to do is the kind of work that should be done arises in many disciplines. There are some 'feminist' methodologies or certain styles of reporting research which are more amenable to supervision by somebody who is sympathetic to such topics and methodologies.

For example, Ayala, a sociology student whose research was on 'non-heterosexual women and work' commented that, although as an undergraduate she had been taught that 'there is no such thing as objectivity', she had discovered as a research student that she and other women were criticized for not being objective in their research proposals. 'Yet,' she argued, 'for feminists it's impossible to separate oneself from one's work. Writing oneself into the thesis and not being invisible is a gender issue.' This particular problem of the relationship between objectivity and subjectivity occurs in many fields.

Problems of communication, debate and feedback

In universities, as in any large organization, some of the important work is done during informal social time. While work can certainly be completed without such social activities, having access to them gives an advantage in terms of being admitted to the 'in' group. Sometimes women students are not included in these informal activities. It may be that they exclude themselves because these social events often revolve around drinks and they are not comfortable with the venue. Or it could be because they have young children to rush home for and other family responsibilities to take care of.

Maybe a woman was not invited because her particular supervisor is one of those men who still feels uncomfortable with women and is not certain how to communicate with them as equals. The only experience that some lecturing staff, as well as a few male students, may previously have had with women is in the roles of husband, father, son, brother or lover in their personal lives, or as manager or boss in their professional lives. Some men still do not know how to play the role of colleague to a woman.

Mapstone (1998) investigated the fact that women are more concerned than men about the potential damage to interpersonal relationships that argument might cause. Her work provides a reason for the fact that it is primarily men who speak in seminars. She explains that women expect to be criticized for expressing disagreement and that this often inhibits them from expressing their true thoughts. Men who argue are regarded as rational whereas women are regarded as disagreeable. Except where equality has been established in a relationship, women tend not to enter into an argument if they can help it.

Her research establishes just one more disadvantage that can work to the detriment of female research students. In the same way as their male peers, they are expected to proffer arguments to support their ideas when those ideas are under attack from people who have higher status. But Mapstone's work suggests that they are likely to have much more difficulty in doing so. Women are less able to perceive argument as rational debate and negotiation.

With this in mind we suggest that you introduce a supervisor management strategy that includes telling your supervisor(s) directly if you think that you have not been given sufficient information to be able to learn from your tutorial. Ask what precisely needs to be done in order to improve the quality of your work. You might ask your supervisor to put you in contact with other female academics in your field. They would not need to be highly placed members of staff but could be research assistants or part-time tutors. You might be able to extend your supervisor management strategy to initiating a discussion about the way you feel you are being treated if the treatment you are receiving is unsatisfactory to you.

Such a statement to your supervisor will not be easy. But it has to be made as soon as you feel the behaviour to be unhelpful – otherwise it will be much worse next time both in terms of what is experienced and what has to be said. Telling well-intentioned supervisors that they are being patronizing may not be as hurtful as you think. You need to explain how you feel in a straightforward way that helps them to understand better their relationship with female students. Of course if you are aggressive, matters will be worsened as they will feel unfairly attacked for trying to be helpful, so do tread carefully.

Scarcity of academic role models

Many female students will inevitably be supervised by male academics. In the majority of cases this works well, but there are times when women students may encounter difficulties as a result of not having a female academic as a role model.

For example, there may be communication difficulties as the following quotation from Veronica, who had two supervisors, one man and one woman, shows.

> It's different talking to a woman supervisor than a man. There's more of a bond between women. If something personal was disturbing me I wouldn't be able to talk to my male supervisor but I do to my female supervisor.

Irene, another woman student, said,

> There's only one woman on the staff, she was definitely a role model for me and my protection from the male–female power relationship. Without her I'd never have stayed.

In some disciplines, the scarcity of successful academic role models for women puts them at a disadvantage when compared with their male peers since it is more difficult to develop an appropriate self-image. Further, it allows prejudice to be manifested. Yvonne, an economist, explained: 'There are some blatant and self-proclaiming misogynists in the department.' Another student of the same department, Shula, told of a specific experience she had had at the time of upgrading:

> My supervisor was happy with what I had written but I met with considerable hostility from an anti-feminist man who wrote two pages of personal vitriol and destroyed any confidence I had. My supervisor tackled the committee about his abuse of power.

Her upgrading was then agreed despite the attack on her work. This kind of incident has resulted in at least one university department setting up a Departmental Gender Subcommittee to deal with 'a macho attitude to work'.

Female PhD students need to find a peer support group that includes other women. It is not necessary to form a 'woman only' group though. (This is something you may find you want to do in addition.) It may only add to your problems, however, if you joined a peer support group where you were the only woman.

Difficulties can also result from situations where female research students are outnumbered by male students. In this situation women have suffered experiences of exclusion and isolation. This could ultimately result in discouraging some from completing the doctorate. If you are in this situation you have to be determined not to let this happen.

Sexual harassment and exploitation

There are also problems for women of having to avoid sexual innuendo in order to maintain an amicable, if somewhat uncomfortable, working relationship. Different people perceive the same situation in different ways. Women students should be aware and beware of this possibility. When a male student goes for a drink with his (male) supervisor he is perceived as an ambitious and sociable person; but when a female student is in the same situation she is in danger of being perceived as flirtatious or even as already being 'involved' with her supervisor.

Carter and Jeffs (1992) looked at the tutor–tutee relationship in professional education. Here recruitment of older students with life or professional experience is encouraged and, at the start of their course, many of the students are nervous, apprehensive and vulnerable. The tutor has power in the relationship which is similar to that which occurs between supervisor and research student.

Carter and Jeffs found that this power is sometimes used in an inappropriate way. They uncovered many cases of sexual harassment and sexual exploitation within the professional training relationship. One student said:

> Within weeks of the course starting X had commenced an affair with one of the students in the group. She was highly flattered by his attention and made no secret of the relationship. It, however, made it very uncomfortable for the rest of us who were aware that in all probability our comments about the course as well as our dissatisfaction about the poor teaching of that lecturer were being carried back to him. The relationship continued until the end of the year when he selected a new student from the incoming first year. The student in our group felt both humiliated and bitter. She never really had much

to do with the rest of us after that and became a very irregular attender.

(1992: 454)

In our opinion the result of such experiences is the corruption of relationships between all staff and students. Innocent and perfectly acceptable social contact between staff and students becomes tainted with gossip and innuendo. The natural growth of friendship is curtailed and even ordinary discourse and collaboration become viewed by staff as professionally dangerous.

All harassment constitutes a particularly invidious form of discrimination. The legal definition of sexual harassment is:

Repeated, unreciprocated and unwelcome comments, looks, actions, suggestions or physical contact that is found objectionable and offensive and might create an intimidating working environment. Sexual harassment takes many forms and can include: leering; ridicule; embarrassing remarks; deliberate abuse; offensive use of pin-ups; repeated, unwanted physical conduct; demands for sexual favours; and physical assault.

The law in the UK does not hold that sexual harassment itself is illegal, but creating an intimidating environment as a result of such harassment is unlawful discrimination.

Sexual harassment is a major cause of stress at work for women and the source of much physical and psychological ill-health. When questioned, men often admit that when they make sexual advances to women it never occurs to them that women might dislike what they are doing. Women say that often harassers genuinely believe they are offering a compliment. Women colleagues often complain that what men call harmless fun or a flattering flirtation is regarded by women as a presumptuous intrusion. Even women whose work includes an awareness of such problems – for example, journalists and broadcasters – find it difficult to talk about their own personal grievances in this area. A typical comment might be: jokes are the worst because they are not as obvious as someone pinching your backside, but they are just as humiliating. You have to respond in a particular way or you are a social outcast. If you do laugh, however, you end up hating yourself. By laughing at a joke you don't find funny, you are accepting whatever ideas the joke is based on.

It is common for the harasser to have a certain degree of power or authority over the victim – for example, a supervisor or other senior academic. But students could find that they have to contend with unwanted behaviour from fellow students as well as members of staff. This makes it very difficult for an individual to tackle sexual harassment, since refusal to go along with the harassment may elicit aggression and denigration of the woman.

It is not unusual for a harasser to inflict harassment on more than one individual. Nor is it unusual that victims of such treatment refrain from mentioning it. There are those who believe that complaining about sexual harassment is making a fuss about nothing. They say that it is harmless fun and the inevitable result of women and men working together. But students are often unaware that others are stressed in similar ways and that there is a common source to their problems. Many universities have appointed an adviser to women students to focus discussion on these issues, so if you are feeling harassment seek her out. You will be able to discuss difficulties with her and discover how widespread the problem is across the university. Most universities have adopted a code of practice which incorporates a professional code of conduct for staff in relation to students.

What all this adds up to is that you, as a female research student, need to develop a degree of social skill and confidence in order to be able to cope with any difficulties that may arise. If necessary attend appropriate courses in assertion techniques, mobilize your student union and join or press for the establishment of an anti-harassment committee. Ways in which you can help to overcome problems of sexual discrimination are given in the action summary.

■ Gay, lesbian, bisexual and trans-gender students

It is estimated that about 1 in every 20 of the population is predominantly gay or lesbian and there is also a minority of people who are bisexual. There will therefore be a considerable number of academics and research students in these groups. Many issues that we have discussed in other sections of this chapter are equally relevant to gay and lesbian students. For example, problems concerning the legitimacy of topics and method-ology are applicable to people researching on sexuality issues; and sexual harassment may arise if either the supervisor or the research student is openly gay or is in the closet.

The effects of stereotyping are considerable. For example, even though statistics show that most sexual abuse of children is perpetrated by hetero-sexual males (often a member of the child's family) media reporting makes it appear that homosexual males are predominantly to blame. Myths such as this only serve to add to the difficulties experienced by gay and lesbian students. As Leonard (1997) points out, while it is women who are more likely to *feel* fear, in western society it is young men – especially those who are from ethnic minorities or are gay – who are more likely to be the subject of violence when, for example, walking home from the library after dark.

Trans-gender people have a very strong desire to be accepted in their new identity but because they are concerned about other's reactions often decide to keep their history secret. The worry about disclosure can affect their work and cause much unnecessary stress.

Increasingly, gay and lesbian people wish to be frank with their friends and colleagues but this honesty opens up greater possibilities for discrimination. Gay or lesbian students who come out may find that their supervisors are nonplussed or antagonistic and this will complicate their relationship. Alternatively, if they remain silent but are subsequently outed they can become targets for harassment. They thus have a risky decision to make.

One way to avoid these problems is to ensure that you keep your emotional life and your professional life apart as far as possible, especially so far as members of academic staff are concerned. You might also try to discover some others in a similar situation for mutual support and, if necessary, get together to influence your university to take these issues seriously. Don't forget that the student union is there to help all students and that includes you.

Heterosexist harassment

Heterosexism is a set of ideas and practices which assumes that heterosexuality is the superior and therefore the only 'normal' and 'natural' form of sexual relationship. Heterosexism works against lesbians, bisexuals, and gay men although, unlike colour or sex, it is impossible to tell by looking whether someone is bisexual, gay or lesbian.

Harassment causes distress, interferes with people's ability to work and can seriously restrict their opportunities. Harassment of lesbians, gay men and bisexuals occurs when people make remarks and comments that stereotype them and imply that there is something 'abnormal' about them. It includes:

☐ physical assault;
☐ circulation of leaflets, magazines, badges and other materials which degrade lesbians and gay men;
☐ heterosexist graffiti and offensive posters on the walls which act as a continual method of humiliation.

Just as with most of the other forms of harassment we have been discussing in this chapter, this kind is an offence with legal sanctions which can be used against the perpetrators when it creates an intimidating environment. It can take many different forms ranging from violence and aggressive bullying to more subtle ways of making people feel nervous, embarrassed or apprehensive because of their sexual orientation. Heterosexist harassment intimidates people in such a way that they can miss out, for example, on sponsorship for trying new ideas due to lack of confidence resulting from being victimized. Ways in which you can help to overcome problems of discrimination against you if you are lesbian, gay, bisexual or trans-gender are given in the action summary.

■ Mature students

Not all students are young, newly graduated and single. Increasingly married people, or those in established relationships, who have children, mortgages and the whole range of responsibilities are deciding to do research work. There are some subjects where these mature students (i.e. those in their 40s and over) are the norm rather than the exception. In architecture, management and social work, for example, it is usual for PhD students to have spent a period as professionals in the field before coming back to carry out their research. But in many subjects mature students are very much in the minority.

They have a number of particular problems to contend with. For some, particularly women, there are much more demanding domestic circum-stances to cope with. Many have to juggle responsibility in caring for children, elderly relatives, etc. All mature students will probably have to combat ageism and the negative images that go with it. They, even more than their younger peers, may be constantly having to demonstrate their intellectual ability. It should be pointed out that at the time of writing, in the UK unlike the USA, ageism is not illegal.

Mature students also have to relate to fellow students who are of a much younger generation and fit in with them. This fitting in can present par-ticular problems because of the common misperception that mature stu-dents are experienced and therefore able to cope. Members of academic staff and students further along in their studies are more likely to behave in protective ways towards younger students than they are towards older ones. Such assumptions of competence may well be true in general but in the rarefied world of the university, where the mature student is new and not fully aware of the rules and how things work, old patterns do not help. New mature students are particularly vulnerable in such situations since their learning must include how to play the role of student again.

Relationships with supervisors can present difficulties too, with the stu-dent often subject to conflicting emotions. There may be resistance to accepting guidance, with students unconsciously feeling that they should know better than their younger supervisors. This may be coupled with a desperate attempt to obtain knowledge without letting the supervisors know how ignorant they feel. As a mature student, you have to make a particular effort to meet the supervisor in an adult to adult relationship.

However, with appropriate determination, these handicaps can be overcome. DSP is particularly proud to have been the supervisor of Dr Edward Brech who has been in the *Guinness Book of Records* as the oldest British recipient of a PhD degree at the age of 85. The UK record is now held by a woman who was awarded the degree at the age of 93. Suggestions for tackling some of the problems associated with being a mature student are given in the action summary.

■ Students with disabilities

Professor Stephen Hawking, the world-renowned Cambridge physicist, is an inspirational example for people with disabilities who wish to progress in the academic world. Indeed many universities have some disabled people on their academic staff who can serve as role models. However, not all academic environments are physically capable of accommodating the full range of students with disabilities. You must therefore discover whether your own particular requirements are satisfied. If you are British or from the EU, explore the possibility of your entitlement to the Post Graduate Disabled Students Allowance at the Department for Education and Skills website *<www.dfes.gov.uk/studentsupport>* or from your LEA.

Disability Legislation

It is now unlawful for institutions to treat a disabled person 'less favourably' than they would a non-disabled person. For example, it is unlawful for an institution to turn a disabled person away from a course, or mark them down in a written assessment because they were dyslexic or an oral examination if they were deaf.

The Special Educational Needs and Disability Act (2001) implemented 2005, requires all publicly-funded higher education institutions to take reasonable steps to:

☐ make physical adjustments to improve access;
☐ provide auxiliary aids, such as induction loops and handouts in Braille;
☐ allow disabled students more than the usual 'one hour at a time' access to computers and permit their use for examinations;
☐ check all new electronic courseware to ensure it is accessible to disabled students.

Note however that the new provisions do not require institutions to lower academic or other standards to accommodate disabled students. An institution would be justified in claiming fair, as opposed to unfair, discrimination in such circumstances. You should be aware of your rights and the university's responsibilities under this Act.

Harassment of people with a disability

Unlike the other forms we have been discussing in this chapter, harassment of people with disabilities is more likely to be the result of thoughtlessness and ignorance than a deliberate intent to hurt. This does not alter the fact that harassment of people with disabilities causes distress, interferes with their ability to work and can seriously restrict their opportunities.

The actual definition of harassment in the case of people with disabilities is comparable to that of sexual or racial harassment. Harassment of disabled people can, like the others, take many forms ranging from violent physical abuse to more subtle ways of making people feel uneasy, uncomfortable or angry because they have a disability. Included in the list of possible objectionable behaviours are:

- [ ] offensive jokes and comments that degrade people with a disability;
- [ ] bullying, humiliating and patronizing behaviour directed at a person because she or he has a disability;
- [ ] physical assault;
- [ ] circulation of leaflets, magazines, badges and other materials which degrade people who have a disability;
- [ ] graffiti.

Ways in which you can help to overcome problems of discrimination against you if you are disabled are given in the action summary

■ Action summary

The overall message for all these groups is to get what social support you can for your disadvantaged interests. In cases of harassment, make sure that the harasser is informed that the conduct is offensive to you.

For part-time students:

1. Choose a research problem that is related to your work.
2. Set aside regular specific periods of time for your PhD work and stick to them.
3. Keep in regular contact with supervisors, peers and the department. At the very least make regular telephone calls or send emails on your progress.
4. Explore the possibility that some financial support may be available from universities and research councils.

For overseas students:

1. Find out as much as possible about Britain and the British

postgraduate educational system before coming, and during your early period here.

2. Join or establish a support network of both new and experienced overseas students.

3. Recognize that it is appropriate for women to be in positions of authority over men if they have the necessary qualifications, knowledge and experience.

4. Use university societies where people from your home country meet together to help minimize the shock of accommodating yourself to the difference in culture.

5. Ascertain whether you can get free language training from your university. If not, enrol in a convenient language school where you will be able to improve your written English.

6. Get to know non-university compatriots for social activities, particularly if these are not to be found at the university.

7. Observe, in the first instance, and participate eventually in situations where the usual criticism, challenge and debate take place, in order to familiarize yourself with how this non-deferential activity is an accepted part of the academic process.

8. Attend a course on assertiveness skills in order to help you to get to the point where you feel confident enough to participate in the academic process.

For students from ethnic minorities:

1. Join or establish a peer support group.

2. Use assertion techniques in situations in which you are not being treated comparably with other (white) students.

3. Whenever necessary enlist the help of your student union representative or a member of staff, possibly from another department, to whom you can explain your experience of unfair treatment.

4. Take time to discover the attitudes of members of staff when choosing the institution for your research work. Gauge that you are able to cope with the level of prejudice that you may expect to find.

5. Become familiar with the definitions of harassment.

For women students:

1. Join or establish a peer support group that includes other women.

2. Discuss with your male supervisor any problems in the male/female aspect of the student–supervisor relationship.

3. Use assertion techniques in tutorials in order to get precise information about how to improve your work or to cope with interpersonal difficulties.

4. Look for role models; if necessary get a woman as a second supervisor.

5. Don't get romantically involved with your supervisor or accept personal favours.
6. Be aware that it is possible for gender issues to affect the outcome of your work in cases where there is some controversy over the research topic, methodology or style of reporting results. If necessary contact others for help.
7. Use your university's Women's Officer, anti-harassment committee or other responsible official for support and remedial action if necessary. If they are not in place, press for their establishment.
8. Keep a record of each incidence of harassment.
9. Discuss the problem with others and you may discover that you are not alone.
10. Contact your student union representative for help if required.

For gay, lesbian, bisexual and trans-gender students:

1. Join or establish a peer support group.
2. Use the student union to influence your college to establish procedures to deal quickly and fairly with complaints regarding harassment.
3. Be aware that it is possible for heterosexist issues to affect the outcome of your work in cases where there is some controversy over the research topic, methodology or style of reporting results. If necessary gain peer support to influence your department to set up a panel to adjudicate on such matters.
4. Don't get romantically involved with your supervisor or accept personal favours.
5. Keep a record of each incidence of harassment.
6. Discuss the problem with others and you may discover that you are not alone.
7. Discover whether your university has a responsible official for support and remedial action.
8. Contact your student union representative for help if necessary.

For mature students:

1. Make contact with and, if necessary, form a network of mature students.
2. In this network, discuss the relevant issues particular to your situation, for example: share experiences and discuss strategies for combating ageism; identify feelings of resistance and resentment; share them with the group as an aid to facing and overcoming them.
3. If your institution does not already have one, lobby for the appointment of a counsellor for mature students.

For students with disabilities:

[1]   Familiarize yourself with your rights and entitlements under government legislation.
[2]   Discuss any problems with your supervisor and head of department.
[3]   Enlist the help of your university's officer for disabled students when you need support.
[4]   Keep a record of each incidence of harassment.
[5]   Discuss the problem with others and you may discover that you are not alone.
[6]   Contact your student union representative for help if necessary.

10

THE EXAMINATION SYSTEM

Each university has a plethora of its own formal procedures concerned with the award of the PhD degree. You will need to conform with the particular rules that apply to your case. Hopefully, you will have sufficient regular informal guidance from your supervisor(s), the appropriate section of the academic registrar's department, and so on to keep you away from possible pitfalls. As with all else in the PhD process, however, in the end it is your own responsibility to see that you conform to the system.

The purpose of this chapter is to make you aware of some of the key points at which the examination system is likely to impinge on you. We can only do this in general terms, since as we have said, the details vary in different institutions. You must study the particular regulations that apply to you.

■ Upgrading to doctoral student status

As an incoming student you will in the first instance usually be registered as a general research student or for an MPhil. After a period, between one and two years into your research work, you have to be recommended for upgrading to PhD student status by your supervisors. This is effectively the first, preliminary stage of the examination process, since you get the important confirmation that your work is expected to develop to PhD standards. The procedure of upgrading can vary from an extremely formal review with written reports to a less formalized process. You need to discover what is required in your case and prepare accordingly.

■ Giving notice of submission

The examination of your PhD is the summit of the process, coming as it does at the end of years of hard work. You start the whole procedure off by giving notice, usually at least three months beforehand, that you intend to submit your thesis for examination. You should realize that you have to make the decision to be examined, in accordance with your professional understanding, although you will discuss the matter fully with your supervisor(s). Formally, you can submit against your supervisor's advice; although this is very risky, it does underline the fact that the decision is yours.

■ The appointment of examiners

After you have given notice of submission, the formal procedures are set in motion for the appointment of examiners. The examiners' task is to represent the academic peer group to which you are hoping to gain access. The usual pattern is for an academic in your department other than your supervisor(s) to become the internal examiner. The external examiner has to be from another university.

The responsibility for recommending the names of the examiners to the appropriate university board is that of your supervisors and head of department. You should expect, though, to be sounded out to give your reactions as to who they might be; and many supervisors, in fact, discuss the issue fully with their students.

It is important for you to know who your examiners are going to be before you actually finish writing your thesis. You should expect that they will be academics whose work you are referring to in your discussion. One rule of thumb is to give first consideration to the British academic whose work is referenced most frequently in the thesis bibliography. If it turns out that writers quoted in the bibliography are not appropriate, then you must study the works of those who are going to be appointed, to see where they can be relevantly quoted. Examiners are only human (you are yourself on your way to being one, remember) and they will certainly expect their work to be appropriately cited and discussed.

■ Submitting the thesis

In submitting your thesis there are many rules and regulations to be followed, which vary by institution. There are rules about the maximum length of your thesis, the language in which it must be written (English, unless permission has been previously obtained in special circumstances), the adequacy of its literary style, the size of the pages, the size of the margins, the type and colour of the binding, the number of copies you have to submit, its material state (suitable for deposit and preservation in the library) and so on. You have to be aware of those regulations which apply in your case.

All institutions require the candidate to submit a short abstract, of about 300–500 words, summarizing the work and its findings, in order to orientate the examiners and, later, other readers to the thesis as a whole. You should spend some time on making the abstract cogent, so that it gives a good impression. This is a professional skill that you should develop for both publications and conference papers.

Since, as we have often reiterated, the aim of the PhD is to get you to become a fully professional researcher in your field, your examination is not limited to your thesis report, although that is the main way in which you demonstrate your competence. In addition to your thesis you should submit to the examiners as supporting material any academic work to full professional standard that you have already published. There are though two provisos: first, the papers must be in the academic field in which you are being examined, although they need not be limited to the specific topic of your PhD. (You may be a keen philatelist but papers in that field cannot help you if your PhD is in plasma physics.) Second, they must not have been taken into consideration in the award of any other degree of any other institution and you will have to make a declaration to this effect. Joint papers which are relevant may be submitted, and in these cases you have to specify precisely your own individual contribution to them.

■   The oral examination – the 'viva'

The oral examination is normally held privately – that is, with only the examiners and the student present. However, some universities allow others to sit in – though not, of course, to take part. If your university allows it, it is a good idea to watch one beforehand. Supervisors may be allowed to be present (in some universities only with the agreement of the candidate) but usually they cannot take part.

The task of the examiners is to establish that by your thesis work and your performance in the viva you have demonstrated that you are a fully professional researcher who should be listened to because you can make a sensible contribution to the development of your field. They are going to argue with you, ask you to justify what you have written in your thesis, and probe for what you see as the developments which should flow from your work.

It can be quite tough because you have got to keep your end up – that is what you get the doctorate for. So you need practice. It is absolutely vital to have had the experience of presenting your work to a professional public beforehand. This 'public' does not have to be big – a couple of academics in your department who are not going to be your examiners but who have had experience of examining would be ideal. Other PhD students should have helped you along the way, as you helped them, and they make excellent examiners in a mock viva.

Just as you need practice in writing during your study years if the thesis is to be well written, so you also need practice in public discussion and defence of your work. This is very important, because it is quite appropriate for the examiners to consider, for example, a particular part of your argument in the thesis to be thin, but to agree that as a result of your discussion in the viva you have justified it acceptably, and thus the thesis will not be referred back for additional written work on this score.

■ Preparing for the viva

You also need to prepare for the oral examination in a systematic way. Phillips (1992) found that, strangely, few students do any real preparation, even though the benefits seem obvious. Useful introductions to it are given in Murray (2003) and Rugg and Petre (2004). But begin by reading the section on the viva in 'How to examine' in this book (see pp. 178–9) which provides information on the form that the meeting will take.

Here is a tried and tested way of revising the complete thesis and preparing for the viva, both at the same time. First you take a maximum of three sheets of feint-ruled A4 paper (try to manage with two if you can). You draw a straight vertical line down the centre of each sheet. You now have two sets of about 35 lines, i.e. 70 half-lines. Each half line represents one page of your thesis. Now you number each half line. One to 35 are the left hand half lines and 36–70 are the right hand half lines on the first sheet of paper.

Next you take your time, say about two weeks, to write on every half line the main idea contained on the corresponding page of your thesis. Here, as an example, is a page of technical description of the methodology from the PhD thesis of one of us (Phillips 1983):

> It may be observed (Figure 2) that the re-sorted grid is presented with two tree diagrams which display the patterns of responses within the grid. These tree diagrams give a visual representation of which elements and which constructs cluster together. In the above grid, construct 1 has been reversed so that what was originally scale point 5 has become scale point 1, scale point 4 becomes scale point 2 and so on, the same is true of construct 3. An example of this is Ewan's

two constructs 'Escape/Has to be done' and 'Boring/Interesting for me'. When one of the two is reversed, it becomes clear that 'Boring' and 'Has to be done' are being used in a similar way. Because of this reversibility, complete mismatching between constructs is as significant as complete matching. A negative match between two constructs is a positive match if the poles of one construct are reversed. 'Matching' in this context refers to elements or constructs that are highly related to each other while 'mismatching' refers to constructs that are negatively related to each other. Elements or constructs that bear no similarity to each other are those where the ratings along them form no particular pattern.

CORE
The grid technique was also used to monitor change over time for each of the postgraduates as they proceeded through their three year course. In order to do this, consecutive grids from one individual were analysed using the Core program (Shaw 1979). This program analyses two grids, comparing each element and each construct with itself and prints out those constructs and elements that have changed the most in the way the postgraduate is using them.

This was reduced to the following:

p. 86   C reversed; matching and mismatching; CORE intr'd.

The pages before and after this were coded as below so that the whole section read as follows on the half lines:

Chapter 4 METHOD – pp. 82–9 sub-section Analysis of Grids
p. 82   Analysis: refers appendix pp. 289–91; interpretation same
p. 83   Reasons for Core and Focus
p. 84   Focus > > > > > 85 diagram of grid
p. 85   diagram
p. 86   C reversed; matching and mis-matching; CORE intr'd
p. 87   Core explained; diagram and eg.
p. 88   Diff. scores; 40% cut off, clusters and isolates
p. 89   calculations; FB new info. from re-sorted grids.

At the end of this exercise you will have achieved two important aims. First, you will have revised, in the most detailed way possible, the whole of your thesis and, second, you will be in a position to pinpoint – at a glance – the precise location of any argument, reference or explanation you wish to use during your viva. Not only will you be able to find your way around your thesis easily but you will probably be able to give a page number to your examiners while they are still thumbing through the document trying to find something that is relevant to the current discussion and they remember having read but can't find at that moment. You can!

In addition to these obvious advantages, you will be able to do last minute revision from the sheets of paper and not the thesis itself. This means that you can go out, spend time with friends and family yet still be able to do some work. Your precious sheets of paper are in your handbag or your pocket to be looked at whenever you feel it appropriate or necessary to do so. The mere process of having produced the summary sheets and knowing that you are familiar with them gives you essential, but usually non-existent, self-confidence when you confront your examiners during the actual viva.

Of course this revision has to be carried out within the context of your overall understanding of your work, as Tinkler and Jackson (2004) point out. At this stage you should be able to answer the question 'What is your thesis, i.e. what is the position that you wish to maintain?' (see p. 41) in one, or possibly two, sentences. You should have a similarly cogent answer to the question 'What is your contribution, i.e. how are the focal and background theories now different as a result of your study?' (see p. 59). Your detailed revision of your work within this focused framework will put you in a good position to defend your thesis at the viva.

■ The results of the examination

People who have not thought much about the nature of the PhD examination usually believe that candidates will either cover themselves with glory and obtain the PhD immediately or fail and leave in disgrace. This is not so; those are the two extremes of a whole continuum of possible outcomes which we can now consider.

☐ The PhD will be awarded immediately after the viva. This is the best outcome and the one to aim for.

☐ The degree will be awarded immediately, but subject to certain corrections and minor amendments, which usually have to be carried out within one month. In effect the examiners say to you: 'If you quickly carry out these changes we will count your revised thesis as the first submission and award the degree.' The changes in this case are usually minor: an incorrect calculation that does not affect the argument, incorrect or inadequate referencing on a particular point, an inadequate explanatory diagram are examples. You carry out these modifications to the satisfaction of your internal examiner and gain the degree.

☐ The examiners say 'Yes, but . . .' They think that your thesis and your defence of it are on the right lines but there are weaknesses that must be remedied, and they therefore require you to resubmit it. They will tell you what the weaknesses are, and why, and you will be allowed a certain period – usually up to two years – to complete the work and resubmit it. Unfortunately, you will have to pay continuing registration fees for that period. If the examiners have been impressed with your performance at the viva, they do not necessarily have to give you another oral examination on the resubmission.

This last result is disappointing, but it is not uncommon and should by no means be regarded as catastrophic. Students usually need a couple of weeks to scrape themselves off the floor and put themselves together again, but the best strategy then is to get on with the extra work as soon as possible. After all, if you are in this position you have learned a very great deal from the examination. The examiners will typically specify in very considerable detail what they think is lacking in the work and what should be done about it. Once you get over the emotional frustration, which admittedly can be considerable, you are in a good position to polish off what is required. But don't take too long to get restarted: the emotional blocks can easily cause you to waste the two years. It is a good tactic, both academically and psychologically, to get a paper from your research published in a reputable journal in the intervening period.

Once you have resubmitted and obtained your degree, then of course it doesn't matter – no one will ever know. What matters is what published papers you can get out of the work. You would be surprised at the number of established academics who have had to resubmit their theses.

☐ The examiners say that the candidate's written thesis was adequate but the defence of it in the viva was not. This is a much less usual result but it underlines the fact that the doctorate is given for professional competence. It is the candidate who passes the degree, not the thesis. If you are in this position you will be asked to re-present yourself for another viva after a certain period (six months to a year), during which you will have read much more widely in your field and gained a better understanding of the implications of your own research study.

It might also be the case that the examiners decide that your research topic is so narrow that the thesis alone will not give them sufficient opportunity to examine your general professional competence. They can then set you – with due notice, of course – a written or practical examination on the subject area of your thesis work. In that event it is possible that they might regard the thesis as adequate, but require you to re-sit the examination after a specified period.

☐ The examiners consider that the candidate's thesis work has not reached the standard required of a doctorate and they do not see any clear way by which it can be brought up to the required standard.

However, the work has achieved the lower standard required of an MPhil, and they can award this degree.

This is a considerable blow; not just because the PhD was not awarded, but principally because the examiners do not see a way of improving it, so it is not likely that the candidate will. It is a result of the candidate's (and, we must say, often of the supervisor too) not understanding the nature of a PhD and how to discover and achieve the appropriate standards. The whole burden of this book is to get you to understand and become skilled at the processes of PhD-getting, so that you do not end up in this situation. In our experience most students who are capable of achieving MPhil standard as a consolation prize are capable, in the right circumstances, of obtaining a PhD.

☐ The examiners may say that the candidate has not satisfied them, and that the standard is such that resubmission will not be permitted.

This is the disaster scenario. It can occur only when the supervisor not only has no conception of what is required for a PhD but does not really understand what research is all about. Of course, it should not occur at all, but it does. However, if the supervisory process and research degree system matched up to anything like the standards we have been discussing in this book, it would not occur. If you did not have the ability to carry out professional research, you would have been counselled on this and advised to leave the system long before getting to the submission stage. You avoid the disaster of failure coming as a bolt from the blue by ensuring that you seek out and learn from those who do know what the process requires.

■ The appeals procedures

Most universities have an academic appeals procedure but the details will vary, and if necessary you must discover what they are for your own institution. They usually enable you to appeal against what you consider to be unwarranted decisions taken against you. For example, under certain circumstances you can be deregistered if the research committee thinks that your work is not progressing satisfactorily, or not progressing at all. You may appeal against this if you provide appropriate evidence, and it will be considered by a subcommittee that contains independent members. The warning note in these cases is always that they would not have occurred if you had not lost contact with your supervisor; and, whatever happens, you must repair this breach or get other supervisors.

Appealing against the results of the examination, particularly when a resubmission is required or an MPhil is awarded, is possible in most universities. It is an option not to be undertaken lightly. You usually have first to demonstrate that your appeal is not 'vexatious', i.e. that you have some prima facie argument for your case. The commonest argument is that the examiners were not really expert in the field and therefore used inappropriate standards for judging the work. Obviously that does not come about in any simple way: chemists are not appointed to examine candidates in psychology, for example. But a social historian, say, might feel that the thesis was found inadequate on sociological grounds, because of the bias of the examiners, whereas it should have been considered more as a contribution to history.

That sort of appeal may be considered. The result will be that additional examiners are appointed to the board to evaluate the thesis. The problem is that with a marginal thesis the *more* the examiners, the *less* likely there is to be a favourable result.

Another common ground for appeal occurs in situations where the thesis has been found to be so inadequate that resubmission is disallowed completely, or only allowed for an MPhil. A student might appeal on the grounds that the supervision has clearly been inadequate and detailed evidence must be produced to support this. Such details might include evidence of inadequate training provided by the department, an insufficiently qualified academic appointed as supervisor with no colleague support, lack of regular contact with an appropriate supervisor due to supervisor's preoccupation with other activities or lack of interest in the topic. Details of special personal circumstances experienced by the student during the registration period (illness, divorce, etc.) might also be grounds for appeal in this situation.

After hearing the evidence, the appeals committee might decide that it is equitable in all the circumstances for the student to be allowed, with good supervision in place, to improve the thesis and resubmit in due course. It is important to understand that it is not possible on these procedural grounds for the appeals committee to decide that the thesis is acceptable for the PhD degree (that is an academic decision to be taken by the examining board), only that an opportunity for further work and resubmission be allowed.

In recent years universities have incorporated a transparently independent element into their appeals procedures. In 2004, the Office of the Independent Adjudicator for Higher Education was established and the first adjudicator, Dame Ruth Deech, appointed. It is now therefore possible for students who feel they have not been fairly treated by their university to appeal to this office. Details are given at its website *<www.oiahe.org.uk>*. The Office can only intervene when all the procedures of the university have been exhausted, and the student has been issued with a 'completion of procedures' letter. The Office cannot deal with issues of academic standards or cases where litigation is pending.

■ Litigation

There have been some cases in recent years where a student has taken the university to court. The contention was that the university, while taking the student's fee, had failed to fulfil its side of the contract by providing only an inadequate service of education. Students on undergraduate and taught masters' courses have received a refund of fees and expenses on these grounds. One PhD student complained to his university about the completely inadequate quality and quantity of the supervisory support that he received. The university upheld the complaints and offered the student more time and money to complete the degree. However, the student decided to go to court, but no further award was made. Again, it should be emphasized that what is in contention in law is the amount of damages (if any) that should be paid, not the academic decision on whether a PhD should be awarded. That decision cannot be made on legal grounds.

■ Action summary

1. You must obtain and study the regulations of the examination system that apply to you.
2. The regulations concern upgrading to doctoral registration, submission of thesis, appointment of examiners, the viva examination, and, in some cases, the appeals procedures. At each point you must ensure that you conform to the requirements.
3. Prepare for the viva by summarizing your thesis, and ensuring that you have a practice mock viva.

11

HOW TO SUPERVISE AND EXAMINE

This chapter is principally addressed to supervisors. We shall be considering a series of strategies for improving supervision. It will help you identify aspects of the role that you may not previously have considered. But this chapter will also give students some insights into the tasks of their partners in this enterprise, thus helping to improve the quality of the relationship on both sides.

To improve your performance as a supervisor, you must understand what your students expect. Once you have this 'inside information' you will be in a better position to develop the skills necessary to teach the craft of research, maintain a helpful contract and encourage your students' academic role development. You will also be in a position, should this prove necessary, to modify these student expectations to make them more appropriate to their particular situation.

■ What students expect of their supervisors

In a series of interviews EMP found the following set of expectations to be general among students regardless of discipline.

Students expect to be supervised

This may sound like a truism but it is surprising how widespread is the feeling among research students of not being supervised. Academics, under pressure to research and publish as well as teach, consult and do administration, may find that doctoral students require too much of their time. Supervisors may come to regard students as a necessary evil. This is very different from the, perhaps idealized, conception of supervisors and students engaged in a high level meeting of minds which they enjoy and from which they benefit.

As an example, Julia, interviewed a year after gaining her PhD in education, was still indignant at the limited help she had obtained from her supervisor. Dr Johnson had arranged to see her only irregularly – indeed there was one period of over six months during which they did not meet. While he made detailed comments on work that she presented, he never discussed with her the overall shape of the study, and as a result she spread her work too widely and thinly. Her research was concerned with mothers' attitudes to breast-feeding, and she tried to encompass both a library-based historical and anthropological study and a detailed attitude survey across two NHS regions.

There was clearly a limit to what she could do, but she felt that she had made a reasonable attempt to cover the whole topic. When she submitted her thesis, it came as a shock to her when the examiners at the oral examination said that she had tried to do too much and that neither component was adequate. On her resubmission, she was told she should jettison the historical and anthropological work and concentrate on bringing the survey work up to the appropriate standard.

Dr Johnson had not suggested this before, although after the oral he was adamant that this was the thing to do. Julia's view is that he had just not given enough thought to the PhD and had therefore not been able to supervise her adequately. Dr Johnson's view was that if Julia had been good enough she would have been able to encompass both aspects of the topic. His supervision was properly directed towards that end until it became clear on the presentation that a different approach was required.

This is an extreme case, but such inadequacies of communication between supervisor and student are not unusual. Dr Johnson should have taken responsibility for ensuring that regular meetings were taking place between himself and Julia. He should also have taken care that these meetings included detailed discussions of the whole project so that he would know whether she was covering adequately the amount of work that they had agreed between them. Most importantly, he should have been supervising her writing by seeing early drafts of the whole thesis. If he had done this systematically he would never have permitted her to get to the point of a final draft that did not appear to be comprehensive enough in all areas of the work undertaken. Finally, he should have informed his student that it was not likely to be passed as it stood.

More subtly, the feeling of not being well supervised can derive from the fact that students define the concept of 'supervision' quite differently from supervisors. For example, Freddy and Professor Forsdike (industrial chemistry) disagreed about the amount of time spent in supervising Freddy's research. Freddy said: 'He really oversupervises, he's in twice a day to see what results I've got.' But Professor Forsdike insisted: 'We don't meet as often as we should, about once a month only.'

What was happening was that Freddy counted every contact with his supervisor in the laboratory as a meeting, while the professor thought only of the formal tutorial appointment as contributing to supervision. What is more, Professor Forsdike reported that Freddy had plenty of ideas and that it was very much a shared meeting. This is very different from thinking merely in terms of 'keeping tabs on results', which is how Freddy interpreted his supervisor's role.

In fact Freddy continued to feel oppressed throughout the three years of his PhD research. He said: 'I feel just another pair of hands for my supervisor. No matter what I do there's always more. I still see him twice a day and he's still on my back trying to get me to do more practical work – but I won't.' However, Professor Forsdike assumed that Freddy needed his support for as long as the postgraduate was prepared to accept it. If the two had talked to each other about this situation it could have been resolved at a very early stage, instead of continuing, as it did almost to the end of the research period. There are, in fact, two different types of meetings. One type is minor and frequent and part of the continuing relationship. The other type is less frequent and more formal, and needs preparatory work on both sides. The difference in purpose needs to be made explicit.

Students expect supervisors to read their work well in advance

From the students' point of view it may appear that the supervisor has read only a little of the work submitted, and at the last minute, and wishes to discuss it in the minimum time possible. Often students' only previous experience of receiving feedback on written work has related to undergraduate essays. They expect comments to be written on the script and to include an overall evaluation. Their idea of a tutorial is to discuss in detail all the points made by the supervisor. But this is not necessarily the best way to set about commenting on work, whether it is a progress report, a description of recent experimental or other research work, or a draft for a section of the thesis.

Most supervisors prefer to focus on specific aspects of the students' work and discuss these in detail. This is because they wish to discourage their students from straying too far from a particular line of research. By ignoring the related, but irrelevant, issues raised by research students they hope to communicate their satisfaction with those areas of concern which should be developed. At the same time they trust that this strategy will dampen the enthusiasm of those students who are sidetracked into exploring all kinds of interesting ideas which will not further the progress of the research or the thesis.

However, this way of dealing with written work can lead to considerable bad feeling and a breakdown of communication between students and supervisors. The following quotation illustrates the problem as it was experienced by Adam and Professor Andrews (architecture):

> *Adam*: After seven weeks of writing he only talked about a very minor aspect of my paper. I realize now that my supervisor is not going to be of any help to me. He doesn't read what I write, so I've realized I'm going to have to get on without him.
> *Professor Andrews*: Each time I choose a single aspect from a paper he has written and suggest that he develops it, I see his work evolving and developing very satisfactorily.

Yet Adam was not at all sure whether he was on the right track and he was unclear about what it was that he was supposed to be doing. It is here that it is essential that communication is clear between the pair. Commenting on work submitted by a postgraduate student means talking around it. The script should form the basis for a discussion. Its function should be to further the student's thinking about the project through an exchange of ideas with the supervisor. The script may be put away and used later as an aide-mémoire for the thesis, parts of it may even be included as it stands. But it is not a complete and final piece of work in which every word merits detailed attention. It is the task of supervisors to make clear to their students how they intend to use written work to further the research.

Students expect their supervisors to be available when needed

It is true that the majority of supervisors believe that they are always ready to see any of their students who needs them, but there are many who are not quite as available as they believe themselves to be. It is good practice for supervisors regularly to take coffee or lunch with their students – or to buy them a drink (not necessarily alcoholic) – in order to facilitate easy communication.

A major reason for lack of availability among those few supervisors who have secretaries with adjoining offices is the loyalty with which their secretaries protect them from the outside world – especially from students. Even if the secretary has been told that research students may make appointments whenever they wish, the postgraduates themselves may have difficulty in going through this formal channel to ask their supervisor something that might be considered quite trivial. The result of this can be long periods without working and with increasing depression on the part of the student who is afraid of bothering the busy and important academic. On the other hand this situation engenders frustration on the part of the supervisor, coupled with doubt about the student's motivation.

Even when supervisors do not have secretaries keeping guard in an outer office and maintaining their appointments diaries, research students still find it difficult to initiate an unplanned meeting – especially if it means having to knock on a closed door.

Sheila found that if she met her supervisor as they were walking down a corridor, or across the campus, she had difficulty in getting beyond the superficial exchange. Requesting a tutorial in these circumstances seemed to be inappropriate, in case the supervisor was in a hurry to get to a meeting or give a lecture. There have even been cases where students and supervisors have travelled a few floors together in a lift and the student has still been unable to say there is a problem or that a meeting is needed. Supervisors ought to be sensitive to these difficulties and maintain regular meetings, ensuring that the date of the next meeting is set during the current one.

When supervisors make it clear that they do not welcome impromptu meetings with their students because of the weight of other commitments, it becomes almost impossible for many students ever to pluck up enough courage to request a tutorial. This means that a student who gets stuck has to waste time waiting for a meeting arranged by the supervisor.

Students expect their supervisors to be friendly, open and supportive

In Chapter 2 we referred to the difficulties experienced, even by mature students, in informal social contact with their supervisors. We also pointed out the supervisors' ignorance of these difficulties. In this chapter the focus is on the more formal aspects of the relationship.

Many of the same tensions are present. Supervisors often feel that if they have established an easygoing, first-name relationship, their students will perceive them to be friendly and open. However, as we have seen, this is not necessarily the case. For example, Charles, who was doing a PhD in astronomy, said:

> It's very difficult to prise things out of Dr Chadwick, so I'm not sure if this meeting today will result in a big step forward for my research. Our meetings are rather silent affairs, as I wait for him to prompt me and he gives very little feedback and only chips in from time to time. I don't get much help, information or encouragement from him. I know that he is my supervisor and I don't want to slight him, but I seem to be avoiding him at present.

Here, Charles is expressing dissatisfaction with tutorial meetings to the point of trying to keep out of view of his supervisor. This made life particularly difficult, as they had rooms just along the corridor from each other.

Dr Chadwick, however, still felt that things between them were reasonably satisfactory:

> Our relationship is friendly, even though I never see him outside the formal interview situation. Our meetings are irregular but fairly often, about once every two or three weeks, usually at his initiative. They last up to half an hour but could be as little as 15 minutes. Most of the time we meet to consider details of the computer program he's working on, so he has to explain the nature of the problem and then we discuss it. These programs will be used a lot and so have to be very efficient.

It is clear that Dr Chadwick does make himself available when Charles requests a meeting and takes it as a sign of success that Charles asks to see him. Although Charles avoids using Dr Chadwick's name when talking to him, the fact that he brings problems along confirms his supervisor in his belief that he is being friendly, open and supportive. Unfortunately, Dr Chadwick is totally unaware of Charles's inability to talk to him about research matters that are bothering him. An effective supervisor, on the other hand, would not merely stick to academic issues but would create regular opportunities to discuss their relationship.

Students expect their supervisors to be constructively critical

This is a particularly sensitive area. It is the supervisor's job to criticize and provide feedback but the manner in which this information is given is absolutely vital. If the criticism is harsh, or perceived as such by the student, considerable damage may be done. It is important to remember also, that giving praise whenever appropriate is one part, often neglected, of providing feedback. During interviews with people who had achieved their PhDs, there were as many unexpected floods of tears (from both men and women) when this topic came up as there were in interviews with those who had dropped out of their PhDs before completing. Doing a PhD is a very emotional, as well as intellectual, experience for most research students.

Supervisors will be concerned with such questions as: Is the work clearly organized? Is the coverage of the topic comprehensive? How does the information relate to prior work in the area? Are the research methods appropriate and described accurately? Is the discussion clear? Will the work make a significant contribution to the discipline? Does it have policy implications? It is very important indeed that students should have learned how to answer these questions and so evaluate their work without recourse to their supervisors by the time they are ready to submit their theses. We have already discussed this in some detail in Chapter 7.

It is essential that in the course of discussions with you, your students gradually become familiar with the criteria against which their work is being measured. As they become better able to mediate for themselves between their efforts and the results, by comparing what has happened with what they expected would happen, they will need to rely less and less on you for feedback. Relying on their own judgement about their work involves confidence, and this will come only from exposure to continual constructive criticism from a supportive and sensitive supervisor.

If students do not receive helpful information of this sort, there is a high probability that they will become discouraged, lose confidence and decide that they are incapable of ever reaching the standard necessary to do a PhD, which, of course, will affect their future careers. The techniques of giving effective feedback are discussed later in this chapter (see p. 155).

Students expect their supervisors to have a good knowledge of the research area

Very often this is the reason that a particular supervisor has been selected. But, especially when students and supervisors have been assigned to each other after registration, it is possible that the supervisor is not expert in the student's area of research. Provided the student has access to others who are expert in the area, it may be more important that the supervisor's style of work and expectations of the supervisory role coincide with those of the student.

Students should be able to use other members of the academic staff as a resource. Between them, these academics will probably have the expertise required by the students at different points during the period of research. Alternatively, the supervisor could ensure that students are well catered for by introducing them to specialists from other universities.

While students consider it essential that supervisors should be well-versed in their areas of research, they do not expect their supervisors to be experts on the particular problems they are exploring within those areas. (The reasons for being awarded the PhD degree include an acceptance that the candidate has become an expert on that particular problem.)

There is more to working together than a common interest in an area of research. The relationship between students and supervisors is a dynamic one that is constantly changing. What is important is that communication about the research is clear and there is knowledge on all sides of how the work is progressing.

Students expect their supervisors to structure the tutorial so that it is relatively easy to exchange ideas

Such an expectation would appear, at first, to be relatively simple, but it is one with which supervisors find it extremely difficult to comply. Creating a comfortable environment in which to discuss ideas and so further the research is not an easy task. We have already seen that there is a discrepancy between the students' and the supervisors' perceptions of degree of familiarity and approachableness.

Students expect their supervisors to have the flexibility to understand what it is that they are trying to say. In understanding students, the supervisor needs to be able to draw out their ideas. This is done through a continual questioning procedure. Students may speak or write in a complex or convoluted manner for fear of being considered too simple, or they may not yet have managed to clarify their thoughts.

There is no pressure on any supervisor to take a course in thought-reading. They may, however, need to learn some simple techniques for eliciting information from people who cannot express themselves coherently.

In addition, they need an uninterrupted period of time in which to concentrate on the discussion. For this reason students' expectation that their supervisors will have the courtesy not to answer the telephone during a tutorial is not unreasonable (but it is always greeted with a laugh when it has been put forward to groups of supervisors). Setting aside a period of time to discuss progress with a research student makes the student feel that they are being taken seriously and conveys the impression that the work under discussion has sufficient merit to be treated with respect. There is nothing more frustrating than to be interrupted in midstream when trying to explain a complex and, as yet, unexpressed idea. Equally, if student and supervisor are engaged in an intense discussion of a specific issue, the line of thought is difficult to regain.

If there are several interruptions the student feels insulted and the work becomes devalued. Any progress that might have been made in the direction of creating a comfortable environment is sure to be lost.

During tutorials supervisors should switch off their mobile phones and arrange for telephone calls to be diverted to voice mail. If, for any reason, a call does come through, supervisors should tell the caller that they are engaged in an important meeting and will call back. It is just bad manners to permit any but the most urgent call to intrude into a meeting that has been arranged and for which work has been prepared.

In addition, supervisors should encourage their students to participate in academic seminars, particularly those provided for research students. These seminars provide a training ground invaluable for developing thinking through discussion, helping students to structure their ideas into a form that facilitates writing. They also enable students to practise the skills necessary for presenting their work at conferences. On occasion you, as a supervisor, should also attend such seminars yourself so that your students get to know you in the role of seminar participant and leader as well as personal tutor. (There is a problem if all supervisors go to all seminars:

students are often then inhibited and less likely to speak up.) Gradually, the seminars should help the students to gain the confidence to openly discuss all the aspects of their research with you in tutorials.

Students expect their supervisors to have sufficient interest in their research to put more information in the students' path

There is a variety of ways in which this can be done. It is important that the supervisor takes into consideration the student's current need for help. For example, in the beginning it may not be sufficient to suggest a reference, leaving the student to follow it up in the library. For some students it may be necessary to give an actual photocopy of the article if it is difficult to obtain in order to get them started. Supervisors can also show their students articles and sections of books from their own collections which are relevant to the point the student has reached.

At a later stage, conference papers reporting the newest developments in the field need to be brought to the student's attention. At this stage the student and the supervisor should both be reading the relevant literature and sending journal articles to each other. In fact, the exchange of papers should be seen as an essential aspect of communication and a source of discussion.

Finally, as we have said, supervisors have a responsibility to introduce their students to others in the field. These specialists should be able to give the students more information than the supervisor alone. Such contacts are important for budding professionals, enabling them to build up a network within which they can discuss their research interests.

Students expect supervisors to be sufficiently involved in their success to help them get a good job at the end of it all!

This expectation is becoming more and more important each year as it gets more and more difficult for supervisors to do anything about it. There are some students who decide it is worthwhile to have an absent supervisor for the period of their research in order to be assured of a good job at the end of it. They are willing to be supervised by busy, jet-setting academics, even though they know that they will be left alone for long periods since their supervisors will be difficult to contact. Research students assume that their supervisor will be able to effect introductions to others, of all nationalities, who are also at the top of their profession. They decide that to have a personal reference from such a well-known authority is worth three years of isolation in learning to do research. At all levels of the academic ladder there are those who agree that it is part of the supervisor's role to help students to find a job once they have completed. Equally, there are those who consider that a supervisor's tasks are at an end when a

PhD degree is awarded. Whichever camp a supervisor may fall into, it may not make very much difference in times when government funding of research is cut, academic employment in general is reduced, and increasingly PhD graduates are looking for employment outside of the university. Encouraging students to participate in UK GRAD Schools <*www.gradschools.ac.uk*> would help in widening their career horizons.

■ Establishing a role model

This is a very important aspect of your task as supervisor. It is not a case of saying 'do as I tell you' but more a case of students gradually learning to 'do as you do', whether that is what you would prefer or not. The way you conduct yourself in your dealings with your research students is therefore vital to their later development. It is crucial for them to see that research is important to you and that you treat it seriously. Nothing could be better for them than your being deeply involved in your own research and writing papers about it that get published in reputable journals. Giving conference papers and attending seminars in your specialized area are activities that benefit your students as well as yourself, without either of you necessarily being aware of it. What it all adds up to is giving potential researchers a mode of behaviour towards which they can aim.

When you postpone a meeting with a research student because of pressure of other work, such as administration or marking examination scripts, it suggests to the student that those areas of your work take precedence over research supervision. Similarly, if your priorities are orientated to undergraduate lecturing, postgraduates will soon understand that doctoral supervision has a low rating on your long list of responsibilities.

Another key task at this early stage in the researcher's career, is that they are taught to develop and respect ethical values, including the unacceptability of plagiarism and falsifying results to make them appear more satisfactory. Professional codes of conduct and high standards of integrity are as important to their learning as how to conduct an experiment or carry out an interview. It is to you, as role model as well as academic supervisor, that this task falls. However, most of this teaching will take place by setting a good example rather than subjecting your students to lectures.

■ Teaching the craft of research

In general, supervisors do not know how to teach how to do research, even though their own research practice may be outstanding. They do not even think of supervision as being a part of their teaching role. Yet it is as important to give some thought to the teaching component in supervision as it is to the research component. Important aspects of the teaching task are: giving feedback effectively, developing a structured weaning programme, maintaining a helpful psychological contract and encouraging students' academic role development. These issues are discussed in turn below.

Giving effective feedback

Giving criticism is one of the main activities that supervisors of doctoral students have to undertake. It is not an easy task, and it is vital that it should be done in a constructive and supportive fashion. If the criticism is overly harsh, or perceived as such by the student, feelings of resentment and hurt can last well into their professional career.

A key beginning point to note is that, if the discipline is not in the tradition of the humanities, it is unlikely that a student will appreciate that the terms 'criticism' and 'critique' include appreciation and praise as well as reproof. Overseas students too, are unlikely to be aware of the wider implications of the terms. We therefore prefer the term 'feedback', which is more neutral and less threatening to students. The word reminds supervisors that they must strongly communicate their recognition of what has been well-achieved as the basis for identifying what is inadequate and needs to be improved.

Giving effective feedback is an activity to which supervisors should give some thought. If it is badly done, it results in one of three unfortunate results:

☐ bewilderment and depression on the part of the student, who does not understand what is being criticized, but realizes that the work has failed;
☐ rejection of the criticisms by the student, who becomes defensive and self-justificatory;
☐ complete acceptance of the criticisms, often with limited understanding of them, which then increases the dependence of the student on the supervisor.

None of these outcomes contributes to the aim of the supervisory process, which is to help the student develop to become a fully professional researcher exercising independent good judgement. If students do not receive helpful information, it is likely that they will become discouraged, lose confidence and decide that they are incapable of ever reaching the standard necessary to do a PhD.

There are a number of useful rules of thumb to be followed in enabling feedback to be more effective:

☐ *Earn the right to include criticism in the feedback.* This may appear a strange rule. Surely a supervisor is entitled to criticize students? Yes, in principle, but in order to avoid the unfortunate outcomes listed above, it is useful for supervisors to remind themselves that they have to establish this right, on a regular basis, as part of the supervisory process. This can be done in the ways suggested below.

☐ *Underline that the purpose of feedback is to make progress.* Establish, and regularly reaffirm, that the doctoral process is a joint enterprise between student and supervisor, and that the point of feedback is to enable the student's knowledge and skills to improve. Create a mutually supportive atmosphere, ensuring that there are no interruptions.

☐ *Give the good news first.* Demonstrate that you are on the side of the student, that you appreciate what has been done, and that you are going to make a balanced evaluation by beginning with a detailed appreciation of the achievements of the work. Point out its strengths, and the improvement achieved compared with the previous submission. This builds student confidence and prepares the way for an open, non-defensive, non-dependent consideration of the inadequacies. The appreciation must be genuine. It is not effective to say: 'Well, it's an improvement, but . . .' and then immediately concentrate on the important criticisms to be made of the work. By the time you are enthusiastically into the four key criticisms, the student will have forgotten the original four words of encouragement.

☐ *Maintain a balance between the appreciation and the criticisms.* Major criticisms of the work should be preceded by major positive evaluations. A good rule of thumb is to match the number and gravity of the criticisms with an equal number of detailed points in appreciation of what has been achieved. If you cannot find four positive things to say about the work, you should consider whether the student is completely inadequate for doctoral level work and should be counselled to withdraw; or whether you, as the supervisor, are being unrealistic as to what can be achieved at this stage of the process and should adjust your expectations accordingly.

☐ *Present criticism impersonally.* Avoid being too personally identified with criticisms, so that the impact on the student is 'This is your criticism of me.' Start by asking students what inadequacies they are themselves aware of. This puts them in a frame of mind more conducive to objective criticism. Preface a major critique by saying 'I'm going to act as devil's advocate here'. Refer to comparable work which the student should emulate.

☐ *Present feedback related to the current piece of work.* Aim to keep comments totally relevant to the piece of work presently being evaluated. Do not refer back to similar mistakes in previous work, since harping on past inadequacies reduces students' confidence. Only refer to previous work in order to demonstrate how far the student has improved. Avoid general comments on the personality or abilities of the student. Relate the feedback specifically to aspects of the work under consideration. So, do not say 'You obviously have a superficial mind; you must get a greater depth of understanding of this.' The comment acts as a general discouragement, whereas what is needed are examples of how the inadequacy is demonstrated in the present work and what tasks the student must undertake to improve.

Again, avoid comments on the student's abilities, such as: 'Your English style is execrable. You should do something about it,' since this comments on a skill inadequacy but does not give any clues about how or what to improve. The comments should be related to the work and should suggest changes to be made. If, like EMP, you believe that split infinitives and prepositional endings to sentences are not appropriate to doctoral writing, then examples might be: 'It is not good practice to split infinitives, as you have done on pages a and b' or 'On page x and page y, it is not a good idea to end sentences with a preposition.' These comments give pointers to what should be changed. You will look for other examples of inappropriate colloquialisms and ungrammatical constructions if, like DSP, you are quite prepared to blatantly split infinitives and think that a preposition is a very useful word to end a sentence with.

☐ *Present feedback clearly; work to minimize ambiguity in criticism; gauge how much the student can usefully absorb on this occasion.* A supervisor should not too obviously enjoy criticizing a student. This is not as easy as it sounds. A great deal of the enjoyment in academic life comes from critiques of fellow academics. This is often regarded as an art form in itself, replete with its appropriate allusions, nuances and put-downs. In the final stages of the PhD process, when the student is about to become a fully professional researcher, this style would be appropriate. In the earlier stages of the research however, critical feedback should be given with regret, be as clear and specific as possible, and be related to the level of development of the student. Damage limitation is important. If you give too much information about what is in need of correction the student may become overwhelmed and think that the task is impossible.

☐ *Pay attention to what your students are saying in response to the feedback you give and then reply to their comments.* Your reaction should demonstrate that you have taken account of what they say in the development of your views. It is important not to be so committed to your own view of the student's work that you are (or appear to be) unwilling to reconsider your views in the light of the student's responses. Always remember that effective feedback is that which is accepted by the recipient as a basis for further work, and you have to demonstrate your ability to accept feedback too.

☐ *Always end a supervision session by reviewing what points have been made, and getting the student to rehearse what now will be done.* This 'action replay' is vital to avoid misunderstanding. Make sure that you agree the date and time of the next supervisory session to re-evaluate the work and progress. The joint establishment of deadlines is important. Getting your student to do further work should not be left open-ended. Finally, students should be encouraged to write a summary of the meeting on one sheet of A4 and, having agreed it with the supervisor, make a copy for the supervisor's files.

☐ *Use a logical framework in presenting feedback.* Apart from being specific about what precisely is wrong with the student's performance, it is also necessary to know what kind of criticism is appropriate at a given point in the student's research career. For example, a detailed critique of grammar and punctuation will not be of very much use if the ideas and general content of a piece of writing are incorrect or confused. You could tell the student that when an unavoidable delay occurs, which prevents the carrying out of an experiment or an interview for example, students should not just stop working. It is necessary to set the wheels in motion to resolve the problem and to continue with some other work such as reading, writing or analysing what has already been done. At the same time a regular check can be kept on developments relating to the removal of the obstacle.

The student needs to be *told* all this as well as whether the work should be longer or shorter, contain more references to published work, have less complex sentences, contain simpler ideas or use less jargon. No matter how obvious it may seem to you, it is essential that you spell out to the student, in very precise terms, just what it is that needs to be redone and why. If all of it needs to be reworked, give explicit advice concerning how the new version must differ from the previous one. It is primarily in this way that students can discover what it is they should be watching for in their own work and so become better at judging what is acceptable and appropriate.

The reason for giving feedback effectively is that through it students can eventually learn how to evaluate their own work and so take over this part of the supervisor's job themselves. In the longer term, they have to be taught how to become independent researchers in their own right.

Supervising a candidate for a PhD involves more than just monitoring the research work. Doing a PhD is a very emotional experience, which involves the whole person. As supervisor you need to be able to communicate with your students about their abilities and achievements, but you also need to discuss their commitment to the PhD and any external circumstances that affect it. Throughout their registration period it is highly probable that you will need to take account of their personal lives.

This is true of anybody engaged in supervising another human being, but unfortunately it is too often the case that managers choose to ignore the 'whole person' and patch over, rather than get to the bottom of, any difficulties that are showing themselves in the individual's work. While this is true of life at work in general, it is even more true of life within the academic community. As we have mentioned above, academics do have some training opportunities but these do not usually include tuition in interpersonal skills and human relations. So it is important that you understand that research students are emotionally more involved with their work than are most people at work. Skill in giving effective feedback and eliciting information that may be relevant to poor performance at work is therefore even more important in the supervisor–student relationship than in the manager–subordinate relationship.

There is much less likelihood of finding those skills within the academic community, however. What is needed here is interpersonal training in how to state honestly and directly what you as supervisor perceive to be the problem, no matter how upsetting you think this may be for the student. It is far worse for the student to think for a long time that everything is reasonably satisfactory, only to discover at a very late stage that the work is not suitable for writing up, or that the thesis will be entered only for an MPhil after all. Alternatively, the student may be aware that things are not as they should be but will imagine all kinds of causes for the problem, including a sudden and inexplicable antipathy on the part of the supervisor. It is far preferable for the student to have some definite information upon which to base decisions about future behaviour than to worry that something isn't quite right without knowing why.

For example, Charles, studying astronomy, wanted to know whether or not to continue. He said: 'I'd like to if I possibly could, but if Dr Chadwick thought I wasn't capable of it I wouldn't be too upset as long as he told me. Nobody seems to want to advise me.'

Dr Chadwick was disappointed with his student's slow progress and lack of initiative. He said: 'He's probably not very organized in his work, although one would hope there's some wider reading going on.'

However, Charles had reported:

> I asked him if he knew of any review articles but he doesn't think there are any. He was busy marking exam papers, so we didn't talk … I still haven't learned how to communicate with Dr Chadwick. There's no rapport between us, none at all. I saw him in the lift accidentally on the last day of last term and all we said was, 'Hello'.

On the other hand Adam, studying architecture, reported at the very end of his time as a research student:

> My supervisor never gave me any indication of what he thought of

me. I decided that he was so bored with what I wrote that he couldn't be bothered to criticize what I did. But really he was hoping that I would be the one to popularize the theories that have been around in his department for some years.

Adam had not enjoyed his years as a research student but was feeling much better as the end came into view and he had some measure of success at a conference.

Professor Andrews explained how the situation had eventually been clarified: 'We had several discussions about the direction his work was taking.' It is sad that this only happened once Adam had received support for his ideas from others, who actually did consider them to be excellent.

These two examples are typical of the situations that develop when supervisors do not keep students informed of how they see their progress through (a) regular meetings and (b) honest feedback regarding their work.

Introducing a structured 'weaning' programme

Supervisors can help research students become progressively more academically independent by introducing a process of weaning into their style of supervision. This weaning process must include helping the postgraduates to become aware that they have sufficient knowledge and ability to trust their own judgement and monitor their own performance. This can be achieved by a structured programme that gradually reduces the amount of dependence as the research student gets further into the work. First, you should set short-term goals (and a close date for a tutorial meeting). Later, students can be left to undertake a more complex piece of work over a longer period. A date for reporting progress by a telephone conversation, email or letter should be set, together with a more distant date for a meeting. If the student has to move from the date originally arranged, an adequate explanation is required. You should also have a very good reason to give your student if you decide to change the original date.

In the final stages the onus should be more on the student to initiate the contact than it was in the beginning, but you should still be aware of a responsibility to chase up a student who does not seem to be keeping to the agreement.

Later in the process students must be helped to develop skills of writing and presenting conference papers, journal articles, seminar presentations, thesis chapters or even reports of work undertaken since the last tutorial meeting. Get to this point by encouraging the following activities:

☐ First the student prepares a rough draft that sets out 'This is what I think', then corrects and rewrites the draft without referring to you.
☐ Next, after discussing the first corrected draft with you, the student

prepares a second corrected draft that sets out 'This is what I and my supervisor think.' Then the student can again give the draft to you for comment.

☐ Finally the student prepares a final draft that states 'This is it', and may keep it as a record. At the end, all well-written records can be used and integrated into the thesis itself.

The way to encourage students to use their supervisors to best advantage is to set goals that initially are short-term but become more abstract and take longer to reach as the student becomes more experienced and develops more confidence. In Chapter 7 we described in some detail the setting of goals within a time management programme (see diagram p. 83). It is important for you, as supervisor, to be aware that the length of time that it takes for research students to become autonomous researchers depends on the type of supervision that they receive. If they are continually set very short-term goals with the requirement that they complete a relatively simple piece of work, they will never learn how to manage their time, tasks and deadlines for themselves. If they are left to their own devices too early, however, or given deadlines that are too far into the future before they are ready for this degree of unstructured planning, then they will not learn how to cope on their own.

Supervisors must adjust the way they supervise to the particular needs of individual students. Some students will take a relatively long time to develop the necessary confidence. They will need to be closely monitored and given well-defined tasks to be completed in a relatively short period, until they are well-established in their research. Other students will need to be given general guidance from quite early on in what they should be doing rather than detailed direction. Supervisors should remember that all students will once again need closer direction when they start the final writing up of their theses.

One student requiring guidance early on was Greg, who was researching in ancient history. Dr Green explained that Greg

usually suggests the meetings, but once last term I was concerned about him and asked to see him. I didn't have to chase him. I just make a passing reference or suggestion and next time I see him he knows the text better than I do. He works extremely well.

She saw her role as that of guide, not only because Greg was able to work well under his own direction but also because he was fascinated by the information he was accruing about the person he was researching and the times in which he lived. Every bit of additional knowledge served to motivate Greg to explore further. His main request of his supervisor was that she be ready to listen to the results of his latest detective work.

A possible paradigm for a structured weaning process in your overall supervision could be:

☐ *Early direction.* The supervisor introduces short-term goals, sets the work to be done, and gives detailed feedback to the student at the end of the period.
☐ *Intermediate weaning.* This phase involves support and guidance rather than direction. The work is discussed with the student, and joint decisions are made about what should be attempted and how long it should take. The supervisor encourages the student to evaluate any work submitted and comments on the evaluation, rather than on the work itself.
☐ *Later separation.* This phase includes an exchange of ideas: the student decides on the work to be done and its time limits. By now the supervisor should expect a detailed critical analysis of the work from the student without prompting.

The timing of these stages will vary according to the developing self-confidence of the students. The main requirement here is that supervisors should recognize the stage that students have reached in their need for support. Supervisors might aim to raise their own level of awareness of students' needs for feedback on their progress. Supervisors also need to teach students, by example, how academics evaluate the results of their own work and use this evaluation as a basis for revision and improvement.

This might be achieved by discussing with their students how the work they have already done affects their plans for further work. In addition, by making explicit the interaction between what they plan to do and what they have already done, supervisors can teach their students to be more cautious and not to get carried away with overambitious projects. Supervisors who are sensitive to the needs of their students and able to teach them to become self-supervising at their own pace will derive greater satisfaction from this part of their work than those supervisors who treat all their students in the same way.

Once students have learned the skills and acquired the confidence necessary to assess their own efforts, their dependence on you as supervisor begins to be superseded by self-reliance. It is at this point that they begin to perceive you not as a tutor but as a colleague.

■ Maintaining a helpful 'psychological contract'

Cast your mind back to the start of this chapter and you will recall that Freddy did not discuss with his supervisor how to conduct the research or to what extent and how often Professor Forsdike should be kept informed of results. In this case the professor's behaviour was depressing Freddy and having an adverse effect on his work. They never discussed this problem, and the situation continued without change for most of the time that Freddy was working toward his PhD. Yet it was so easily avoidable; all they had to do was to talk to each other about the context as well as the content of Freddy's work.

A similar lack of communication existed between Adam and Professor Andrews. If Adam had assumed that his supervisor had read the paper (even though privately he believed this not to be the case) he could have asked why Professor Andrews had not bothered to mention more than a small section of it. The conversation would have been opened up enough for the professor to convey his knowledge of the content and express his doubts about the scope of what Adam had done. Such questions from Adam, asked in a positive manner, would have changed their relationship completely. Professor Andrews would have been more expansive in his comments, and Adam would not have spent most of his postgraduate years believing that he was almost totally unsupervised. Of course, if Professor Andrews had put even minimal written comments on the draft, the student would have known that it had been read. Putting a tick at the bottom of each page as you finish reading it will inform your student that nothing has been missed.

It is so easy for postgraduates to become discouraged that a significant part of your job as supervisor is one of keeping morale at a reasonable level. The process of learning to do research and becoming a fully professional researcher involves periods of doubt and disillusionment, when it seems that the only thing to do is to give up. There are periods when moods are volatile, and a certain subtlety is needed to help a student through the difficult times.

Do not be taken in by rationalizations no matter how persuasive they may be. It is not helpful to concede that there is 'no need' for a meeting just now or to forgo some evidence of work in progress, because you feel sorry for the student. Of course, you should be supportive when support is needed. But when you discover that there are continually new and ever more important reasons why the student should be given more time, you will need to be firm if the student is not to fall by the wayside.

If there is a good reason for a year's break, then set it out formally as a break within the institutional framework. This will be more helpful in the long term than building up increasing gaps in work on an informal basis. It is damaging to the contract between you for the student to live with uncertainty or lack of constraints. Therefore it is essential that at regular intervals you:

☐ offer a statement of your expectations, within the oral contract that has already been agreed;

☐ ask your students what their expectations are;
☐ agree a compromise incorporating any changes.

Handling the situation in this way would ensure that the student felt the supervisor was neither uncaring nor lacking in control. It would underline the fact that the supervisor and the student are in a partnership.

In order to maintain the psychological contract at an appropriate level it is important that you play your role as supervisor in a firm way. If you let your professional judgement be swayed by a fear of seeming to be too tough at a time of difficulty in a research student's career, you will not be providing help at a time when it is most needed. The help you need to provide is to chart a course for the student, avoiding the extremes of, on the one hand, easing the path completely and, on the other, leaving the student to founder, simply so that you might appear more sympathetic. It is not your sympathy that the student needs, but your expertise.

■ Encouraging students' academic role development

It is not sufficient for supervisors merely to ensure that postgraduates' research and their reporting of it are progressing satisfactorily. As PhD students get closer to the goal of gaining the research degree, so too do they get closer to recognition as a full professional. But becoming a full professional means more than having completed a research project to a satisfactory standard: it means being able to contribute fully to academic life. It is part of the supervisor's job to help students prepare for this.

This preparation entails encouraging your students to give seminars on their research and related topics and to attend seminars that others are giving. It means helping them gain the confidence to question and comment on what has been presented by the speaker. Research students should also gain experience of attending conferences, speaking from the floor (as they have learned to do in seminars) and giving papers of their own.

These papers may be of an appropriate standard for publication, in which case you, as the supervisor, must initiate the students into the secrets of getting their work published in reputable journals. You could also give them a helping hand by introducing them to your own network of contacts and encouraging them to get in touch with colleagues who are working in their area of interest. In addition, you should facilitate their progression into academic life by trying to give them occasional tutoring work and letting them know when further teaching possibilities are offered – for example, a weekend or summer-school post.

Giving such support to your students will not take up very much of your time and energy. When there is a conference you want to go to, all you have to do is mention it to them and perhaps sign an official request for help with their expenses. Similarly, inviting them to lunch with you once or twice when you are meeting a friend from another university does not make much of a demand on you, yet it has dividends for the students out of all proportion to the effort needed.

■ Supervising non-traditional students

Supervisors need some understanding of, and sympathy for, the difficulties that non-traditional students face. By non-traditional we mean any of those student groups covered in Chapter 9. There we discuss these problems fully, primarily from the point of view of the student. In this section we discuss these issues from the perspective of the supervisor, assuming that you have made yourself familiar with the appropriate section of Chapter 9. By becoming aware of issues that these students are facing, supervisors will be in a position to offer support and information when, for example, overseas or disabled students have to be pointed in the direction of appropriate people or organizations for assistance.

Part-time students

Part-time students are now in a majority in many disciplines where appropriate arrangements are made for their requirements. But in those disciplines where they are still in a minority, supervisors should ensure that they are not disadvantaged. Even when they are no longer a minority, part-time students still have particular difficulties because most of their life is spent *not* as a student.

Problems of access

Opening hours of academic and support facilities in the university are not necessarily consistent with part-timers' need to use them. Library times, for example, should be extended so that students who are not available during usual working hours can still gain access to books and journals. Access to such amenities as computers, use of the Internet and assistance from statistical services is more difficult for them than for full-time students

Part-timers may also suffer from a lack of opportunity to meet others because of the restricted time they have available to spend at university. As well as limiting their exchange of information with peers, they can be further disadvantaged if communication of changed locations or cancelled seminars does not reach them in time. There are also limits to their being effectively represented at staff–student or postgraduate meetings owing to their contact hours being outside the university's normal working hours. As supervisor you should ensure that arrangements are made for them to have all the access that they need.

As we point out in Chapter 9, part-time students may have to arrange to work fewer hours and therefore rely on less income. Supervisors must ensure that the Registry is satisfied that the student will not suffer extreme hardship nor be overlooked for possible financial support.

Organizing work

In the case of part-time students, time allocation is a common cause of stress. The main psychological difficulty experienced by them is that of having to switch from everyday work to research work in order to proceed. To keep this to a minimum the research problem should be related to the student's paid work, if at all possible.

Guidance and help concerning how best to manage their work might include the advice we give to all students in Chapter 5 on writing the thesis that, when they do leave their research work, they should leave it in the middle – mid-sentence, mid-idea, mid-design – rather than at a natural break. Not only does this make it easier to return later and continue more quickly but it also adds internal pressure to return in order to complete that which they have started but have not yet completed.

Supervisors should always remember that part-timers need reinforcement of their student identity and a supportive framework for their studies.

Overseas students

Overseas students, paying higher fees, are an important postgraduate presence in British universities. They inevitably have extra problems, particularly if they come from non-English speaking backgrounds. In the first place they might experience extreme loneliness, especially if they are the only one from their home country at the university. They have to make huge adaptations to study at our universities. They have to work in a foreign language, adapt to an alien culture and experience a different tradition of learning from that with which they are familiar.

They come from a large variety of countries, all of whom may be experiencing different difficulties so that, as Geake and Maingard (1999) observed, there are more individual differences among such students than between them and native English-speaking students. For example, students from some countries, have to observe dietary restrictions or are forbidden to enter licenced premises, and so it is even more difficult for them to socialize. Therefore supervisors, as well as becoming aware of their common difficulties, must be sensitive to differences among them.

For example, when meeting with students from some cultural back-grounds, supervisors must be prepared for differences in non-verbal com-munication such as smiling, nodding or shaking the head at what might appear to them to be an inappropriate moment. They could be disconcerted by avoidance of eye-contact when speaking to Malaysian students, and yet discover the need to maintain eye-contact for longer than is necessary in the British culture when holding the attention of their Arab students.

They may discover that Asian students remain silent when supervisors expect a response, but for different cultural reasons. While Japanese stu-dents may fear giving an incorrect answer and so 'losing face' by being wrong, Chinese students may believe they will be considered arrogant and bad-mannered if they seem to answer too confidently about their work. Supervisors may also experience unexpected problems in regard to the extent of personal space and the acceptability of touching, which may depend upon the gender or religion of the student. The attention given to time constraints or the apparent neglect of them, is another issue that often requires adjustment of previous norms on the part of the student – with the understanding help of the supervisor.

There are other important cultural differences. Eastern students have to be helped to understand the major contrasts between the Asian and the western attitudes to knowledge. The much higher importance of conserv-ing wisdom in eastern culture is counterposed with the greater emphasis on extending ideas in the West. Eastern academic traditions emphasize consensus and harmony in place of the western tradition of challenge and argument. Hickson and Pugh (2001) discuss all these issues of culture clashes fully in relation to expatriate managers around the world, but the same problems face the expatriate research student.

It seems self-evident to state that a basic problem for students from non-English speaking backgrounds is the language. Problems with speaking and writing English are very discernible, yet it is easily overlooked that listening to and reading English are also language skills. So we blithely encourage students' participation in academic discourse which must be informed by analysis, critical and reflective thinking, speculation and syn-thesis of ideas and information. It is important to be conscious of their difficulties and be realistic in helping them to develop. There is the add-itional complication that, to a student who is not a native English speaker, academic writing is almost a different language from everyday spoken English. While it is not the supervisors' responsibility to teach students mastery of diverse aspects of English, it is their responsibility to ensure that their own students have access to whatever language training they need.

Even with language training there is also, for many supervisors, the difficult decision to make as to how far to go in editing students' written work – or even in rewriting it. Some copyediting and the correction of spelling and grammatical errors is the lot of the supervisor in regard to all students, but with non-English speaking students the question arises as to how much further this can go before the work ceases to be regarded as the student's own. Knight (1999) makes the point that a relatively small amount of rewiting (e.g. one small section of one chapter) would be justified on grounds of giving an example for the student to learn from, but it would be difficult to defend a greater amount of rewriting.

Nevertheless this is a temptation to which many supervisors are exposed, as it seems to be the easiest way of progressing the research. The use of copyeditors, which university regulations do not normally proscribe, raises the same issue. How far is work by another allowable before the necessary statement that the thesis is genuinely the work of the candidate becomes compromised? There are no definite rules, and this is a judgement that has to be made in every case.

We think it right that supervisors should very carefully restrict their contribution, if the examination process is not to be undermined. It is thus important that they establish early in the research that their contribution on this front will be strictly limited, so that students can do the necessary learning during the course of the research. It would be patently unfair for students to be confronted with this problem in its entirety only at the writing-up stage of their project.

The unprepared supervisor may also be surprised to discover problems arising out of the use of quotations and the need to ensure that they are appropriately referenced. In many non-western cultures, for example, the practice of meticulously giving credit for quotations used is not common, and therefore students may be unwittingly guilty of plagiarism. There is the notion that if it has been written well by someone else and is in the public domain, then use it. This view may seem strange to us now, but we should remember that it was not that long ago that it was considered perfectly appropriate for a professor, for example, to take material from his student's report and simply include it in his own published papers. The current western view of the intellectual property rights of students and other academics is now much stronger and the supervisor has to ensure that the student internalizes it.

Financial problems can loom large, because students from non-English speaking backgrounds lack the required language skills and work experience and consequently end up in poorly paid jobs. Climatic differences and ill health are further burdens. Such students also encounter problems in negotiating with unfamiliar bureaucracies. Sometimes worries about families and friends in situations of political unrest in their home countries add to the strain.

Finally, overseas student expectations of supervisors may be inappropriate. It is true that many British students are not very well-informed about the role of the supervisor when they first register for their research degree. But overseas students often expect an unrealistically high level of contribution from their supervisors towards the research and the thesis. They have to be helped to understand better the role of the supervisor in order to survive within British universities. Ryan and Zuber-Skerrit (1999), based on work in Australia, is a collection of insightful analyses and case studies highly relevant to the problems of supervising overseas students in both Britain and Australia.

Having these extra problems to cope with, students from other cultural backgrounds might find all this academic re-socialization a threat, rather than a challenge, to their own academic competence. Supervisors need to be aware of the difficulties and differences and provide the greatly needed sympathy and support.

Ethnic minorities

Only about one in ten of doctoral students is from an ethnic minority. Therefore, it is important for supervisors to be aware of the more unusual difficulties which such students have to face.

The typical isolation experienced when working toward a PhD, and discussed in some detail throughout this book, is intensified in the case of ethnic minority students. They may experience discrimination by staff and other students, which can take the form of unfounded perceptions that emphasize deficits in abilities and underachievement due to their background and culture, and incorporate ideas that, for example, black individuals cannot be as clever as their white peers. They can feel isolated from their peers; isolated from white students with whom relationships are often strained, isolated within largely white institutions, and isolated from parents and parental cultures. Black individuals are conspicuous by their absence from this level of education in the UK, so there is a clear lack of role models for students from a wide range of ethnic minorities. This serves to make relationships with staff more difficult for them than it is for most other students. Gundara (1997) gives a full discussion of the cultural issues involved.

Black students may have to deal with racist taunts, but other minorities also have problems. Jewish students contend with anti-Semitism and disabled students struggle to establish their independence. Muslim students, both home and overseas, may find themselves confronted by unexpected problems. Since 9/11 (the events in New York on 11 September 2001) the world has become more afraid than ever of the possibility of attacks by terrorists. This fear has developed into a form of Islamophobia which manifests itself into a suspicion of Arabs and conveys in particular a stereotype of Muslims as potential terrorists.

Many of the suspects held captive by the Americans, as well as some who succeeded in their suicide bombing of the World Trade Center, were known to be university students. This mistrust of people who fit such a stereotype may result in harassment of students from these ethnic minorities especially when newspapers, radio and TV broadcasts are full of items about the police stopping and searching young Muslims. The suspicion is likely to be greatest in politically-sensitive subjects such as nuclear physics or aeronautics.

Even before the current rise in Islamic extremism, University Jewish and Israel societies were also facing difficulties. Worries about the threat of harassment or attack prevented some Jewish students from joining. In a few universities they were unable to join these societies because of student union anti-Zionist action which had resulted in their closure.

For these reasons many minority students may be feeling cut off from the main group which would have given them the much needed peer support we recommend for all students. It is doubtful that students will tell their supervisors about any of these problems so supervisors need to demonstrate their understanding of the problems and endeavour to provide greater than usual social and emotional support.

Women students

Even though women research students are no longer a small minority in most subjects, there can still be problems of gender difference in the supervisor–student relationship. Women are clearly visible and should not be treated as token presences in order for the department to prove that they are not sexist, but do practice equal opportunities. Supervisors should ensure that the allocation of scarce resources such as money for conference attendance or part-time, paid research or teaching work does not discriminate against any group.

You as a supervisor should be aware that there are a number of different ways in which female students may need extra support. In a review of the literature on gender differences in behaviour in small groups, Conrad and Phillips (1995) found clear evidence that in mixed working groups men tended to dominate. You should therefore make particular efforts to encourage your female students to speak up in seminars and discussions.

In the not unusual situation of a male academic supervising a female student, it may be the case that the supervisor believes (wrongly) that women are more emotional than men or feels that they would not know how to cope with tears if they occurred, and so limit their criticism. In this situation female students may not receive detailed feedback on their work. Then the male student is given an advantage denied to his female colleague through no fault of her own. He will know what to do to avoid making the same mistake again; she will not. The moral is: do not hold back important negative feedback from your woman student because of being afraid that she may cry. (Men may cry too!) All such feedback must, of course, be given with skill as we describe above.

In Chapter 9 we refer to the rights that students have if they feel that they are being harassed or treated in any way that makes them feel uncomfortable. We tell them how to recognize inappropriate behaviour on the part of fellow students or staff. In order to ensure that you do not inadvertently put yourself in a position where you can be accused of such behaviour with any of your students, you must beware of unwittingly acting in an inappropriate or overly sexual manner. This might happen if a supervisor were to stroke the head or put an arm round the shoulders of a student who was worried or unhappy. It could be that a woman student (or a student from a less tactile culture) would misinterpret such an action and be upset by it.

Finally, beware of becoming emotionally involved with your female students. We believe that it is as important for supervisors to beware of such relationships as it is for their students. As Delamont *et al.* (2004) note, the power dimension to supervision complicates the notion of any con- sensual sexual relationship between student and supervisor. It is clear that the power resides with academic staff and, as feelings change from heady romantic love at the start of the relationship (and possibly the research) through disenchantment, anger and jealousy as time progresses, it can become difficult to communicate satisfactorily. The result is that the work, as well as the people, suffer.

Gay, lesbian, bisexual and trans-gender students

Supervisors should be aware that harassment is an issue that may occur at any time and can take many forms. Non-traditional students are more likely to be the victims and this is particularly the case with gay, lesbian, bisexual and trans-gender students.

The whole area of 'coming out' in academic environments has to be managed with the help of staff who are neither ignorant nor homophobic. Discuss with your student any problems in the gender aspect of the student–supervisor relationship. In all these cases, it would be extremely beneficial to them if you were able to help find role models in academia.

Field trips could present a problem in this regard. Clearly women, gay, lesbian, and disabled students may require more thought when making arrangements. Leonard (2001) gives the example of openly lesbian geol- ogy and geography students who have experienced problems with sleep- ing arrangements on such trips. These difficulties may happen in other disciplines too, for example archeology, anthropology or zoology – any discipline involving field work. If you are supervising students who you know to be in one of the minority categories it would be a good idea to suggest that they check such arrangements before setting out.

You may find yourself in the unusual position of supervising a trans- gender student. As we pointed out in Chapter 9, people who have crossed the gender divide have a very strong desire to be accepted in their new identity. This can be due to their concern regarding other people's reactions or because they want to leave their past experiences, which were alien to them even when they were living them, behind and start afresh as though they had never undergone such a major transformation. You should show your awareness of the currently practising highly successful trans-gender legal and medical specialists.

As before, we warn of the difficulties of becoming emotionally involved with non-traditional students. Leonard (2001) relates the case of a bisexual academic, accused of sexual harassment, who used as her defence of her affairs with both male and female students, that teachers should use every means at their disposal to excite them. She argued that permitting the transfer of power through sexual, as well as intellectual stimulation, was beneficial to students, making them more productive and confident as scholars. We utterly disagree with this view and would suggest that the fact that the supervisor in question was having to defend herself against a sexual harassment charge points to its glaring limitations. We believe that all supervisors need to be aware of the position of power in which they are placed and treat their students in a completely professional manner.

Mature students

Universities have been quite successful in recruiting a wider range of people who are returning to do a research degree after some years out of education. We no longer have the situation where most of the academic staff are younger than their mature students. The average age of academic staff has remained in the early forties for some years and you, as supervisor, may find that you have someone of the same age as a research student.

However, these mature students often have family responsibilities to contend with and some may also be coping with financial difficulties. In fact some mature students might suddenly discover that they have been thrust into a socioeconomic level of relative poverty. It may be that you can help by interceding on their behalf for payment of fees over an extended period of time or advising on the application for a hardship grant.

As we have stated in Chapter 9, there are departments where mature students are the norm but it is also true that there are many departments where they are very much in the minority. You should be aware that at least some of your mature students will find that they have to fight ageism and the stereotypes that go with it.

They, more than their more conventional colleagues, will feel that they have to prove their ability to work at this high level. Do beware of being more supportive and protective of your younger students under the misapprehension that the older ones have had so much life experience that they can probably manage all right on their own. This is far from the truth. Mature students certainly need your help at least as much as the others. They have the additional difficulty of learning all over again how to play the role of student and how to interact with an academic superior who may be their own age or, worse still, younger than them.

Another problem for mature students, especially those from overseas, is leaving family behind, but so is bringing their family with them. It is up to you, as their supervisor, to recognize the stress incurred by either of these situations and point them in the direction of appropriate support agencies.

Finally, you should be aware that even now there is still no legislation against ageism in the UK, although the USA has had laws against it since the 1960s. This group of students needs your protection as much as the other groups discussed in this section.

Disabled students

In Chapter 9 we referred to The Special Educational Needs and Disability Act (2001) which makes it unlawful for institutions to treat a disabled person 'less favourably' than they would a non-disabled person. It requires universities to take 'all reasonable steps' to ensure this.

Since there is a small but distinct minority (about 4 per cent) of students who are disabled, you may find that you need to familiarize yourself with the Act and find out how it is being applied in your university. It will put you in a good position to be of help to them if required. You should also suggest that they explore their rights to a Post Graduate Disabled Students Allowance or other government support.

In summary of the whole of this section, we would say that non-traditional students are inevitably vulnerable in a system that is not immediately geared to their needs. Once you, as a supervisor, have accepted the importance of familiarizing yourself with both the potential problems and the routes to solving them, you will be in a position to offer support and information to help them.

■ Supervising your research assistant

The tasks facing the supervisor which we have been analysing become more complicated if the student is also a research assistant. PhD students who are also research assistants have declined in numbers in recent years. This is the result of regulations brought in by research councils and funding bodies who have discovered that often their thesis work and the scientific research they are paid to do are not necessarily the same.

Consequently the work that they are doing is either not suitable or is too focused for a PhD thesis.

However, if you do find yourself in the position of supervising your research assistant, there are two roles which both the team leader/ supervisor and the research assistant/student have to play. These are not entirely congruent. Understandably the research team leader must have as a main priority the completion of the research programme for which the assistant is a human resource. This resource must be managed in the most effective way for the achievement of the goals, in much the same way as any subordinate in an organization. At the same time the subordinate, in the capacity of student, is entitled to the same service of supervision as all other doctoral students.

In our experience, for many supervisors the management task wins out easily over the student supervisory one. If the student's thesis is on a different topic this gets squeezed out. If it is cognate to the team's research, then there is generated a tension as to what can and cannot be counted towards the PhD, and where the time priorities should be put.

Effectiveness in this situation requires three elements of good practice from the supervisor. The first is to get agreement, as early as possible in the project, on what is the precise nature of the PhD study and how it differs from the remainder of the research programme. The second agreement needs to be on what amount of time it is appropriate for the student to spend on thesis work – perhaps a minimum and maximum per week as a guideline. Third, supervisor–managers should recognize that they have these two roles. In their understandable commitment to managing research projects to a successful outcome, they must not neglect the important educational service, as described in this chapter, which they need to give as supervisors of their students.

■ Outcomes of good supervision

In concluding our discussion of supervision, we may reflect on what would constitute a satisfying result of good supervisory practice for both the student and the supervisor. Such an outcome would include:

- ☐ a doctorate of quality completed on time;
- ☐ advancing the topic as a result of the research;
- ☐ a paper presented at a conference, so that the student has faced external criticism;
- ☐ meeting other professionals, allowing the student to argue with and impress them so that they may be used as possible additional referees;
- ☐ a paper published in an academic journal, so that the student has experienced the journal refereeing process;

☐ a commitment by the student to postdoctoral research and publication;
☐ a stimulating experience for both the student and the supervisor, which has started the student on a research career.

If you give just a little of your time to thinking about helping your students to get a foot on the academic ladder, you will be rewarded by having students who not only like and admire you, but also will in later years make you proud to acknowledge that at one time you were their supervisor.

■ Training for supervision

Training for supervisors to increase their effectiveness is now the norm for new staff, and more experienced academics are also encouraged to attend. Most universities fund sessions to help staff deal with key stages in the management of research degree projects. Topics such as the university's guidelines on higher degrees, the role of the internal examiner, ethical issues in research, how to aid students in formulating their research question, and other problems in supervision are commonly discussed.

We strongly encourage all supervisors, whether new to the role or experienced, to attend at least one such group because of the considerable benefits to be gained. You will meet other academics from different departments and disciplines of your university and have the opportunity to share experiences with them. You may well pick up some tips on the supervisory process and discover that some of the difficulties you face are not only shared across subjects but are the responsibility of the institution as a whole rather than you, the supervisor. In addition you will become more confident that you are a good role model for future researchers.

In conclusion, bad supervision breeds bad supervision. Over the years research students will continue to feel neglected and depressed if their needs are ignored. If, on the other hand, today's supervisors act conscientiously in their work, we will have a more contented group of PhDs who will be more successful in their own future careers.

■ How to examine

Supervisors are not allowed to be the examiners of their own students, but they are often called upon to examine others. They act as internal examiners for students of their colleagues and external examiners for students of other universities. How should they set about this important task?

First, we must reiterate that it is not possible to set rules and regulations that allow the standards for a PhD to be established in a mechanical or bureaucratic way. In general, examiners look for conceptual understanding, critical ability and an explicit and well-structured argument. There is usually basic agreement within a discipline concerning what they are looking for in a good candidate.

Even so Phillips (1994b) found that supervisors and examiners cannot easily talk about the level of competence required for a good PhD. They tend to see each as a unique product not open to generalizations. They claim to recognize when a thesis is really bad, but say that only experience teaches them to know what is interesting and exciting.

The regulations of the university usually include phrases like 'making a significant contribution to knowledge or understanding' and 'demonstrating a capacity to undertake independent research'. These have to be applied in a large range of situations which will inevitably involve a great deal of judgement on the part of the examiner concerning the particular case, in the particular discipline, at the particular time.

Examiners, like students, have to be aware of what standards are being applied in their discipline by regularly reading and pondering upon newly successful PhD theses. They need also to be aware of articles being published in journals in their field to be able to recognize what currently counts as a contribution to the discipline worthy of publication. The examining process may be helpfully compared to refereeing articles submitted for publication to journals. These give an idea of standards at the forefront of the discipline. They help examiners to cope with such questions as: Does the thesis show impressive depth? Does the student demonstrate excellent critical understanding of the issues involved? Has the student creatively integrated the research material to indicate attractive future lines of work? These are questions which often have to be reformulated into: Does the thesis show *enough* depth? Does the student demonstrate *adequate* critical understanding? Has the student *sufficiently* integrated the research material to indicate future work? As in any examining situation, while examiners hope and look for excellent work, even at this high level they are soon faced with the question: Is this good *enough*? It may be helpful to reflect that, just as a First and a 2.2 are both regarded as acceptable honours degrees, so a PhD thesis may be considered acceptable even if it is not consistently excellent.

However, students are often confused about what is required of them and would like guidelines on method and form at the beginning. Even when departments do provide some information, students can feel frustrated that what they have been told does not accord with what they were hoping to hear. One student expressed what many were feeling when he said: 'At the seminar where the basic outline of a thesis was recommended there was an emphasis on the problems of having to reduce an exotic, once in a lifetime experience to a dry as dust thesis format' (Phillips 1994b). In such a situation supervisors have to help students come to terms with the fact that there is a standard form to which the thesis must adhere.

One topic that is often raised in the discussion subsequent to the oral defence, is the problem of dealing with the candidate who has clearly been the victim of inadequate supervision. By implication the supervisors involved feel that they too are being examined and become very defensive in arguing that what has been done is adequate for the PhD degree. Indeed it was for this very reason that supervisors were eventually precluded from being internal examiners as used to be the procedure in most universities. Examiners have to face the question: Is it fair that the candidate be penalized for what is patently a failure of the supervisor? The answer has to be that, since standards have to be maintained, sympathy for the candidate is properly limited to allowing the conditions for the resubmission to be as generous as possible.

As we noted in Chapter 3, research councils put considerable pressure on universities to complete the process of doctoral education and get candidates to submit their theses within four years of registration. As a result they have pushed up the percentage of students who submit within this time frame. But this change has lead some to wonder whether the time limitation has caused a rush to submission and therefore an increase in the proportion of candidates who are referred for further work, since this is acceptable under the research councils' rules. At the time of writing, we do not have adequate information on whether this is the case.

A less fortunate outcome would be pressure on examiners to allow borderline theses to pass on the argument that the university department needs to achieve a satisfactory number of successes for research council appraisal purposes. These pressures must be stoutly resisted, if for no other reason than that the research councils strongly proclaim that it is not their purpose to drive PhD standards down, only for them to be achieved more efficiently.

As we discussed in Chapter 10 on the examination system, the aim of the PhD process is to get the student to the stage of being a fully professional researcher. The PhD examination reflects this. The degree is awarded on the candidate's academic achievement which includes the thesis itself, defence of it at the oral examination and any supporting material in the discipline that the candidate has carried out and published. The viva is thus a key part of the examination, and it is inappropriate to decide that the thesis itself justifies the award of the PhD degree before it has been defended. This is for two reasons.

First, it is one of the functions of the viva for the examiners, through their questions, to satisfy themselves that the thesis is genuinely the work of the candidate. They even have to sign a declaration to that effect. Second, as we explained in Chapter 10, one of the possible, though rare, outcomes of the process is the examiners' decision that the written thesis was adequate, but the defence of it at the viva was not. The PhD will not then be awarded and a new oral examination will be set up, after a certain period, to allow the candidate to get a better understanding of the implications of the research and thus to conduct a better defence. (We should note that this is the British position. In Australia at the present time, the general practice is to rely primarily on the written material with a supplementary oral defence only in some cases. However, the policy is in the process of change, and some form of oral defence is becoming more common.)

The oral examination

The oral examination is what remains of the original formal public disputation that took place on the presentation of a thesis in the Middle Ages, after which the audience voted on whether to award the doctorate and admit the candidate as a member of their faculty. Now the oral examination in Britain consists of a discussion prompted by questions and comments from the two or, occasionally three, examiners.

There are considerable variations in the conduct of the viva. Candidates' descriptions of their experience of the viva range from a pleasant after-tea chat to a persecutory inquisition. We give what we consider to be a useful structure for the examination that avoids these two extremes.

We must begin by pointing out that most students are given little or no information about what to expect in the oral examination. However, some recent publications have tried to rectify this situation by going into some detail which can help both candidates and examiners concerning what to expect (Leonard 2001; Murray 2003; Tinkler and Jackson 2004).

As Tinkler and Jackson (2004: 2) point out, the oral examination 'is a source of concern and confusion for many supervisors and examiners'. Since nobody talks about it formally, much of what candidates believe happens is told to them not by their supervisors but by other research students. They may not even know how many people will be present. They usually learn that there will be general discussion of the whole thesis, and they have sometimes heard stories of enormously long PhDs being criticized on just one small detail. Students expect something really tough, with examiners who try to take their work apart in order to give them the opportunity to defend it. They see it as a battle and most are terrified.

This confusion regarding what will happen means that candidates are unsure about what it is that they need to prepare. It is good practice therefore for an experienced examiner (who may well be the supervisor) to discuss with the student the form that the examination will take, who will be present, how long it will last, etc. illustrated with examples from previous experience.

In fact the oral examination, as the PhD degree itself, is not a battle since the examiners and the candidate are on the same side. The examiners are trying to haul the candidate on board as a fully professional researcher, and they have to satisfy themselves that the applicant is ready for that status. The examiners (one internal and one external) will ask questions which require the candidate to respond, to defend the thesis and thus to demonstrate the research professionalism expected.

Only these three will participate in the examination. (If, on particular multidisciplinary topics, two externals are appointed, then the four will participate.) The usual presence of the supervisor, who is not officially allowed to participate in the discussion, serves two purposes. The first is to provide a friendly face to the candidate in an inevitably tense situation at the beginning of the session. The second is to allow the supervisor to become fully appraised of any required amendments if a resubmission is called for. It is the supervisor's responsibility to oversee subsequent changes.

It is common for internal examiners to chair the meeting. They thus have the responsibility to ensure that the discussion is conducted in a clear and orderly fashion. Before the candidate is called in, the examiners will normally begin the meeting by discussing the procedures they will use. For example they will agree an order of asking questions, at least for the beginning of the examination. They will allocate between them who will ask the lead questions on each aspect of the work, although as the discussion progresses each examiner may well wish to contribute on all the topics. This is preferable to a free-for-all where nobody in the room is sure who will speak next or on what topic. This structure of the meeting is important, and should be communicated to the candidate, since it allows everyone to feel more confident.

As in all formal interview situations, it is good practice for chairpersons to begin by asking a couple of simple questions to allow candidates to gain confidence by hearing the sound of their own voice being attended to seriously. Rather than, 'Did you have any problems getting here?' the opening cliché in this situation is, 'How did you come to study this topic?' Oral examinations should not last longer than two and a half hours. If it is necessary to go on beyond this time, then the chairperson should suggest a break to allow the examiners to review what has taken place and the candidates to renew their energies.

■ Action summary

[1] Be aware of the expectations that students have of supervisors and try to fulfil them. If you are not able to fulfil some of them, or think them inappropriate, do not simply neglect them. Raise them as issues for discussion with your students.

[2] Be aware that you inevitably act as a role model for research students.

In this respect, the most important single contribution that you can make to their success is to demonstrate continually that you take research seriously in your own academic life.

3. Be aware that supervision, like undergraduate teaching, has to be considered as an educational process and thought must be given to the most appropriate teaching approaches. Look for ways of designing learning situations for the student and improving your ability to give effective feedback in a trusting relationship.

4. Since students can easily become discouraged, a significant part of a supervisor's task is keeping their morale high. It is important to demonstrate that you understand their problems, emotional as well as intellectual.

5. Set up a helpful climate in which there are outline agreements on what the student and the supervisor have to do. If progress is not being made, do not let the position slide. Review the agreements in discussion and renegotiate them if necessary.

6. Look for ways of supporting your research students in their academic careers – for example, by arranging for them to give departmental seminars, present conference papers, discuss their research with leading academics from other institutions, write joint papers for submission to journals, etc.

7. Be aware of the pitfalls that can occur when you are supervising non-traditional students. Try to familiarize yourself with their situation and to anticipate possible predicaments that might occur. Do not expect to solve their problems but do give them support and understanding and point them in the direction of those who are able to help them.

8. If you are supervising your research assistant, ensure that you act to give a service of student supervision, in addition to the management of your research project.

9. Prepare for the task of examining by analysing accepted PhDs in your field in order to ascertain what are the current standards of professional research required for the doctorate.

10. Ensure that the oral examination has a clear structure that is communicated to the candidate.

12

INSTITUTIONAL
RESPONSIBILITIES

This chapter is aimed at university decision-makers. The success of doctoral students, with its consequent reflection in the institution's research ratings, is affected to an important extent by the context in which they have to work. Since a considerable proportion of university research is carried out by postgraduates, it is clearly incumbent on institutional authorities to ensure that they provide an environment which facilitates good work by research students.

In previous editions of this book we have argued for universities to devote greater consideration to the needs of research students, and in particular that universities should take their responsibilities to their doctoral students as seriously as they take their responsibilities to their undergraduate students. Within the last decade, pressures from the Funding Councils, the Research Councils, the Quality Assurance Agency and other bodies have, to a considerable extent, brought this about. There is still more to be done, as we discuss below. But the issues of the appropriate education, professional development and practical support of PhD students are now taken seriously. So also is the concept of increasing the effectiveness of supervisors through training and guided experience.

The public policy shifts that are acting as drivers for change can be usefully summarized under four headings (Stainton-Rogers 2004):

1 *The need to ensure that doctoral graduates are competent professionals.*
   Instead of the objective being simply for the student to produce a thesis, the aim now is for the student to be developed into a competent professional researcher. So there is the intention that in the course of carrying out the specific research project, the student not only learns discipline

based technical knowledge and skills, but also develops generic skills of, for example, computer literacy, communication and work planning. These skills are much more widely applicable and thus will improve the student's postdoctoral employment prospects in industry and the public sector as well as in academia. The opportunity to learn and exercise them should be provided by the university.

2 *The need to provide a high quality graduate community within a research-rich environment.* It is now felt to be inadequate for an individual research student to be working in isolation, having one or two supervisors whose primary task is teaching. Having little or no contact with other academics or students, the opportunity for important learning – both explicit and tacit – of values and skills that contribute to the education of an effective professional researcher who is proficient in state-of-the-art practices, will be limited. Universities should develop groups of researchers in an environment that values research highly, and that has the appropriate financial and other support to be productive. Doctoral students should primarily be recruited to be associated with such groups.

3 *The need to adopt the principle of reflective learning.* Students should be aware of their own learning and take responsibility for it. This is achieved by their undertaking personal development plans (PDP) which list their prior achievements, their aspirations and therefore the learning that they need to carry out. A progress file with evidence recording these achievements should be kept. The use of a system of documents to support reflective learning should be standard university practice.

4 *The need to widen participation and establish equitable student support.* There has been a steady increase over the years in the proportion of part-time research students. Overall they are now in the majority, although there are large variations across faculties and disciplines. This trend should be encouraged as being economically more viable, with the corollary that appropriate study, research and financial arrangements are made for such students. Those students that are full-time should receive grants or studentships which, when combined with payment for a limited amount of tutoring and demonstrating, provide realistic financial support.

Clearly, not all of these policies are without controversy and there are bound to be tensions as the changes evolve. But the 2004 QAA Code of Practice for Research Degree Programmes sets out a number of clearly defined precepts (or commitments) which the university must undertake if it is to be supported by public funding. A capable supervisory team, an adequate research environment, success indicators such as targets for completion times and rates, effective monitoring and feedback mechanisms, among other provisions, all have to be in place. These are considered to form an agreement between the student and the university and should be set out in a letter of contract.

In this chapter we outline what we see as the present responsibilities of the university in providing structures, policies, regulations and resources in order to fulfill these guidelines. We then cover the responsibilities of the department in providing roles and practices to achieve a supportive environment for research students. Universities must ensure that their policies and practices in regard to PhD students continue to improve.

■ University responsibilities

A university-wide graduate school for doctoral students

The conditions that universities are now required to provide when accepting research degree students are best satisfied by establishing a university-wide graduate school with which all such students are associated. This provides institutional recognition that PhD students are an integral component of the university for whom resources are available.

The graduate school has a number of tasks. The first is to provide support for students, by helping faculties and departments carry out good doctoral education. This includes: providing facilities for departments to support doctoral research activities, mounting a university-wide structured induction procedure, contributing an informative (and readable) university research student handbook, and supplying, where necessary, English language tuition.

The second task of the school is to provide support for supervisors, including provision of resources for training (particularly in the non-technical, relational aspects of the supervisor's role) and in recognition for teaching credit of supervisory activity.

In the present period of considerable change, a third key task of the graduate school is to provide a forum in which policies and practices for the maintenance and improvement of the educational experience of all PhD students in the university can be established. This should include providing guidelines for supportive research environments, developing supervisory arrangements that provide access to experienced supervisors, and establishing good feedback mechanisms. All these tasks are expanded on below.

■ Participation in a regional hub

In previous editions of this book we have advocated the advantages of universities participating in collaborative relationships with others in the same region. In the past few years, with the support of the UK GRAD programme, such a series of regional networks, referred to as 'hubs', has been set up. They cover the whole country as listed on the UK GRAD website <*www.gradschools.ac.uk*>.

The hubs are a collaborative effort between the participating universities, with some support from the research councils. For students, they aim to provide advice on access to materials and to facilitate linking between institutions to increase the provision and quality of programmes offered. The hubs also offer assistance in encouraging networking between academia and regional employers as a contribution to increasing the career options of doctoral graduates.

For staff, they host 'training the trainer' courses and 'good practice workshops' which provide opportunities for both new and experienced supervisors to develop their skills, as we advocate below (pp. 187ff). For those responsible for the design of doctoral education, they offer meetings on a number of topics such as 'stretching your postgraduate skills training budget'. The Yorkshire and NE Hub workshop 'showcases a variety of postgraduate skills training options available to suit all budgets'. Universities should make resources available for their members to participate in hub activities.

As part of the future development of hub activities universities might also engage in more collaborative research and coordination so that students from other universities can attend relevant seminars at their local university. This could be extended to include lectures and access to computers and other technical equipment on campus. During the long summer vacation, when university facilities are underutilized by more conventional students, study rooms and libraries could be made accessible to additional postgraduates. It would involve little or no expense to offer these facilities on a reciprocal basis, always provided that a good relationship had been developed between the home and the local university.

■ Support for students

Facilities for departments to support doctoral research activity

Every department should have the space and resources to provide a room with desks, available for the use of research students. This would serve as a common room that postgraduates in other faculties and departments would be able to use as a location point for contacting people in related but different areas. The institution should ensure that there are adequate facilities for research students including, for example, laboratory space and apparatus, access to a technician, as well as the more general resources of adequate library and computing services.

In order to encourage successful research and a feeling of belonging to an academic community, universities must set aside financial resources for research students' use. These would be relatively modest, probably not more than would be required to support such activities as the occasional postal survey for social science or business students, additional cultures for biology students, microfiches for history students, conference fees, photocopying and travel costs.

It is also important that facilities and resources available for full-time students are at the disposal of the increasing numbers of part-time students. Library hours, for example, may need to be extended so that students who are not on campus during usual working hours can still gain access to books and journals. The availability of computer facilities and specialist statistical help may similarly need to be extended.

A university-wide structured induction procedure

All institutions should adopt a university-wide structured induction procedure for newly registered research students. After an induction conference, every new research student should be required to attend a regular series of meetings (weekly, fortnightly) led by members of staff from the university research school. It is important that new students know that there are identifiable academics who have a major responsibility for them.

The meetings should continue over the first six months. In the beginning they should cover informative topics about the university: how to make the best use of the library services or the academic computing services; where to find relevant academics or research students in other departments. If we are members of universities, we forget how hard it is to join such large institutions and how easy it is to become lost. 'Leave them to their own devices to settle down' is a most inefficient and punitive strategy for this stage of the proceedings.

As Phillips (2001) advocates, later meetings should cover such process topics as the relationship between students and their supervisors, expectations and fears of the research student's role, the importance of working to deadlines – in fact most of the issues with which this book has been concerned. As recommended by the research councils, sessions encouraging the development of the generic skills of communication, personal effectiveness, team working and career management, should be part of this programme. As well as helping the student at the time, these skills will increase employability on graduation.

Such a programme achieves, at the very beginning, the raising of awareness of the processes involved in undertaking a three-year period of research training. Students may be told about the different stages through which they can expect to pass. This will not protect them from experiencing boredom, depression and the rest but at least they will be able to recognize what is happening to them when it does happen and this will be valuable. Invited speakers to the group could include a newly successful

PhD graduate, an administrator from the registrar's department with responsibility for the formal system, and so on.

Such a series of meetings enables students to identify others in a situation similar to their own and so makes them feel part of a community, rather than reinforcing the differences between disciplines and faculties. It introduces them to the common problems of being a research student and provides them with some knowledge and skills to tackle these. Finally, it creates a network and enables them to choose whether they wish to continue meeting as a group, perhaps without any member of staff, to discuss their progress and their problems. The specific problems of overseas students should also be included in the programme.

A handbook for university research degree students

The handbook for university research degree students should be regularly updated. It is an important part of communicating the nature of research degree study and the university framework within which it takes place. Key information would include: a description of the university structure, regulations for registration, upgrading, fees, examinations, awards and a code of practice for supervisors and research students. This should be prepared with the participation of research student representatives of the student union. The code spells out what is legitimately expected by students of supervisors (e.g., appropriate expertise of the supervisor in the subject and topic, minimum frequency of supervisory tutorials, prompt and constructive response to submitted written work) and, in turn, by supervisors of students (e.g., to work conscientiously and independently, to keep a lab record of experimental work, to present written work at the agreed time).

It is also the responsibility of the institution to provide within its regulations an ethical and professional code for staff to follow. This should provide guidelines particularly relevant to research students, such as ethical aspects of experimentation and data collection, the inadmissibility of plagiarism and data falsification. Issues of harassment and establishing appropriate relationships between staff and students should be included. Remember too that it is only through ethnic monitoring that universities can tell whether they are treating students fairly and if they are really providing access to research degree study for a diversity of students from different backgrounds. Correctly implemented it can help to inform not only against barriers to access but also against barriers to successful progression once access is gained.

English language support where necessary

Where students from non-English speaking backgrounds are accepted for a research degree it is the responsibility of the institution, not the individual supervisor, to provide English language training. The university should make provision for this by offering classes to all who need them. Native English speakers may sometimes benefit from these classes too.

The importance of being able to write in acceptable English is often not emphasized at the point of selection into the system. It is unacceptable to take high fees from overseas students without providing an appropriate service in return. Indeed, British universities have an unfortunate reputation in some countries for the double standard involved when students with inadequate English are awarded a doctoral degree. Resources need to be allocated to remedy this situation.

Students need to have impressed upon them very early in the period of registration that they must improve their command of English. It is important for them to be aware of precisely the level of written English needed for an acceptable thesis. Too often, it appears that any focus on the standard of written English required is left until the empirical research work is almost completed, which is too late.

Support for non-traditional students

With the increasing diversity of students, institutions should ensure that the academic environment is free from harassment or discrimination. Universities must establish policies and practices to support their less traditional research students. These should cover such issues as those discussed in Chapters 9 and 11. Policies to encourage the development of equality, integration and affiliation between all students are needed, together with procedures that provide support for victims of, and complaints about, harassment in all its forms.

A particular problem for gay, lesbian, bisexual and trans-gender students is the fact that, unlike other non-traditional students, they have to decide whether or not to declare themselves openly. The elimination of heterosexist harassment can be assisted by creating a safe atmosphere, where such students feel that they can be open about their identity.

■ Resources for supervisors

The training of supervisors

Training is needed in order to help academics to develop more effectively in their roles as supervisors. We take this view as a result of participating over a period of years in discussion groups attended by supervisors from many different universities, where we have seen the benefits they gain in knowledge and skill.

A majority of universities are accepting this responsibility and allocating resources to enable training groups to be mounted for new supervisors, but only a minority arrange them for all supervisors, experienced as well as new. We believe they should be available to all supervisors, even though we accept that, realistically, experienced supervisors are less likely to take advantage of them.

During the training there should be the opportunity for supervisors to think about issues specific to managing research; to listen to what specialists in the area have to say and to discuss with their peers any doubts or problems they may have.

Some supervisors believe that they are doing a good job, while some presume that others are doing better. Some think that everyone is using the same framework and are astonished to discover large variations in practice. Some may be surprised to learn that others are as unsure about what constitutes good supervision as they are themselves. The topics covered will vary but should include improving selection of research students, and the skills involved in giving effective feedback, supervising students' writing and inculcating appropriate academic standards. Such training permits staff to work toward a general improvement in standards.

If adequate resources were allocated by all universities to enable this activity to take place, the role of the academic supervisor would become more clearly defined and the standards improved.

Teaching credit for doctoral supervision

One important prerequisite to improving supervisory capability is the allocation of teaching credit for doctoral supervision. Traditionally academics have been expected to accept doctoral students as an addition to other duties. They have not been given any teaching compensation for this activity because it was held that the higher status gained by having such students was sufficient reward in itself. This has sometimes resulted in research students being treated in a perfunctory way because supervisors feel that any supervision is being done out of the goodness of their heart and supplementary to their 'real' duties.

There is thus a vital need for supervision to be recognized as an important staff role and to be counted into the time spent on teaching duties, in a similar way to lecturing and attending to the needs of undergraduate students. Supervision of research students should be accounted for in staff planning schedules and budgeted for accordingly, both in staff time and financial costs.

Guidelines should also be established on the appropriate limit to the number of research students that one academic may supervise. This is a particular concern with lead supervisors who will be expected to spend considerable time with their students. Universities vary in their practice with a maximum of anything from three to 10 being allowed. We consider six to be an appropriate maximum but, for this to be effective, it assumes that there is good back-up support from the research tutor and other academics in associated roles.

In some institutions credit is already given, but the amount varies from department to department. Other institutions inappropriately regard supervising PhD students as research work rather than teaching and so give no teaching credit. A system of teaching credit should be devised and applied to all supervisors. Such a development can only take place in the context of a system that attempts to monitor all the work of academics in order to ensure that the teaching and administrative tasks are distributed fairly – and this needs to be established.

Knowing that the supervisory role is taken seriously, and is one of the factors in considering promotion, would encourage supervisors to support students in the manner put forward in this book. Making resources available to ensure that supervision is an integral and recognized part of an academic's responsibilities would greatly improve the effectiveness of doctoral education.

■ Faculty/departmental doctoral research tutor

The role of the faculty/departmental research tutor needs to be supported throughout all parts of the university in order to ensure the proper functioning of the doctoral system. This support should allow a considerable amount of the academic's time, say a half, to be devoted to this post with consequent reduction in teaching duties.

There are a variety of titles which may appropriately be used for this role including sub-dean for research, convenor of the doctoral programme or director of research. We shall refer to it as doctoral research tutor. As it is a departmental responsibility to implement this role, its functions and duties are described below.

■ Providing appropriate regulations

Selection of doctoral students

Universities should have a policy to encourage their faculties to think more broadly when considering applications from people who do not have the standard qualifications for entry to a research degree. This should include ethnic monitoring. Such monitoring is a precondition for challenging tacit assumptions and helping universities to meet the goals and targets of their equal opportunities policies, even though as Bird (1996) points out, there are still people who perceive the whole monitoring exercise itself to be racist.

All that we know about selection is that we do not know how to select very efficiently research students who will be successful. In classic studies Hudson (1960) and Miller (1970) discussed the poor predictive quality of final undergraduate examination results. Whitehand (1966) recommended tests of problem solving, rather than knowledge, for selection of research students.

Even though this has been a topic of discussion for more than 40 years, little or nothing has been done about it. The current guidelines for improving standards in doctoral programmes propose a much wider range of objectives for successful PhD graduates. In addition to research skills, they include skills in research management, communication, networking and team working, career management and personal effectiveness. Yet the guidelines still propose the traditional method of selecting students who have performed well in undergraduate examinations in spite of the fact that the skills required there are based largely on memory rather than curiosity and exploration.

We reject those who have the enthusiasm, determination and persistence to apply themselves to research just because they have not managed to achieve at least an upper second in their degree. That is an arbitrary requirement. Even experienced supervisors have difficulty in describing the embryonic qualities that will gradually develop into the more mature characteristics that are required of a successful research worker. Clearly more research on this topic is needed.

■ **Monitoring of students' progress**

Many universities have regulations that ensure the effective monitoring of research students' progress. These include annual reports on each student, which are reviewed by a thesis advisory panel that may consist of, for example, the head of department, the research tutor and the supervisors. It is then submitted by the department to the research school. Each department also has a responsibility to submit a summary report and evaluation of all its doctoral students to an overall university body. Regulations for breaks in studies, suspension of registration and an appeals procedure that is seen to offer students an unbiased review of their cases, all have their part to play in facilitating students' progress and the optimal use of resources.

In addition, many universities also support a 'student portfolio' by providing a pro forma document that is designed to assist students monitor their own progress throughout their degree programme. It enables them to keep a record of all their personal development activities, including courses attended, together with any validating documents. It covers discipline-based research skills, project-based skills, and generic skills as outlined above It can be used as a point of reference in discussions with supervisors to identify any gaps in training needs. If properly organized, it assists in job applications after the PhD has been obtained. In our research for this latest edition of *How to Get a PhD*, we have found it impossible to obtain statistics from universities relating to PhD student submission, referral, success and failure rates. We would strongly recommend that, in future, such statistical records on student progress be maintained. This will enable policymakers to compare empirically the effectiveness of changing practices over time.

■ Upgrading from MPhil to PhD registration

It is important to have formal procedures in operation to determine whether and when upgrading from MPhil to PhD occurs. Departmental guidelines indicating how the procedures will be interpreted can then be made explicit to students at an early point in their period of registration.

Research students are usually registered for a generic degree or an MPhil and then retrospectively upgraded to PhD registration. The procedure adopted in upgrading students from MPhil to PhD status is important as it is, or could be, the first step in the examination process and will, therefore, give some clue to the standard set by the institution. It provides information on the development of any potential problems for a given student before the problem grows out of proportion. It is also possible to use the upgrading process as an opportunity to teach and prepare the student for what is ultimately required.

Phillips (1992) found that there is wide variety in the way that this part of the process is handled. Some departments have extremely formal upgrading procedures in operation. These include mandatory written papers and a panel interview based on the written work. Others are less structured and a more relaxed discussion between the candidate and supervisors takes place, usually with some written work forming the basis for discussion.

While both these approaches include talking about a document produced by the candidate, we think it important that the university should set up a common procedure for upgrading. The procedure must require written work from the student which is formally presented and then evaluated by the supervisor and at least one other member of the department. In this way only students whose work is of sufficient potential will be allowed to proceed to the PhD.

■ Appointment of external examiners

Examiners represent the academic peer group to which the doctoral student aspires. The thesis is the demonstration that the candidate has made a research contribution of a sufficient standard to be admitted and to have the title conferred. The British system attempts to equalize the standards across all universities by requiring at least one external examiner from another institution to be appointed. To maintain integrity it is important for the regulations to state that external examiners must be in a position to make an independent assessment. There can be a tendency, particularly in disciplines that are relatively small in academic numbers, for the supervisor to propose a professional colleague who may turn out not to have sufficient independence.

Two examples known to us will illustrate the dangers. The first was a proposal that the external examiner be a professor at another university who was intending to make a job offer of a postdoctoral fellowship to the candidate. This would, of course, be conditional on the student passing the degree. In the second case the external examiner proposed seemed a very appropriate academic in the field. It was purely by chance, since they had different professional names, that the approving committee discovered that he was the husband of the supervisor. In neither of these cases was approval given.

■ A forum for review of the PhD

The nature of doctoral education, like all higher education, is subject to change. A representative academic forum gives an opportunity for these issues to be debated. Four important issues, which would appear to be on the agenda of many universities, will be considered here.

The PhD as a series of projects

A radical reform of the PhD system would be to move away from the award of the degree on the basis of one piece of research. The argument is that the attempt to evaluate academic competence on the basis of a large 'big bang' project is unrealistic – particularly as it takes place at the initial stages of the researcher's career. At the beginning it would be much more sensible to require the students to demonstrate their range of professional skills through a series of smaller projects. Thus the PhD should be awarded on the basis of, say, four conceptually linked projects, each of which is carried out to the standards of publishable papers in refereed academic journals.

In our view this is a development that should be encouraged. It fits in well with the approach that we have been putting throughout this book on the professional nature and meaning of a doctorate. For most beginning professional researchers, it would make a much more realistic introduction to the academic work which they can be expected to contribute at the outset of their careers. Useful, publishable academic contributions are more likely to result from such a series of appropriately related studies. Indeed it would not be unrealistic in this approach to require the project papers, or some of them, actually to have been published in reputable journals before the degree is awarded. The definition of 'reputable' would be the responsibility of the examiners.

In fact this approach would extend the application of the award of 'PhD by published work'. This route to the doctorate is offered by many universities, normally to full-time staff only, and without the benefit of supervision, although an 'advisor' is often appointed (Powell 2004). Some universities extend the eligibility to all their own graduates, and a few (e.g. Leeds Metropolitan, Teeside) offer this route to any graduate. The project route, with supervision in place, could advantageously be offered as an optional alternative to the more traditional 'big bang' PhD.

Intellectual copyright and appropriate recognition for doctoral students' work

With the realization that knowledge is the key resource in modern society, issues of the ownership of such knowledge are becoming increasingly contentious. The law of intellectual copyright, which attempts to protect the rights of knowledge generators, including researchers, is continuing to develop fast. The proper treatment of the research and writing produced by doctoral students is one aspect of this topic that is the subject of much debate.

In law, all authors – including doctoral students – are entitled to the copyright benefits from their written and published work. In addition, they are all entitled to exert their 'moral rights' of recognition and integrity. Recognition (called 'paternity rights' in law, even if the author is a woman!) means that they are entitled to be named as the authors of any writing that they produce, and this protects against plagiarism. Integrity means that they are entitled not to have their work changed on publication in ways of which they disapprove. The first contentious issue is that some universities ask doctoral students (even though they are not employees) to sign away their copyright and moral rights. The argument is that the provision of resources for the carrying out of the research entitles the university to own the outputs, as it does the outputs of employees. This is somewhat of a grey area, still to be tested in court. As it is unlikely that written research material (as distinct from inventions and patents) will generate much income, it would appear to be rather invidious for universities to insist on taking these rights from students.

A second issue that has come into much greater contention is that of the appropriate recognition in published papers of the relative contributions of student and supervisor. Should a supervisor be named as joint author of a paper on the basis of carrying out doctoral supervision, even without making a contribution to authorship? Or is an appreciatory footnote the appropriate recognition for supervisory guidance and support? Some departments are placing pressure on research students to include their supervisors' names on journal papers, regardless of whether or not the supervisor has made contributions to the writing. In the UK these pressures have been exacerbated by the research assessment exercise, which seeks to assess the research output of universities funded by the higher education funding councils. A joint paper with a student counts equally as one of the four that each academic can submit for assessment. Although it is technically possible to submit a published paper by the student alone as one of the four on the supervisor's list, this is rarely done, and its impact on the assessment is more dubious. Thus if supervisors need to improve their lists, they may insist on joint papers with their names included. How justified is this practice?

There are large variations between the cultures of different disciplines here, as we discussed in Chapter 1. For example, in the sciences the supervisor may typically have developed a line of study, obtained a studentship from a research council based on previous work, and appointed a student to carry out the designated research. In these circumstances the argument for joint authorship is apparent. In the social sciences and the humanities, research students often come with their own topics within the field in which the supervisor is expert, and academics give a service of research supervision in much the same way as they give a service of undergraduate teaching. In this situation joint authorship appears less justified, unless the paper is actually jointly written.

Conflict arises when students are unaware of the appropriate conventions and supervisors appear to press arbitrarily for their names to be included as authors. It is important therefore to have a full discussion early in the doctoral research, so that agreement can be obtained on the appropriate practice. Some universities have established guidelines on such matters. For example the University of Hong Kong guidelines state that:

☐ All those who have genuinely and significantly contributed to the work (and only those) should be listed as authors. All should agree to the inclusion of fellow authors' names and their ordering before publication.
☐ Authors should be listed in relation to their contribution to the work, with the primary author being the one who has done the most work.

☐ Authors' names should not be included unless they have at least the knowledge and competence in the subject of the paper to give an unaided seminar presentation on it.

(Butler 1995)

Given that conflicts may arise, clear guidelines are needed on student recognition and those from Hong Kong might well serve as a starting point for discussion. In the UK the situation would be eased if papers published by doctoral students were counted in the assessment exercise in their own right.

The PhD in a practice-based discipline

In practice-based disciplines such as art, music or design and technology there is an ongoing debate on the form of a PhD. Since knowledge is advanced in these disciplines largely by means of professional and artistic practice, an original, creative artefact may be appropriately included as a part of a PhD submission. This is now accepted in most universities.

The debate concerns the extent to which an 'artefact' such as a sculpture (represented, if necessary, by photographs or a videotape) or a musical composition (represented by an audio recording) can be accepted as stand-alone evidence of the contribution to knowledge and the development of the discipline that justifies the award of a PhD. In fact, there is a gradual shift towards the artefact being the main focus of the doctoral research with explanatory text only as a supporting document.

As in any subject area, PhD candidates must be able to defend and explain in what way their doctoral work constitutes an original contribution to the extension of knowledge in their field; they must also be able to understand and to communicate the research context in which their work belongs. This is the crucial difference between an artist's private practice – developing their own work just for themselves – and practice as research (sometimes referred to as 'research through practice').

What place do videos, computer programs, crafted objects and so on have as a contribution to actual research? Currently in the practice disciplines, discussion centres on the extent to which doctoral students should be required to account verbally for their research, rather than letting the finished work (performance, exhibition, composition etc.) speak for itself.

At present, the approach is to require both artefact and text. The debate centres around what the weighting should be between them. It is usual to insist on a permanent and publicly accessible form for each part of the thesis. The creative part must be fully open to examination by illustration, exhibition or multimedia presentation. Some argue that the developmental process of the work be made public, perhaps by including all the rough drafts that eventually led to the finished product, thus externally demonstrating the thinking involved. The presentation of this developmental history might even be considered acceptable in lieu of an analysis in words.

However, institutions require that, in addition to the creative component, students must show that they have a theoretical as well as a practical understanding of their area. They must be able to provide a rationale for the work undertaken. If there has been no previous academic work in the field, then it is incumbent on candidates to cite relevant thinking from other areas or to espouse a specific theoretical approach. In addition, the project needs to be set within a larger context involving current issues. It is important to demonstrate how the research being presented expands on what has already been done. This contribution could change previous work by using different materials or develop it with new tools.

Questioning previous work or clarifying its meaning and impact are also important contributions. As in any PhD, there is also a need to convince the examiners that the candidate understands what is involved in conducting the research. This would include, for example, describing difficulties encountered in the research and strategies undertaken to overcome them together with a statement of possible future directions of work.

It is the responsibility of universities to define what constitutes an acceptable PhD submission but, to date, we know of none that accept a completed artefact without any supporting written document.

Professional doctorates

Since the 1990s a new version of the doctorate has been established in many universities. It is known as the professional doctorate – or sometimes as the 'taught doctorate' – although the latter name does seem to be a contradiction in terms in view of the fact that the doctorate is awarded to recognize an individual's contribution to the development of the field, rather than just what has been studied.

Professional doctorates have been designed to recognize a greater level of professional skill than the master's degree, which is a licence to practise. Just as the PhD requires a contribution to the advancement of the academic field, these doctorates require candidates to demonstrate a contribution to the advancement of professional practice. As Gregory (1997) put it: if the PhD is for 'professional scholars' then these degrees can be said to be for 'scholarly professionals'.

The degrees have been named for the professional activity. The fields in which they have been established most frequently are business and management studies, education and engineering. Candidates for the Doctor of Business Administration (DBA), the Doctor of Education (EdD) and the Doctor of Engineering (EngD) are expected to demonstrate that they have made an original contribution by undertaking an effective application of theory and knowledge in a professional setting.

The fact that these degrees have been instituted in the last decade has meant that the current focus on specifying educational outcomes in the design of programmes has had a major impact. All the programmes involve students in carrying out specified activities on the way to the final project in order to develop their research and professional skills. These modules typically include advanced taught courses, surveys of research and professional developments in the field, a research proposal, etc. Each of these modules is subject to assessment and satisfactory completion is required before the candidate can proceed to the final project (which may be called either a dissertation or a thesis).

The final project is typically the application of professional knowledge and skill to the solution of a practical problem in a real world setting. The supervisory team will include an academic from the university and a practitioner from the relevant organization in which the application takes place. (The examining board will also include academic and practitioner representatives.) Since successful completion of the earlier projects is required and taken into account in the award of the doctorate, the word length requirement of final dissertation project is shorter than that of the PhD. Typically the word length limits are set at 50,000 words for these doctorates, compared with 80,000 to 100,000 words for the PhD.

An issue in these doctorates is the level required to demonstrate an original contribution to professional practice, and thus justify the degree of Doctor. As we argue in Chapter 5, problem-solving research of itself requires a candidate to demonstrate a higher level of professional skill to make a contribution, certainly at the PhD level. Strangely the student here is often required to spend less time on the final project.

What does originality mean in this situation? The question inevitably arises as to whether a competent application of current professional skills and techniques to a real-world situation of itself shows sufficient evidence of originality. The obvious answer to this question is no, a master's degree is the appropriate qualification for an effective practitioner. Something more is required to demonstrate a contribution and justify a doctorate. So a key component of the final thesis required in many cases is a self-analysis of the work carried out and a reflection on the use of academic knowledge in a practical situation. Successful candidates will be skilled and experienced professionals who have not only practised but pondered on and analysed the use of their academic and practical knowledge. The lessons learned from this reflection are evaluated as a contribution to professional practice.

How does the thesis of the professional doctorate compare in level to the PhD? Although the regulations of many universities in regard to the EngD require that the dissertation be of PhD standard, most are silent on this issue in relation to other professional doctorates. Its advocates (e.g. Scott *et al.* 2004; Mills *et al.* 2004) maintain that its professional orientation means that it is a different activity from the PhD, with the implication that it is different but equal. At the time of writing the levels are still being established by custom and practice, but it is already clear that, while the preparatory modules are more structured and rigorous than is often the case for a PhD, in many instances the research component of the professional doctorate may not be as demanding.

However the processes involved in studying for a professional doctorate, such as issues of relationships with the supervisor, time management, the problems of part-time study, etc., will be quite comparable to those for the PhD as discussed in other chapters in this book.

■ Departmental responsibilities

Departments are a key factor in successful doctoral education. Senior academics should be considering the department's role in terms of the following questions: How are departments helping their postgraduate students to learn and to succeed in their research? What strategies have been introduced to counter isolation and enable students to learn from people other than their supervisors? Have self-help groups been established to assist students in learning from one another? Are arrangements in place for students to develop their conceptions of what constitutes excellent research in their discipline and their role as researchers?

The departmental research tutor

Each department should ensure that they receive resources to establish a research tutor role. Tutors should have this administrative responsibility formally recognized as part of their overall workload.

If a lecturer is appointed, this has the advantage that students perceive the research tutor as accessible. This is important because small problems, if confronted at an early stage, can be prevented from erupting into major difficulties that threaten the very continuation of the student's progress. If a senior lecturer or professor is appointed, there is a real probability that students will hesitate to go to the research tutor with their concerns.

The problem when the tutor is a lecturer is in ensuring that all members of the department take the role seriously. This is vital for the role to be effective because there will be situations where the research tutor will be taking issue with senior colleagues about their treatment of one of the research students. The appointment of a senior member of staff as research tutor recognizes the importance of doctoral education in the work of the department. There are fewer problems of status in acting on behalf of a student but more problems of approachability.

There are a number of tasks for the tutor to carry out. In order to ensure that at least one person has an overall picture of the students entering the department, the tutor should be involved in all applications and accept-ances. The maintenance of standards requires that all British students be interviewed and, wherever possible, overseas applicants too. The tutor, either in person or by nominating a colleague to take his or her place, should participate in the interview process.

To help in maintaining student progress the tutor should operate a sys-tem for six-monthly monitoring of students' work via supervisors. This would involve distribution of departmental report forms (based on the university annual monitoring forms) noting all the responses and taking any action necessary. Regular reports to the staff group on the overall position of the department's research students should be provided.

Actions based upon the report forms might include counselling a stu-dent, supporting a supervisor and negotiating with a colleague. Joint meetings with student and supervisors together might also be appropriate.

An important but delicate aspect of the tutor's work is the monitoring of the relationship between the student and the supervisor(s) in order to ensure that it develops well. This covers the ability and motivation of the student and the interest and commitment of the supervisors. The tutor may have to act as a conciliator or arbiter when interpersonal conflicts occur.

The tutor will need to liaise with supervisor colleagues to ensure that there are sufficient resources provided to back up the proposed research. These could include equipment and the cooperation of the lab technician for example. Help in obtaining access to fieldwork sites, such as schools or industrial organizations, may be given.

An important task of the tutor is to interpret the university guidelines, as discussed above, concerning the upgrading from MPhil to PhD. This requires maintaining a consistent standard, which is communicated to all students so that they are aware of what is required of them. When there are different practices in operation, students understandably become extremely anxious about whether or not they will be upgraded. This can inhibit their ability to study.

It is good practice therefore for the research tutor to set up the situation where all new students in the department get an opportunity to discover what a PhD looks like. They should be required to read and evaluate recently accepted PhD theses in order to understand what it is they are aiming for. If asked to do this on their own, students often emerge from the document depressed, and convinced that they will never be able to write anything even remotely resembling it in either length or quality. Being asked to carry out a task, in pairs or small groups, helps students to come to terms more easily with what is required. The task should include:

- [ ] a summary of the research – one always has to set out what is being criticized before being able to go ahead with the criticism;
- [ ] a description of the contribution of the research and why they believe the examiners decided it was worthy of the PhD degree;
- [ ] An identification of criticisms of the work and inadequacies in it, which would lead them to do the study differently.

This analysis should be presented in a departmental doctoral seminar, so that students may begin to acquire the confidence of presenting their ideas to others for feedback. It also begins the process of enabling students to feel that the task they are undertaking is something of which they are capable.

The research tutor must become an expert in the administrative arrangements needed for submission and examination of the final thesis. The tutor is then in a position to help colleagues who deal less frequently with this stage of the process.

Finally, the research tutor has a major part to play in all the activities described in the following sections.

Improving the selection of students into the department

Selection of students into the department is very important indeed and should be carried out systematically. In order to widen the pool of possible applicants, we suggest that there should be a special open evening for research students at which prospective supervisors talk about their research interests and the facilities that can be offered.

All departments are looking for students who have the potential to succeed in completing their research and writing their theses to the required standard within given deadlines. Selection would be improved if a wider range of characteristics were to be taken into account. For example, degree classification should not be taken as the only indicator but special weight should be given to performance in undergraduate student projects.

In addition to interviewing, classic tests of problem solving and flexible thinking along the lines of those developed by Wason (1960, 1968) should be considered for use. The aim of such tests is to diagnose the approach that the candidate takes to solving problems. The correctness of the answer is only of secondary importance in identifying research potential. These procedures should ideally also include a personal interview.

A short test of writing in English is also an effective aid to selection. Asking applicants to summarize a research report, or any published paper, while in the presence of the member of staff (to ensure that it is their own work) is a way of ascertaining that they have the necessary command of the written language to commence study.

An additional problem with the increasing number of research students is a tendency for them to be allocated to supervisors. This is a trend that should be avoided. Academic staff should have the full support and encouragement of their department to be involved in the selection of their own research students. Regardless of any prior contact, each applicant should be interviewed by any potential supervisors and another member of the academic staff of the department, usually the research tutor.

The procedures might also involve a formal research proposal together with some evidence of having knowledge of the subject area. Some departments insist that no new student be accepted without a clear-cut research proposal. Others consider the research proposal to be more suited to the upgrading procedures once the student has been working for a year or more towards the research degree.

There is no reason why we should expect candidates to be in a position to write acceptable research proposals prior to receiving any training. In fact, it is unlikely that a well-constructed research proposal would be possible before the student has spent some time developing the necessary skills in a research environment. Therefore, if institutional regulations require it at time of entry, applicants will probably need some help in preparing the proposal from a member of staff of the department they are hoping to join. In addition, some guidance on which aspect of a topic is likely to be looked on favourably by a particular member of staff would make sense at this stage.

If the candidate is able to provide a proposal at the time of the selection interview, it is of great assistance to the staff making the decision whether or not to offer a place. The proposal would allow the selectors to ascertain whether there is anybody available and willing to supervise the specific topic, and whether the candidate is aware of what is involved in constructing and conducting the research and has sufficient background knowledge to commence work at the level required.

Even though part-time research students are in a majority overall, there is considerable need for more awareness of the difficulties experienced by them, as discussed in Chapters 9 and 11. These difficulties occur in many areas, but in particular, time allocation and financial pressures during the period of study are common causes of stress for many part-time students. Enquiries into sources of support during the period of study must therefore be given special attention in order to ensure that nobody is accepted until the department is satisfied that the applicant will not suffer undue financial hardship as a result of registering as a student.

Selection of supervisors

An important departmental responsibility is the setting up of adequate criteria for the selection of supervisors. There are two factors involved, and they do not necessarily correlate: first, the academics' past experience of research and present level of research activity in the chosen field, and second, their past experience of supervision and present degree of commitment to the supervision of research students.

Ideally only supervisors who are high on both aspects would be selected – and even so they will normally require some training, as described above, to be fully effective. The fact that the supervisor is an enthusiastic and successful practitioner of research, and is seen to be so, is a very important input to the successful completion of the PhD by the student. Students who experience their supervisors as being very involved on non-research activities – teaching, administration, policy, consultancy – at the expense of doing research, very soon come to devalue their research work and are less likely to finish. Active researchers are also necessary to give the contemporary professional knowledge and skill that PhD students need to acquire.

Experience of supervision to successful completion of the student's PhD is such an important factor that at least one of the supervisors must have achieved this. If this is not the subject specialist, a common way to attempt to combine these needed strengths is the setting up of a super-visory team of a first and a second supervisor. It is becoming more and more unlikely for a student to have a single supervisor, no matter how established in the subject, who has not had this experience.

■ Guidelines on appropriate supervisory behaviour

It should be departmental policy to provide guidelines concerning departmental expectations of supervisors, which may be established across the university, and should stipulate:

☐ the maximum number of students that a supervisor may supervise (particularly as a lead supervisor);

☐ the maximum amount of time a member of staff might reasonably be expected to take to respond to written work presented by the student (as recommended in Chapter 8);

☐ that research students and supervisors agree a contract between them, including the minimum number of meetings per annum (as recommended in Chapter 8);

☐ that the student be informed of relevant university and departmental regulations and administrative requirements in good time for them to be adhered to;

☐ that the student be provided with early information regarding satisfactory or unsatisfactory progress;

☐ that supervisors introduce their students to a variety of people and ideas within the academic community;

☐ that advice be given on ethical and welfare issues and how to overcome related difficulties;

☐ that supervisors refer their students to these guidelines and any other official documents relevant to their status as postgraduate research students.

In addition the departmental tutor should work to encourage the good supervisory practices described in Chapter 11.

■ Support groups for research students

Social isolation is a major contributory factor to research student dissatis-faction, withdrawal and late submission of work. Non-completion has as much to do with feelings of isolation and alienation as it has to do with any lack of intellectual ability. Support and encouragement from fellow doctoral students helps to alleviate these persistent problems. Therefore the context in which the students are working becomes vitally important and departments should ensure that their research students are not suffering social isolation.

In order to achieve this, departments should make it easy for their stu-dents, including the non-traditional ones, to meet regularly with others in their situation. The research tutor needs to set up meetings for the research students so that they have a feeling of belonging to a university and are able to develop a sense of identity as a member of a research community. This entails accepting demands on them as individuals to perform and to conform to deadlines.

Research students have to be constantly reminded that they are not working in isolation and that there are people who are interested in their work and their progress. This will help to develop their commitment. A contributory factor in non-completion is the belief by students that they are letting nobody down if they decide not to continue. This is not the case as they would be letting the department and the university down. Indeed, if they have research council funding, the university would be penalized because of their non-completion.

By arranging for students to meet their peers, departments can help them to discover that they can help themselves and others in a variety of ways. Considering gender differences in communication and debate, however, it is very important that departments consider ways of intro-ducing self-help groups in such a way so that the groups are appropriate for all students.

■ A departmental doctoral programme

A departmental doctoral programme has two key characteristics that attempt to improve the standard of doctoral education:

☐ There are many students, organized by faculty, department or research unit, who combat isolation by providing a support group of peers.
☐ It provides a common educational core of both discipline-specific and generic skills.

The precise content of the core studies needs to be hammered out by each discipline, but to be effective it must be seen by the students as contributing directly to their professional development as researchers and thus to be concerned with skills as well as knowledge.

Unless the core of studies leads to the award of a degree such as the MRes, the courses should not be examined. This underlines the fact that their purpose is only to help students prepare for their research work.

However, the effectiveness of a doctoral programme depends upon how stringently departments interpret the requirement for taught courses. In some departments the considerable number of taught courses students are required to take in the first year effectively precludes them from starting on any research at all until the second year. Yet students want to proceed with their research rather than take courses the relevance of which they question. They particularly do not want to study subjects in their discipline that are unrelated to their research topics. Therefore exemptions from courses should be permitted if a good case is made on the basis of previous work. However, no research student should be permitted to proceed to the project work for the PhD degree without first having acquired (whether through an introductory taught course, or prior to registration) a comprehensive knowledge of research methodology and analysis.

The core teaching arrangements should include the induction programme for new students described above, opportunities for students to present seminar papers on their work, and regular discussion of the issues that arise in getting a PhD of the kind discussed in this book.

The resources required to provide a core teaching component can be made available only if there is a group of research students as part of a doctoral programme to receive it. Programmes have the added benefit that they enable research students to become an identifiable section of a department. Participants in a programme are thus in a more advantageous position to press for greater recognition of the needs of both research students and supervisors. The existence of a programme makes it easier to obtain physical space and material resources for students, to arrange teaching credit recognition for the work of supervisors, and to facilitate changes between supervisors should this become necessary. The departmental research tutor should act as programme director to monitor the progress of students and be an extra resource to help things along when required. The resulting structure provides a clear framework for students to identify with and from which they can receive social support.

■ The doctoral cohort system

One of the ways of getting the social and intellectual support benefits of a scientific research programme is for a department to elect to run an annual doctoral cohort. In this system students are selected to work in a specific area: for example, stress in alloys (in a department of materials science) or stress at work (in a department of industrial psychology). Within the selected area students define their own problems, which can therefore be more distinctive and farther apart than in an integrated programme of research as described above. The cohort is led by two members of staff with an interest in the chosen topic area, and these two people act as supervisors to all members of the group until such time as this is no longer appropriate.

The group meets regularly every two weeks, say, to talk about what they are doing. The format is that of a workshop in which one member's progress, problems and thinking are discussed by the staff and other students. They provide feedback, help, information and comparisons from their own experience. In this way there is a constant sharing and exchange of views and the group becomes a support network. In addition, people can discuss problems by email, telephone, or meet outside the formal group, as they wish. This system is particularly appropriate for part-time students since it provides reinforcement of their identity as students and a supportive framework for their studies.

Early meetings of the cohort cover induction issues; later meetings serve to determine when any member of the cohort needs to be linked to a particular member of staff and so become a more traditional PhD student.

It may be that even after all members of the cohort have been assigned to individual supervisors (and the cohort leaders may act in this capacity) they still wish to meet as a group. The structure and development of the group need to be kept as flexible as possible to accommodate the needs of different cohorts, but the format is always the same during the early stages of its life.

This system has many advantages. Its main limitation is that it is only viable in large departments with many doctoral students. Smaller departments will have difficulty in recruiting applicants who wish to study closely related topics.

In general there is little doubt that the concept of a doctoral programme, flexibly adapted to the needs of particular departments and students, is a most promising way forward, for the reasons listed at the beginning of this section. There are inevitably potential hazards which need to be guarded against in this development, the most formidable of which is the view that PhD students should be trained *only* in doctoral programmes. In our view this would be an unwarranted restriction. Individual students, well supervised, have an important place, if only to set limits to the centralization of research resources that is currently so prevalent.

This chapter has addressed some of the issues that we consider vital to the survival of the PhD as a developing system. At a time when academic policy-makers are seriously trying to improve this aspect of higher education, it is crucial that policies be defined that work to the advantage of the whole system.

■ Action summary

1. Ensure that the university fulfils the responsibilities it has undertaken by the fact of accepting PhD students.
2. Provide support to doctoral students through the establishment of a research school, a structured induction procedure, facilities for departments, additional essential information and any necessary language tuition.
3. Provide resources for the training of supervisors, allocation of teaching credit for doctoral supervision, and the creation of a part-time post of faculty or departmental doctoral research tutor.
4. Provide appropriate regulations for doctoral education and a forum for the regular review of the nature of the PhD.
5. At the departmental level, establish the role of doctoral research tutor with a brief to monitor and improve the functioning of doctoral education.
6. Regularly review the selection methods and criteria for acceptance of students into the department.
7. Develop guidelines on the selection of supervisors and on appropriate supervisory behaviour.
8. Encourage collaborative groups and meetings among students.
9. Establish a departmental doctoral programme.

■ Conclusion

The ideas in this book are all based on systematic study and practical experience, over many years, of the PhD in operation. Taken as a whole they form the basis of a coherent reappraisal of the system and thus make a contribution to the developments currently being introduced. As well as improving the quality and completion rate of doctorates, these policies would greatly improve the experience that individual students have of actually doing a PhD.

APPENDIX

This questionnaire has been designed as a tool to allow you to consider realistically your own personal situation as a PhD student. The items have all been stated positively so that ideally each one of them should be marked 'Strongly Agree' (SA). Those items that are not marked SA or 'Agree' (A) act as a diagnosis of what could be improved in your situation. After first completing the questionnaire individually, it would be sensible for you to share your diagnosis with fellow doctoral students in order for you to help each other to work on strategies and tactics for improvement.

■ Self-evaluation questionnaire on research student progress

In order to focus your views on your progress towards a PhD, please give your opinion on the statements below. As you go through the question-naire, please list on a separate sheet the reasons for your opinion.

SA = strongly agree
A = agree
U = undecided
D = disagree
SD = strongly disagree

My progress

P1 I am fully committed to getting my PhD whatever the problems I encounter.

SA A U D SD

P2 Under no circumstances will I take a new job before finishing my PhD.

SA A U D SD

P3 I understand clearly the standards that I will be required to achieve in my thesis.

SA A U D SD

P4 I am confident that I can make 'an original contribution to knowledge' in my thesis.

SA A U D SD

P5 I have a plan for my work which I stick to, and so can evaluate my progress.

SA A U D SD

P6 I regularly set myself realistic deadlines and achieve them.

SA A U D SD

P7 My research work is directed towards making a contribution by having an argument to maintain (i.e. a thesis).

SA A U D SD

P8 I take every opportunity to produce written work (reports, draft papers, draft chapters) in order to improve my writing skills.

SA A U D SD

P9 Overall, I am satisfied with my progress towards the PhD.

SA A U D SD

Support from my supervisor

S1 My supervisor is an experienced researcher with a good knowledge of my research area.

SA A U D SD

S2 I am confident that my supervisor understands the level of work required for a PhD, and neither under nor overestimates it.

SA A U D SD

S3 I am in regular contact with my supervisor, who is always available when needed.

SA A U D SD

S4 I get a great deal of help from my supervisor, who is friendly and approachable.

SA A U D SD

S5 My supervisor always reads my work well in advance of our meetings.

SA A U D SD

S6 My supervisor has not 'taken over' my research, but allows me to develop it independently.

SA A U D SD

S7 I am always punctilious in keeping appointments with my supervisor.

SA A U D SD

S8 My supervisor is equally punctilious in keeping appointments with me.

SA A U D SD

S9 I have a good friendly relationship with the departmental secretary which helps to keep me in contact with my supervisor.

SA A U D SD

S10 Overall, I am well satisfied with the quality of supervision that I am receiving.

SA A U D SD

Support from my department

D1 The department provides adequate physical and financial resources for my research (e.g. lab or other working space, equipment, library access).

SA A U D SD

D2 The department provides opportunities for research students to meet and receive support from each other and I have taken advantage of them.

SA A U D SD

D3 The department provides a stimulating seminar programme for doctoral students to which I contribute.

SA A U D SD

D4 The department provides opportunities for good professional contact with academic staff which I have taken up.

SA A U D SD

D5 The department provides opportunities for social contact with academic staff which I have taken up.

SA A U D SD

D6 The department encourages and supports attendance at conferences and other academic gatherings which I have taken up.

SA A U D SD

D7 The department organizes meetings to discuss the nature of the doctoral process and the relevant university regulations applying to my research work which I have attended.

SA A U D SD

D8 Overall, I am satisfied with the support I receive from my department.

SA A U D SD

REFERENCES

Bird, J. (1996) *Black Students and Higher Education*. Buckingham: SRHE and Open University Press.

Butler, R. (1995) Communication to the electronic conference, 11 February. *<postgraduate@mailbase.ac.uk>*

Carter, P. and Jeffs, T. (1992) The hidden curriculum: sexuality in professional education, in P. Carter, T. Jeffs and M. K. Smith (eds) *Changing Social Work and Welfare*. Buckingham: Open University Press.

Conrad, L. and Phillips, E. M. (1995) From isolation to collaboration: a positive change for postgraduate women? *Higher Education*, 30(3): 313–22. Reprinted in O. Zuber-Skerritt (ed.) *Frameworks for Postgraduate Education*. Lismore: Southern Cross University Press.

Delamont, S. and Atkinson P. (2004) *Successful Research Careers*. Maidenhead: Open University Press.

Delamont, S., Atkinson, P. and Parry, O. (2004) *Supervising the Doctorate*. 2nd edn. Maidenhead: SRHE and Open University Press.

Francis, J. R. D. (1976) Supervision and examination of higher degree students, *Bulletin of the University of London*, 31: 3–6.

Geake, J. and Maingard, C. (1999) NESB postgraduate students at Southern Cross University: plus ça change, plus c'est la meme chose, in Y. Ryan and O. Zuber-Skerritt (eds) *Supervising Postgraduates from Non-English Speaking Backgrounds*. Buckingham: Open University Press.

Gregory, M. (1997) Professional scholars and scholarly professionals, *The New Academic*, 6 (2): 19–22.

Gundara, J. (1997) Intercultural issues and doctoral studies, in N. Graves and V. Varma (eds) *Working for a Doctorate*. London: Routledge.

Hartley J. (2004) On writing scientific articles in English, *Science Foundation in China*, 11 (2): 53–6.

Hickson, D. J. and Pugh, D.S. (2001) *Management Worldwide: Distinctive Styles Amid Globalization*, 2nd edn. London: Penguin Books.

Hockey, J. (1994) New territory problems of adjusting to the first year of a social science PhD, *Studies in Higher Education*, 19: 177–90.

Hudson, L. (1960) Degree class and attainment in scientific research, *British Journal of Psychology*, 51(1): 67–73.

Knight, N (1999) Responsibilities and limits in the supervision of NESB research students in the social sciences and humanities, in Y. Ryan and O. Zuber-Skeritt (eds) *Supervising Postgraduates from Non-English Speaking Backgrounds*. Buckingham: Open University Press.

Kuhn, T. S. (1970) *The Structure of Scientific Revolutions*. Chicago: University of Chicago Press.

Leonard, D. (1997) Gender issues in doctoral studies, in N. Graves and V. Varma (eds) *Working for a Doctorate*. London: Routledge.

Leonard, D. (2001) *A Woman's Guide to Doctoral Studies*. Buckingham: Open University Press.

Mapstone, E. R. (1998) *War of Words: Women and Men Arguing*. London: Chatto & Windus.

Medawar, P. B. (1964) Is the scientific paper a fraud? in D. Edge (ed.) *Experiment*. London: BBC Publications.

Miller, G. W. (1970) *Success, Failure and Wastage in Higher Education*. London: University of London Institute of Education/Harrap.

Mills, G., Bunker, V. and Castle, A. (2004) Professional doctorates in healthcare disciplines at the University of Portsmouth, *Journal of Graduate Education*, 3(2): 82–5.

Murray, R. (2002) *How to Write a Thesis*. Buckingham, Open University Press.

Murray, R. (2003) *How to Survive your Viva*. Maidenhead: Open University Press.

Phillips, E. M. (1983) The PhD as a learning process. Unpublished PhD thesis, University of London.

Phillips, E. M. (1991) Learning to do research, in N. C. Smith and P. Dainty (eds) *The Management Research Handbook*. London: Routledge.

Phillips, E. M. (1992) The PhD: assessing quality at different stages of its development, in O. Zuber-Skerritt (ed.) *Starting Research: Supervision and Training*. Brisbane, Queensland: Tertiary Education Institute, University of Queensland.

Phillips, E.M. (1993) The concept of quality in the PhD, in D.J. Cullen (ed.) *Quality in PhD Education*. Canberra: Centre for Educational Development and Academic Methods (CEDAM).

Phillips, E.M. (1994a) Avoiding communication breakdown, in O. Zuber-Skerritt and Y. Ryan (eds) *Quality in Postgraduate Education*. London: Kogan Page.

Phillips, E. M. (1994b) Quality in the PhD: points at which quality may be assessed, in R. Burgess (ed.) *Postgraduate Education and Training in the Social Sciences: Processes and Products*. London: Jessica Kingsley Publishers.

Phillips, E.M. (1996) The quality of a good thesis, in O. Zuber-Skerritt (ed.) *Frameworks for Postgraduate Education*. Lismore: Southern Cross University Press.

Phillips, E.M. (2001) The induction of graduate research students, in P. Frame (ed.) *Student Induction in Practice*, SEDA paper 113. Selly Park, Birmingham.

Phillips, E.M. and Zuber-Skerritt, O. (1993) Perceptions of educators and potential employers of the research training needs of postgraduates in business and management, *Journal of Management Development*, 12(5): 12–20.

Popper, K. (1972) *The Logic of Scientific Discovery*, 3rd edn. London: Hutchinson.

Powell, S. (2004) *The Award of the PhD by Published Work in the UK*. Lichfield: UK Council for Graduate Education.

Rugg, G. and Petre, M. (2004) *The Unwritten Rules of PhD Research*, Maidenhead: Open University Press.

Ryan, Y. and Zuber-Skeritt, O. (eds) (1999) *Supervising Postgraduates from Non-English Speaking Backgrounds*. Buckingham: Open University Press.

Salmon, P. (1992) *Achieving a PhD: Ten Students' Experience*. Stoke-on-Trent: Trentham Books.

Scott, D., Brown, A., Lunt, I. and Thorne, L. (2004) *Professional Doctorates*. Maidenhead: SRHE and Open University Press.

Snow, C. P. (1958) *The Search*. London: Macmillan.

Stainton-Rogers, W. (2004) Policy shifts in PGRS supervision and training. Internal memorandum, Open University, Milton Keynes.

Tinkler, P. and Jackson, C. (2004) *The Doctoral Examination Process*. Maidenhead: SRHE and Open University Press.

Torrance, M., Thomas, G. V. and Robinson, E. J. (1992) The writing strategies of graduate research students in the social sciences, *Studies in Higher Education*, 17(2): 155–67.

Wason, P. C. (1960) On the failure to eliminate hypotheses in a conceptual task, *Quarterly Journal of Experimental Psychology*, 12: 129–40.

Wason, P. C. (1968) Reasoning about a rule, *Quarterly Journal of Experimental Psychology*, 20: 273–81.

Wason, P. C. (1974) Notes on the supervision of PhDs, *Bulletin of the British Psychological Society*, 27: 25–9.

Watson, J. D. (1968) *The Double Helix*. London: Weidenfeld and Nicolson.

Watson, J.D. and Crick, F.H.C. (1953) A structure for DNA, *Nature*, 171 (25 April): 737–8.

Whitehand, J. W. R. (1966) The selection of research students, *Universities Quarterly*, 21(1): 44–8.

INDEX

abstract, 60, 137
abstraction, 56
academic role development, 164–5
academic writing, 167
access, 165–6
advice, 95, 101
ageism, 129, 173
aims
  examiners, 28–9
  research councils, 29–30
  students, 25–6
  supervisors, 26–8
  this book, 5
  universities, 29–30
appeals procedures, 142–4
appendices, 60–1
assertiveness skills, 118, 121
attendance, 13
attitude, 101–3
Australia, 178

bachelor's degree, 20
background theory, 57–8
bisexual students, 127–8, 133,
  171–2
black students, 169
borderline theses, 177
boredom, 76

brilliance, 77
British government, 53
British Universities degree structure,
  20–1
British University Research Assessment
  Exercise, 8

Cambridge, 21
casual teaching, 91–2
chapter headings, 60–1
Code of Practice for Research Degree
  Programes (QAA), 182
codes of conduct, 154, 182, 186
Commission for Racial Equality, 120–1
commitment, 101–3
communication barriers, 105
  supervision, 146, 148
  women students, 123–4
conclusions, 59–60
conference papers, 153
conferences, 152
confidence, 79, 151, 156, 161, 164
conformity, 97
constraints, 52
contacts, 153
contracts, 106, 113, 183
contribution, 59–60, 194
copyeditors, 85, 168

copyright, 193–5
critical examination, 49
criticism, 99, 110, 150–1, 155
cultural diversity, 117–19, 166–7

data
    collection and analysis, 85
    critical examination, 49
data theory, 58–9
deadlines, 87–9, 158, 161
degree structure, 20–1
departmental doctoral programme,
        204–5
Departmental Gender Subcommittee,
        125
departmental rating, 7
departmental responsibilities, 198–202
dependence, transfer, 74
disability legislation, 130
disabled students, 130–1, 134, 169, 173
discrimination, 112, 119, 126, 128, 130,
        169
dissertation, 44
distance supervision, 12–13
Doctor of Business Administration
        (DBA), 196–7
Doctor of Education (EdD), 196–7
Doctor of Engineering (EngD), 196–7
doctoral cohort system, 205–6
doctoral education
    nature of, 2–4
doctoral programme, 204–5
doctorates
    meaning, 20–1
    professional, 196–8
doctor's degree, 20–1
DPhil, 21
drop-out rate, 29

Eastern academic traditions, 167
eliciting, 152
eligibility, 10–11
employment, 43–4, 153–4, 182, 191
English language, 116–17, 186–7, 200
English reserve, 119
enthusiasm, 71–2, 101–3
environment, 182
equal opportunities policies, 189

ethical values, 154
ethnic minorities, 119–21, 132
    supervision, 169–70
ethnic monitoring, 186, 189
euphoria, 78–9
evaluation, 23, 58, 59, 86, 147, 150,
        158, 162
examination system, 135–44
examiners
    aims, 28–9
    appointment, 136, 192
examining, 175–9
excitement, 101–3
exploitation, 125–7
exploratory research, 51–2, 53
external examiners, 192

facilities, 184–7
feedback, 147
    effective, 150, 155–60
    women students, 123–4
female academics see women
field of interest, 82, 84
field trips, 171
finance, 116, 182
Flesch Reading Ease score, 68
focal theory, 58, 84
footnotes, 66
format, 67
frustration, 76–7
funding bodies, 173, 181
future development, 8

gay students, 127–8, 133, 171–2
generalizations, 49
generic skills, 182, 185, 204
goals
    completion of task, 77–8
    long and short-term, 86–7
grants, 11–12

handbook, 186
harrassment
    disabled people, 131
    heterosexist, 128–9
    racial, 120–1
    sexual, 125–7
heterosexist harrassment, 128–9

historical studies, 59
holists, 64
honesty, 100–1
humanities, 3, 67
hypotheses, 50
hypothetico-deductive method, 50–1

impartiality, 68, 122
independence, 74, 97–8, 192
induction, 185–6
inductive method, 50
institutional change, xiii
institutional responsibilities, 181–206
integrity, 154, 192
intellectual property rights, 168, 193–5
intelligence-gathering, 47, 48, 49
interest, increasing, 73–4
internal examiners, 136
internet groups, 90–1
interruptions, 152, 156
interviews, 199, 200
involvement, 73–4
isolation, 18, 72–3, 115, 166, 169, 203
IT, 13
ivory tower myth, 17–19

Jewish students, 169, 170
joint papers, 137, 194
journal articles, 153
Journal of Graduate Education, 91

knowledge, 151, 167

language, 67, 116–17, 186–7
league tables, 29
lesbian students, 127–8, 133, 171–2
limitations, 49
literature review, 8, 57–8
litigation, 144

master's degree, 20
mature students, 129–30, 133, 172–3
meetings, 97, 99–100, 149, 152, 158, 185
method section, 65
methodology, 50–1, 122
mismatches, 30–1
monitoring progress, 190–1

moral rights, 193
morale, 163
motivation, 33–5, 102
MPhil, 10, 135, 142
    differences from PhD, 24–5
MRes, 10, 11, 12, 24
Muslim students, 169–70
myths, 17–19

names, 119
National Post-Graduate Committee, 91, 92
Nobel prizes, 79
non-traditional students, 165–73, 187
notice of submission, 136

objectivity, 156
Office of the Independent Adjudicator for Higher Education, 143
open evenings, 200
Open University, 9
openness, 48
oral examination, 137–8
    cultural differences, 118
    examining, 178–9
    preparation, 138–40
    results, 140–2
originality, 54, 61–3, 197
other researchers, 79–80
overestimating requirements, 35–7
overseas students, 114–19, 131–2
    cultural differences, 117–19
    racial harrassment, 120–1
    settling into Britain, 115–16
    supervision, 166–9
    using English, 116–17
Oxford, 21

part-time students, 9, 112–14, 131, 165–6
peer support groups, 89–90, 182
personal development plans (PDP), 182
personal relationships, 17–18
    inappropriate, 110–11, 171
personal voice, 68
PhD, 21
    differences from MPhil, 24–5

form of thesis, 56–70
  understanding, 56–7
  getting down to it, 65–6
  how not to get one, 33–45
  nature of qualification, 20–32
  not understanding, 35–9
  see also doctorate
pilot study, 84
plagiarism, 154
position, 42
power relationships, 124, 125, 126, 171, 172
practical aspects, 80–5
practice-based disciplines, 195–6
presentation, 98, 99, 138, 160
problem-solving research, 52, 53, 200
process, 71–93
  duration, 82–5
  stages, 82, 84
procrastination, 65
professional doctorates, 196–8
professional researchers
  becoming one, 22–4
professional skills, 22–4, 54
professionalism, 36
progress
  monitoring, 190–1
  reports, 97, 100–1
project route, 192–3
proposal, 8, 84, 201
provision, range, 9
psychological aspects, 71–9
psychological contract, 162–4
public policy, 181
publication, 68–9, 137, 141, 164

qualities
  of supervisor, 149–50
Quality Asssurance Agency, 181, 182
questions, 150

racial harrassment, 120–1
racism, 119, 169
range of provision, 9
reading by supervisor, 147–8
real-world applicability, 53
realities
  myths and, 17–19

recognition, 107
redrafting, 63–4, 98–9
references, 60–1, 136, 153
reflective learning, 182
refunds, 144
regional hubs, 183–4
registration, 135, 141, 143
regulations, 56, 61, 85, 110, 136, 173, 176, 189–90
reporting on progress, 97, 100–1
requirements
  overestimating, 35–7
  supervisor's (lack of) knowledge, 39–40
  underestimating, 37–9
research
  analysis, 48
  basic types, 51–2
    which one?, 52–4
  characteristics, 46–7, 48–9
  the craft, 54–5
  how to do it, 46–55
  interative process, 17
research assessment exercise, 194
research assistants, 173–4
research councils, 92, 173, 177, 181
  aims, 29–30
research groups, 182
research students
  aims, 25–6
  becoming one, 1–6
  number, 188
  psychology of being one, 4
  qualities required, 34
  relationship with supervisor, 15, 104, 171
  starting out, 16
research support, 11–12
resources, 12, 187–9, 204
responsibilities
  diffusion, 95
  institutional, 181–206
results, 140–2
review forum, 158, 192–8
rewriting *see* redrafting
role models, 119, 124–5, 130, 154, 169, 171

science, 3, 36, 58, 65
scientific method, 50
scientific research programme, 9–10
Scottish universities, 21
secretaries, 148
selection
    of students, 189–90, 200–1
    of supervisors, 201–2
self-doubt, 4, 6
self-evaluation questionnaire, 207–10
self-help, 89–90
self-management, 2–3, 5, 117, 162
seminars, 107, 118, 152, 164
serialists, 64
sexual harrassment, 125–7, 172
skills, 190
    assertiveness, 118, 121
    generic, 182, 185, 204
    professional, 22–4, 54
social sciences, 3, 36, 59, 67
sonata form analogy, 56–7
speakers, 185
Special Educational Needs and
        Disability Act (2001), 130, 173
specialists, 151, 153
standards, 176, 190, 199
stereotyping, 127, 128, 169–70
structure, 60–1
student portfolio, 190
student union, 128
styles, 67–8, 122
submission, 136, 136–7
summaries, 59–60, 107, 140, 158
supervision, 145–80
    distance, 12–13
    inadequate, 39–40, 142, 143, 146, 177
    non-traditional students, 165–73
    successful outcomes, 174–5
    training for, 65, 175, 187–8
    university disciplines, 3–4
    variation in perception, 146–7
supervisors
    aims, 26–8
    changing, 108–10
    and deadlines, 87–8
    dependence on, 74–5
    educating, 101–3
    expectations, 97–103, 145–54

inadequacy, 39–40, 142, 143, 146,
        177
    knowledge (lack) of requirements,
        39–40
    losing contact with, 40–1
    managing, 94–111
    qualities, 145–54
    reading the thesis, 147–8
    relationship with student, 15, 104,
        171
    resources, 187–9
    selecting, 14–16
    suitability, 39–40
    training, 65, 175, 187–8
supervisory behaviour guidelines,
        202–3
supervisory team, 4, 94–5
    limitations, 95–7
support, 89–90, 118, 125, 131, 162, 182,
        203
surprise, 102
Sussex, 21
symmetry of potential outcomes,
        84

the system
    getting into it, 7–9
taught doctorates see professional
        doctorates
teaching, 91–3
    assistantships, 92–3
    casual, 91–2
    research, 154–5
teaching credit, 188–9
Teaching Universities, 21
teamworking, 18–19
telephone calls, 152
testing out research, 52, 53
thesis
    formulation, 66–7
    lack of, 41–3
    term, 42, 44
time frame, 11, 83, 166
time management, 80–1
topics, 84, 122, 141
training, 65, 175, 187–8
trans-gender students, 127–8, 128, 133,
        171–2

trial exercises, 54
tutorials, 9, 105–8, 147, 149, 151–3
tutors, 189, 198–200
two-way learning, 104

UK GRAD schools, 91, 154, 183
underestimating requirements, 37–9
universities
  aims, 29–30
University of Hong Kong guidelines,
    194–5
university responsibilities, 183
upgrading, 135, 191

viva *see* oral examination

weaning process, 160–2
websites, 91, 143, 154, 184
whole person, 158–9

women, 118–19, 122, 123, 129
women students, 121–7, 132–3
  academic role models, 124–5
  communication, debate and
    feedback, 123–4
  sexual harrassment and exploitation,
    125–7
  supervision, 170–1
  topics and methodology, 122
work context
  choosing, 13–14
workshops, 184, 205
World Wide Web, 90
writers, types, 64
writing, 63–7, 67–8, 85, 160, 200
  as process of rewriting, 63–4

York, 21
Yorkshire and NE Hub workshop, 184

Related books from Open University Press

Purchase from www.openup.co.uk or order through your local bookseller

HOW TO SURVIVE YOUR VIVA

Rowena Murray

The oral examination is a new type of communication event. It requires the highest standard of communication skills. Writing a thesis or dissertation requires students to pull their ideas together into a unified whole; oral examinations take it all apart again.

Typical questions, and strategies for answering them, are provided in order to help participants prepare and practise.

The book features:

- Real examples of questions and answers
- Narratives of experiences
- Planning tools
- Preparation framework
- Specific verbal strategies to use in the viva to do justice to the thesis
- User-friendly writing style
- Reading list

This is the first book to provide comprehensive coverage of the viva. It is an essential handbook for all involved in oral examinations: students, supervisors, tutors and examiners, including undergraduate, masters and doctoral examinations.

Contents

Introduction – What is a viva? – Roles and responsibilities – Countdown to the viva – Questions – Answers – Interactions – Practice – Outcomes – A new type of communication event – Bibliography – Index.

176pp   0 335 21284 0 (Paperback)   0 335 21285 9 (Hardback)

THE UNWRITTEN RULES OF PhD RESEARCH

Gordon Rugg and Marian Petre

A breath of fresh air – I wish someone had told me this beforehand.

PhD student, UK

This book covers things the other books don't tell you about doing a PhD – what it's really like and how to come through it with a happy ending! It covers all the things you wish someone had told you before you started:

- What a PhD is really about, and how to do one well
- The 'unwritten rules' of research and of academic writing
- What your supervisor actually means by terms like 'good referencing' and 'clean research question'
- How to write like a skilled researcher
- How academic careers really work

An ideal resource if someone you care about (including yourself) is undergoing or considering a PhD. This book turns lost, clueless students back into people who know what they are doing, and who can enjoy life again.

Contents

Preface – A challenge – About this book – Acknowledgements – So you want to do a PhD – Procedures and milestones – The System – Supervision – Networks – Reading – Paper types – Writing – Writing structure – Writing style – The process of writing – Presentations – Research design – The viva – Conferences – What next? – Useful principles and the like – Useful terms – Some further reading.

222pp   0 335 21344 8 (Paperback)   0 335 21345 6 (Hardback)

THE DOCTORAL EXAMINATION PROCESS
A HANDBOOK FOR STUDENTS, EXAMINERS AND SUPERVISORS

Penny Tinkler and Carolyn Jackson

- What is the viva and how can students prepare for it?
- What should supervisors consider when selecting PhD examiners?
- How should examiners assess a doctoral thesis and conduct the viva?

The doctoral examination process has been shrouded in mystery and has been a frequent source of anxiety and concern for students, supervisors and examiners alike. But now help is at hand. This book sheds new light on the process, providing constructive ways of understanding the doctoral examination, preparing for it and undertaking it.

This book stands alone in the field due to the extensive research undertaken by the authors. During a four year project, interviews were conducted with candidates and academics from a wide range of disciplines through the United Kingdom. Outcomes and ideas from the research have been united to provide the most comprehensive information available.

Real life accounts and case studies are combined with useful advice, tasks and checklists to create an illuminating handbook. This user-friendly book is a vital resource for anyone involved in the doctoral process. No doctoral candidate, examiner or supervisor should be without it.

Contents

Acknowledgements – Introduction to the PhD examination process – Understanding the doctoral viva: what is it for? – Understanding the doctoral viva: how does it work? – Viva preparation: long term – Selecting examiners – Who attends the viva? roles and obligations – Examiners: should you examine? – Examiners: assessing a PhD thesis – Viva preparation: short term – Viva preparation: final stage – In the viva: candidates' perspectives – The viva: tips and issues for examiners – Post viva – References.

192pp   0 335 21305 7 (Paperback)   0 335 21306 5 (Hardback)

HOW TO WRITE A THESIS

Rowena Murray

This is the book that all PhD supervisors and their students have been waiting for: the first comprehensive overview of the many different writing practices, and processes, involved in the production of a doctoral thesis. Crammed full of explanations, shortcuts and tips, this book demystifies academic writing in one fell swoop. Everyone who reads it will be massively enabled as a writer.

> Professor Lynne Pearce, Associate Dean for Postgraduate Teaching,
> University of Lancaster

Rowena Murray's down-to-earth approach both recognises and relieves some of the agony of writing a PhD. The advice in this book is both practical and motivational; sometimes it's 'PhD-saving' too. By using Rowena Murray's techniques of regular snacking, instead of occasional bingeing, I managed to rescue my PhD from near-death at a time of work overload.

> Christine Sinclair, part-time PhD student and lecturer in Educational
> Development, University of Paisley

This book evolved from 15 years' experience of teaching thesis writing. The contents have been tried and tested with postgraduates and academics. Early chapters explore the ambiguities and subtleties of thesis writing in detail. Later chapters are more compact, listing steps in the writing process. All chapters provide examples to illustrate techniques and activities to progress writing.

When you write a thesis, be ready to develop new modes of writing. The harsh reality is that if you like to work to goals, you are likely to have to submit to floundering around, reconstructing your well laid plans.

If you are the kind of person who hates to be driven by goals, or does not see the point of them, you will have to submit to deadlines and milestones that may seem like millstones. This book will help you cope with the challenges inherent in writing your thesis.

Contents

Introduction – How to write 1000 words an hour – Thinking about writing a doctorate – Starting to write – Seeking structure – The first milestone – Becoming a serial writer – Creating closure – Fear and loathing: revising – It is never too late to start – The last 385 yards – After the viva: more writing? – References – Index.

304pp   0 335 20718 9 (Paperback)   0 335 20719 7 (Hardback)